Praise for *Usability Testing Essentials*

"Have you been inspired to try usability testing, but not sure exactly how to go about it? Carol Barnum's book will take you step-by-step through all you need to do. Plus, she gives you a solid background in the context and history of testing—and adds a valuable chapter on international testing. Carol is highly regarded as a teacher, an academic, and a practitioner, and all three of her roles shine through in this book."

—Caroline Jarrett, User Experience and Usability Consultant,
Effortmark Limited, author of *Forms that Work*

"Carol Barnum's *Usability Testing Essentials* delivers just what the title promises. Readers who are new to usability studies will find here all they need to know to design and execute a test, analyze the test data, and provide an effective report with recommendations for clients. But even usability experts will find the book chock full of ideas, insights, and suggestions that will improve their practice and their teaching in this increasingly important area of study. Barnum's expertise on the subject shines through on every page, but the book's greatest strength is its careful attention to analyzing test results—a topic that earlier texts have tended to gloss over much too quickly."

—George Hayhoe, PhD, Mercer University School of Engineering

"*Usability Testing Essentials* will guide you through both conducting a usability evaluation and making the decisions that will make it a useful and effective part of any user experience project. Carol Barnum places usability evaluation into the larger context of user-centered design. It is a valuable resource for anyone getting started in usability and an excellent companion to both *Letting Go of the Words* and *Forms that Work*."

—Whitney Quesenbery, WQusability

"Carol Barnum has done a wonderful job of distilling her research, consulting, and teaching experience into this very lively, practical book on how to do usability testing. You get up-to-date, step-by-step help with lots of variations to suit your own situation. You see each part in action through the running case study. If you have a global market, you'll especially want to review Chapter 10 on international usability testing. This is a great addition to the usability toolkit.

—Janice (Ginny) Redish, charter member of the UPA, author of
Letting Go of the Words: Writing Web Content that Works

"Carol is a rare breed, both an academic and a practitioner. Her voice of experience comes across clearly, backed by references that illustrate where and who our methods came from. Newcomers to usability testing will find a solid introduction; while those more experienced will find unexpected insights into the field."

—Carolyn Snyder, Snyder Consulting

Usability Testing Essentials

Acquiring Editor: Mary James
Assistant Editor: David Bevans
Project Manager: Marilyn Rash
Designer: Joanne Blank

Morgan Kaufmann is an imprint of Elsevier
30 Corporate Drive, Suite 400, Burlington, MA 01803, USA

Notices
Knowledge and best practice in this field are constantly changing. As new research and experience broaden our understanding, changes in research methods or professional practices may become necessary. Practitioners and researchers must always rely on their own experience and knowledge in evaluating and using any information or methods described herein. In using such information or methods they should be mindful of their own safety and the safety of others, including parties for whom they have a professional responsibility.

To the fullest extent of the law, neither the Publisher nor the authors, contributors, or editors assume any liability for any injury and/or damage to persons or property as a matter of products liability, negligence or otherwise, or from any use or operation of any methods, products, instructions, or ideas contained in the material herein.

Library of Congress Cataloging-in-Publication Data
Barnum, Carol M.
    Usability testing essentials : ready, set...test! / Carol M. Barnum.
        p. cm.
    ISBN 978-0-12-375092-1
1. User interfaces (Computer systems)—Testing.   2. Web-based user interfaces—Testing.   3. Human-computer interaction.   I. Title.
    QA76.9.U83B3634 2010
    004.01'9—dc22   2010023393

British Library Cataloguing-in-Publication Data
A catalogue record for this book is available from the British Library.

Printed in China
10 11 12 13 14   10 9 8 7 6 5 4 3 2 1

For information on all MK publications
visit our website at *www.mkp.com*

Usability Testing Essentials

Ready, Set...Test!

Carol M. Barnum

Amsterdam • Boston • Heidelberg • London • New York • Oxford
Paris • San Diego • San Francisco • Singapore • Sydney • Tokyo
Morgan Kaufmann is an imprint of Elsevier

For Carolyn, George, Ginny, and Whitney

*with deep appreciation for your insights, encouragement,
and vision for what this book could be*

Contents

Foreword

In 2008, I decided to put together a panel at the annual conference of the Usability Professionals' Association. The topic was *Discount Testing by Amateurs: Threat or Menace?*

At the time, I was about to go out on a limb by writing a book[1] based on the premise that everyone involved in creating websites should be doing their own usability testing.

Not surprisingly, the idea of amateurs doing the work of professionals was viewed by some members of the usability community as a potential threat to full employment and high standards, although these concerns were rarely discussed in public. So I thought it would be a good idea to bring the debate out in the open—preferably *before* I spent what promised to be a painful year writing my book.

Randolph Bias kindly agreed to take the contrary position ("Testing by amateurs is a very bad idea for many reasons"), but we needed someone to sit in between us and argue for a sensible, balanced viewpoint. It had to be someone very smart, with a lot of credibility in the profession. I immediately thought of Carol Barnum.

To help people get in the spirit of the thing and hopefully take sides, we even made up a series of buttons with inflammatory phrases like: "Steve, you ignorant slut!" and "Randolph, you ignorant slut!"[2] Carol's button was easy to write.

Even though I've had the pleasure of knowing Carol for more than a decade, I think I first started thinking of her as the voice of reason in

Vote Carol, Voice of Reason

---

[1] *Rocket Surgery Made Easy: The Do-It-Yourself Guide to Finding and Fixing Usability Problems,* New Riders, 2010.
[2] References to a Dan Aykroyd catchphrase ("Jane, you ignorant slut") from an old *Saturday Night Live* sketch where he and Jane Curtin are news analysts whose debates are, well, acrimonious.

2002 when I read a paper she'd written about one of the perennial questions in our field: How many participants do you need in a usability test to discover most of the problems?[3]

In it, she took an argument that threatened to go on forever and finally made sense out of it, recapping all the research (some of the most insightful of which was done by her own students at Southern Polytechnic), neatly summarizing the various viewpoints, and drawing what I thought were incredibly insightful conclusions.

Ever since then, she's been one of my go-to people when I need a sounding board on usability-related issues.

You may be wondering why I'm here recommending Carol's usability testing book if I just published one myself. But mine is a very short book that only covers the basics of one "flavor" of testing. I was ruthless in leaving out whole topics—important topics—because I had a very specific objective: to get people started.

But I only felt free to be this ruthless because I knew that once people got a taste of usability testing they'd want to know more, and I could point them to books that *do* go into detail on all the important topics.

And even though Carol's book wasn't written yet, I included it in my list of recommended reading anyway (a very short list—I only recommend books that I think are excellent) because I knew it would be one of the best.

I'm glad it's finally here. And I'm glad I was right: it's excellent.

I knew it would be.

Steve Krug
Brookline, Massachusetts

[3]The "magic number 5": Is it enough for Web testing? *Proceedings of the 1st European UPA Conference*, London, September 2002.

Acknowledgments

A book does not spring to life like spontaneous combustion. It smolders for years, taking on energy from the world around it. Then it finally bursts into flame. The energy I have gotten from the many people who have helped light the spark and keep the fire going for this book comes from my many students in usability testing courses at Southern Polytechnic and in workshops and training sessions for usability practitioners around the world. In addition, energy comes from my clients in the Usability Center at Southern Polytechnic, who have partnered with me in pursuing a common goal of understanding their users' experience.

I am grateful for all the insights I have gotten from teaching and working with clients and their users and for the samples I can share from client and student projects. I have included as many of these samples as space permits in this book. And there's more on the book's companion website.

For the excellent feedback I received on the proposal for this book, I wish to show my appreciation to my reviewers: Laura Downey, George Hayhoe, Mike Hughes, Caroline Jarrett, Katie Leonard, Ginny Redish, Alison Reynolds, and Whitney Quesenbery.

For my dear friend and colleague, Steve Krug, who generously agreed to write the Foreword, I cannot adequately express how much I appreciate his contribution. It should come as no surprise to those of you who know Steve and his work that he would *want* to do the Foreword. Still, it surprised, pleased, and touched me.

And for the amazingly thorough, instructive, informative, challenging, and insightful reviews I received from my four colleagues for the chapter-by-chapter review of the book—George Hayhoe, Whitney Quesenbery, Ginny Redish, and Carolyn Snyder—I am deeply grateful, so much so that I have dedicated the book to them. The book you are reading would not be the book it is were it not for the vision of these colleagues and friends in helping me see the light.

And to Morgan Kaufmann—particularly Mary James, David Bevans, Marilyn Rash, and Rachel Roumeliotis—for shepherding me through the process: thanks for all your support.

About the author

Carol Barnum became a usability advocate in the early 1990s. It happened when she heard (and saw) the word "usability" in a session at a Society for Technical Communication conference. Technical communicators have always seen themselves as the user's advocate, but here was an emerging discipline that championed the cause of the user!

It was love at first sight.

In 1993, Carol attended the second Usability Professionals' Association conference, where she was thrilled to mix and mingle with several hundred usability folks on Microsoft's corporate campus. Those two conferences sparked a desire to combine her love of teaching people how to be clear communicators with a new-found passion for helping companies understand how to promote good communication between their products and their users.

In 1994, she opened her first usability lab in a windowless basement at Southern Polytechnic State University. Since then, Carol has relocated and rebuilt the lab into a great three-room complex, with plenty of light and plenty of room for a team in the control room; visitors in the executive viewing room; and, of course, participants in the participant room. Working with many different clients over the years, she has greatly enjoyed helping them unlock their users' experience with software, hardware, documentation and training products, mobile devices, web applications, and, of course, websites.

In addition to being the director of the Usability Center, Carol directs the graduate programs in Information Design and Communication at Southern Polytechnic and teaches a variety of courses, including usability testing, information design, and international technical communication.

Carol is a sought-after speaker and trainer, receiving the top presentation prize at the first European Usability Professionals' Association conference, and top ratings at UPA, STC, and IEEE's Professional Communication conferences. She has traveled the world—England, Ireland, New Zealand, Australia, China, and India—speaking about usability testing. And closer to home, she was an invited keynote speaker at the World Conference on e-Learning in Quebec, Ontario, and at World Usability Day at Michigan State University.

She is the author of five other books and numerous articles and book chapters covering a variety of topics, including the impact of agile on usability testing, the "Magic Number 5" and whether it is enough for web testing, using Microsoft's product reaction cards for insights into the desirability factor in user experience, e-learning and usability, and issues affecting international and intercultural communication and information design.

Carol's work has brought recognition from the Society for Technical Communication (STC), including the Rainey Award for Excellence in Research, the Gould Award for Excellence in Teaching Technical Communication, and the designation of Fellow. Her first book on usability testing won STC's highest-level international publications award. Carol served seven years on the Board of Directors of STC and is also a founding member of the editorial board of the *Journal of Usability Studies*.

Image credits and permissions

Figure 1.1. Used with permission from Peter Morville.

Figures 1.2 and 2.1. Used with permission from Jakob Nielsen.

Figure 2.2. Used with permission from EyeTech Digital Systems, Inc.

Figures 2.3, 2.4, 2.7, 2.9, 2.11, 2.12, 4.4, and 7.2. Photos by Lisa M. Zunzanyika.

Figure 2.5. Used with permission from Kelly Goto, Gotomedia.

Figures 2.13 and 2.14. Used with permission from Optimal Workshop, the development arm of New Zealand-based user experience consultancy Optimal Usability, which developed these two tools.

Figure 3.1. Used with permission from Bev Arends.

Figure 3.2. UX Stencil © Todd Zazelenchuk & Elizabeth Boling. Used with permission. *www.userfocus.co.uk/uxstencil*

Chapter 3 sidebar. Five steps to a (user-centered) expert review. Used with permission from Whitney Quesenbery and Caroline Jarrett.

Figures 4.2 and 4.3. Used with permission from Susanna Fox, study co-author and Associate Director, Pew Internet & American Life Project.

Chapter 5 sidebar. How many one-hour sessions are optimal for a day? Used with permission from Cliff Anderson.

Figure 6.9. Copyright © Digital Equipment Corporation, 1986. From Brooke (1986).

Figure 6.10. Adapted from the work of James R. Lewis (1995). Used with permission.

Figures 6.11 and 7.1. Permission is granted to use this Tool for personal, academic, and commercial purposes with the following attribution: Developed by and copyright © 2002 Microsoft Corporation. All rights reserved.

Chapter 7 sidebar. What makes a good moderator. Adapted and used with permission from Chauncey Wilson.

Chapter 8 sidebar. Affinity matching tips and tricks. Adapted and used with permission from Tara Scanlon.

Figure 8.2. Photo courtesy of IEEE and Whitney Quesenbery; used with permission.

Figures 9.10 and 9.11. Health study. Used with permission.

Figures 9.12 and 9.23. Used with permission from Ginny Redish.

Figures 10.6 and 10.7. Photos by Daniel Szuc and Josephine Wong, Apogee—*www.apogeehk.com.* Used with permission.

Figures 10.3 and 10.4. Used with permission from Enquiro Search Solutions, *www.enquiro.com*

Case Studies. Used with permission of authors. Holiday Inn China website usability case study used with permission of sponsor, Karen Bennett, Manager, User Experience, Distribution Marketing—IHG.

Introduction: Getting started guide

Usability is invisible

Do you love your mobile phone? Your MP3 player (you know the one)? Your e-book reader? Your laptop or tablet PC? Your search engine of choice? Your GPS system (or the application in your smart phone)? Your bank's online banking application or its ATM?

There's a reason for that. Usability.

When usability is inherent in the products we use, it's invisible. We don't think about it. But we know it's there.

That's because the products that have built-in usability suit us. We don't have to bend to the will of the product. It works the way we want it to work. Perhaps we had to learn a few things, or more than a few, to get going, but we don't mind because the effort was small and the rewards are great. Rewards like

- ease of learning
- ease of use
- intuitiveness
- fun (let's not forget the importance of fun)

Usability Testing Essentials. DOI: 10.1016/B978-0-12-375092-1.00012-X

But what happens when usability is *not* inherent in the products we use? Here's one example that many of us can relate to: We check into a hotel and need to set the alarm clock for an early morning meeting. But we don't trust the alarm clock to work properly. Or we think we can do this simple thing, so we set the alarm, only to find out it doesn't wake us up at the time we think we set it.

Did you know that one major hotel chain, Hilton hotels, decided to do something about this problem? It tested more than 150 alarm clocks on the market and didn't find *one* that passed the "ease-of-use" test. So, Hilton designed its own alarm clock shown here. Other hotels are now doing the same thing.

For an interesting review of this alarm clock by Donald Norman, the author of *The Design of Everyday Things* and a usability specialist, see *www.jnd.org/ dn.mss/the_hilton_hotel_ ala.html*

Can you think of any products you've purchased that were just too complicated? Maybe you struggled to figure out how to make them work. Did you know that the average U.S. consumer will struggle for *20 minutes* to try to make something work?

Things shouldn't be that hard to learn to use. Time wasted trying to learn to use products means lost time for consumers and lost sales for companies when dissatisfied customers return products that don't seem to work. But are these products always broken? A study by Accenture found that 95% of product returns actually worked perfectly.

Reported by Arar in *PC World,* June 2, 2008.

Maybe you have experienced bad or inadequate product design, but you didn't return the product for some reason. Maybe it was because you felt you didn't have a choice or that nothing better was available. Does the remote control for any of your electronic devices come to mind?

Shouldn't all products be designed with you in mind? Silly question. So what's the answer to build usability into every product?

It's you.

U R usability

If you are a software or web developer, engineer, interaction designer, information architect, technical communicator, visual or graphic designer, trainer, user-assistance specialist, instructional technologist, or anyone else who has a hand in the development or support of a product of any type, then you are the face of usability. Your passion for the user, advocacy for the user, and actions on behalf of the user can and do influence the usability of the product.

Despite your desire to support the needs of users, you may not yet be doing usability testing. Or, you may already be doing usability testing but would like to formalize or standardize your practice, perhaps even expand it. This book gives you the essentials to begin or add to your expertise. With a strong foundation in strategies for success and models to show you how, you will develop the core skills you need and add to those you already have.

How to use this book

The idea behind this book is to give you the tools and techniques you need to get going or to advance your knowledge of what you're already doing. That's why the book is called *Usability Testing Essentials*. The subtitle—*Ready, Set . . . Test!*—is meant to suggest that you should pick your starting point.

Begin wherever it makes sense to you. If you're new to the field or perhaps a student, it probably makes the most sense to begin at the beginning of the book and read the chapters in the order in which they are presented. However, if you have some experience or have read about this topic before, you can jump in at the chapter or chapters that most interest you.

Maybe you need this book now because you're getting ready to do your first usability test. Or maybe you've done some informal usability testing, but you're looking for a methodology that you can apply to standardize your testing practices. In these cases, you might want to start with Chapter 5 on planning a test, or jump into Chapter 7 on conducting a test.

Here's how the chapters are organized:

Chapter 1, *Establishing the essentials,* does just that. It gives you the essentials to define usability and usability testing so that you start with a vocabulary you can use. With a quick look back at traditional testing practices, the chapter moves you forward to what's typically being done today in both small, formative studies and large, summative studies.

Chapter 2, *Testing here, there, everywhere,* looks at your testing options, including testing in a lab, testing without a lab, field testing, and remote testing—both moderated and unmoderated.

Chapter 3, *Big U and little u usability,* puts usability testing into the context of a user-centered design (UCD) process so that you have the big picture. In this chapter, you get a quick look at a toolkit of techniques you can use before and after usability testing to help your organization grow its understanding of the user experience. Special attention is given to heuristic evaluation because it's often the most widely used tool in the UCD toolkit and is a frequent companion to usability testing. This chapter also gives you strategies to make the case for user-centered design by presenting some approaches for cost-justifying the use of these techniques.

Chapter 4, *Understanding users and their goals,* starts the preplanning process by focusing on users and their tasks. Of course, users are the linchpin for everything related to usability. This chapter starts off by reviewing the things we know about users in general. Then it looks at the things we know about web users in particular, especially the things we know about them because of their age or generation. Because it's so important to get it right when it comes to your users, this chapter provides information on applying what you know about your users to create personas and scenarios.

The heart of the book is in *Chapters 5 through 7: Planning, Preparing, and Conducting a usability test.* In some cases, you may have the time to plan, then prepare, then test in three separate steps. In other cases, you may have to compress the planning and preparing stages into one, with testing following right on the heels of preparation. Still, whether the timeframe is weeks or days, you will want to plan your test, then prepare for it, then conduct it. That's why there is a chapter for each of these stages.

What to do with all of those findings from a usability test? *Chapter 8, Analyzing the findings,* helps you make sense of what you have learned from users. *Chapter 9, Reporting the findings,* reviews the approaches—formal and informal—for sharing your findings with others.

Chapter 10 delves into *International usability testing.* Interest in learning about users from other countries and cultures is increasing, along with a growing number of studies about users from different cultures. This chapter focuses on the unique aspects of international usability testing. Although it is the last chapter in the book, this placement is not meant to suggest that this topic is an afterthought. In fact, the main case study used throughout the book is a usability study of a Chinese hotel website, conducted in the United States, which shows that international usability testing can take place wherever you are.

Special features you can use or skip

Within the chapters, you will find some special features that you can use or skip, as suits your needs. These include:

- *References*—Although this book is well researched and well documented, it is designed to let you access the information you need without getting bogged down with references. The references are mentioned in margin notes, with full citations listed at the end of the book.

- *Margin notes*—I also use the margins to give you suggestions about relevant sources or to point you to another chapter for more information. If you're skipping around in the book, this may be particularly helpful to you.

- *Boxed sections*—These are either extended examples or sidebars of helpful hints or useful information. Case studies and extended examples are boxed in green and sidebars are boxed in purple. The colors will help you identify them so that you can use them or skip them.

A few words about words

Words can be slippery, especially when you're using the vocabulary of a relatively new discipline. So, to be clear about the way in which I use some of the core words in this book, here's what I mean for each:

- *Usability testing*—the process of learning *about* users *from* users by observing them using a product to accomplish specific goals of interest to them.
- *Usability test*—a single testing session.
- *Usability study*—the total number of testing sessions.
- *User*—the person who is the "customer" for the product; that is, the person for whom the product is designed. Also called the "target" or "end" user. In usability testing, we recruit the target user, who becomes a *participant* in the study. For some, the word *user* has become controversial in that there is some sensitivity surrounding its association with illicit drugs. Others prefer to refer to users as *people* or *humans,* as in the term *human-centered design.* I am sticking with *users* to mean the people we need to learn from so that we can build our knowledge about their experiences into the products we design for them.

  One word of caution: Avoid calling your users "test subjects." This term is a holdover from the olden days of experimental design. Today, we are not working with test subjects; we are working with people who test our products for us so that we can understand their experiences. Some usability experts call them "testers" because they are testing a product.

- *Participant*—refers to the testers, or users. When we refer to them as participants, we focus on their role in the study as the target users.
- *Product*—a catch-all term to refer to any element or component of the design that contributes directly or indirectly to the user's experience. A product can be hardware, software, a web application, or a website. It can be an e-learning course, or a company's intranet, or a computer game, or an interactive voice response (IVR) system. It can be a print document such as a manual, getting started guide, quick reference, or assembly instructions. It can be the packaging that starts the "out-of-box" experience. It can be the experience of calling customer support or engaging in a live chat session. In usability testing, the product is the "thing," or process, that is being tested.

- *Interface*—the part of the product that the user interacts with to accomplish tasks. It's the place where the user, the device, and the application interact. Sometimes the word *interface* is used in place of *product,* particularly when testing takes place on a computer or handheld device.

But wait, there's more on the companion website

Because the growth of our profession expands almost faster than we can keep up, there certainly will be changes by the time this book is in your hands. You will find the latest developments and updates on the book's companion website at *www.mkp.com/testingessentials*. It includes:

- Complete reports from the examples and case studies shown in the book, plus other reports
- Forms, checklists, templates, and so forth
- Resources for additional information

For *instructors,* you will find a special section containing:

- A sample syllabus and sample assignments
- An instructor's guide
- Questions and topics for discussion
- Exercises for classroom or homework use
- Activities for developing a usability testing project

Establishing the essentials

1

Communication equals remembering what it's like not to know.
—Richard Saul Wurman

Information Anxiety, 1989

From the moment you know enough to talk about a product—any product, whether it's hardware, software, a video game, a training guide, or a website—you know too much to be able to tell if the product would be usable for a person who doesn't know what you know. As Jakob Nielsen, a strong advocate of usability in product design, puts it, "Your best guess is not good enough." That's why usability testing is essential.

Usability Engineering, 1993

With usability testing, we get to see what people actually do—what works for them, and what doesn't—not what we think they would do or even what *they* think they would do if they were using your product. When usability testing is a part of design and development, the knowledge we get about our users' experience supports all aspects of design and development.

This chapter presents the essentials of usability testing, which include the need to

- focus on the user, not the product
- start with some essential definitions:

Usability Testing Essentials. DOI: 10.1016/B978-0-12-375092-1.00001-5

○ defining usability

○ defining usability testing and differentiating the two main types of testing:
  – formative testing
  – summative testing

- know when to conduct small studies
- know how to conduct small studies, which include:

  ○ defining the user profile

  ○ creating task-based scenarios

  ○ using a think-aloud process

  ○ making changes and testing again

- know when to conduct large studies
- think of usability testing as hill climbing

Focus on the user, not the product

When you focus on the user and not the product, you learn what works for your users, as well as what doesn't work, what pleases, what puzzles, and what frustrates them. You understand your users' experience with the product to determine whether the design matches their expectations and supports their goals.

Usability testing gives you this access to your users using your product to perform tasks that they would want to do, which are matched to goals that are realistic for them. In the testing situation, you have the chance to elicit their comments, to observe their body language (in many cases), to discover their wishes and hopes for the product, and to learn how well the product supports them in their goals. The mantra of usability testing is, "We are testing the product, not you." Many people begin a testing session with this statement. Even if you don't make this statement to the participant, it's important to remember that this is the focus of testing.

Start with some essential definitions

To have a common vocabulary to talk about user experience, we need a common set of definitions for the essential words we use.

These include:

- usability
- usability testing
- types of testing
  - formative
  - summative

Defining usability

The best-known definition of *usability* is the one from ISO, the International Organization for Standardization (9241-11): "The extent to which a product can be used by specified users to achieve specified goals with effectiveness, efficiency, and satisfaction in a specified context of use."

Although this definition is rather formal, as you might expect for one that has become a standard, I like it because it encompasses the three critical elements of

- *Specific users*—not just any user, but the specific ones for whom the product is designed.
- *Specified goals*—these specific users have to share the goals for the product, meaning that the product's goals represent their goals.
- *A specific context of use*—the product has to be designed to work in the environment in which these users will use it.

I also like this definition because it focuses on the critical measures of usability:

- effectiveness
- efficiency
- satisfaction

Effectiveness and *efficiency* support the user's need to achieve a goal for using the product with accuracy and speed. Frequently, this also means that the product supports the user in a way that is *better* than the current way in which the user works. This is the value-added part of usability. If the product doesn't add value to the way in which the user currently performs tasks or needs to learn to perform tasks, then the user will have no use for the product. For instance, if the user perceives that the online bill-paying feature offered by her bank is not worth the effort to set up and use, then she will continue to write checks, put stamps on envelopes, and mail in her payments. Her rejection of the new product may be because it does not appear to be efficient, even if it proves to be effective.

Beyond effectiveness and efficiency, however, is the critical criterion of *satisfaction.* Although measures of effectiveness and efficiency are, to some extent, determined by the user's perceptions of these qualities, there is no denying that the measure of satisfaction is derived wholly from the user's *perception* of satisfaction. Is the user satisfied with the display of the information on the page or screen? Is the design pleasing to the user? Is the overall experience a positive one? If users think that the answer to these questions is "yes," their interest in using the product will often trump recognized problems affecting effectiveness and efficiency. Why? Because satisfaction = desirability. And the "desirability factor" is often the elusive brass ring that developers, especially marketing teams, are seeking in new products.

Satisfaction was clearly important when the ISO standard was developed, but it has become even more important today—some would say it is the most important measure of usability. That's because users *expect* products to be usable. Meeting users' expectations for satisfaction can determine whether users will resist, repel, or even rebel against using the product.

For Quesenbery's article about using the 5Es, see *www.wqusability.com*

If the ISO definition seems a bit too formal for your tastes, you might find Whitney Quesenbery's definition more to your liking. Quesenbery, a well-known usability consultant, distills the definition of usability into the following easy-to-remember dimensions of usability, which she calls the *5Es:*

Dimension	Definition
Effective	How completely and accurately the work or experience is completed or goals reached
Efficient	How quickly this work can be completed
Engaging	How well the interface draws the user into the interaction and how pleasant and satisfying it is to use
Error tolerant	How well the product prevents errors and can help the user recover from mistakes that do occur
Easy to learn	How well the product supports both the initial orientation and continued learning throughout the complete lifetime of use

Peter Morville, a well-known information architect and co-author of the "polar bear" book, put together many of these concepts of usability in a visual form, which he calls the *user experience honeycomb* (Figure 1.1). It was originally intended to explain the qualities of user experience that web designers must address, but it can just as easily show the experience that all product designers should address.

Information Architecture for the World Wide Web: Designing Large-Scale Web Sites, 2006

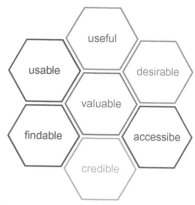

Figure 1.1 The facets of user experience are presented as the user experience honeycomb.

The facets in the honeycomb include both behavioral measures and the intangibles of "valuable," "desirable," and "credible" that users determine through their use of the product. You can use the honeycomb as the basis for discussion about what elements are most important to build into your products so that the user experience is a positive one. You can also use the honeycomb to determine what facets you want to learn from users when you conduct usability testing.

For an explanation of the honeycomb, see Morville's "User Experience Design" column at *http://semanticstudios.com/ publications/semantics/ 000029.php*

Defining usability testing

When I refer to *usability testing,* I mean the activity that focuses on observing users working with a product, performing tasks that are real and meaningful to them.

Although much has changed in the approaches we may take to doing usability testing, even including the possibility of *not* observing users when conducting remote unmoderated testing, the core definition remains basically unchanged. Changes in technology, including access to users anywhere at any time, coupled with changes in the scope of testing (from very big to very small studies) mean that the definition of usability testing needs to stretch to encompass the methods and practices that support testing in many different environments and under many different conditions. As you will see in this book, the simple definition I use can make that stretch.

Using this definition for all usability testing, we can now look at subdividing testing into two types, depending on the point at which it is done and the goal for the study:

- *Formative testing*—while the product is in development, with a goal of diagnosing and fixing problems; typically based on small studies, repeated during development.
- *Summative testing*—after the product is finished, with a goal of establishing a baseline of metrics or validating that the product meets requirements; generally requires larger numbers for statistical validity.

With these essential definitions for talking about usability testing, we can now start to apply them.

For those of you who want to take a small detour first, you might want to take a peek at a brief history of usability testing practice in the sidebar. I've put this history in this first chapter because there are still people who question how you can get good results from small studies. I find that I frequently need to explain how—and why—usability testing works when you see only a few users. If you need the ammunition for this argument, you'll get it from this brief history.

Take a peek at a brief history of usability testing—then and now

"Those who don't know history are destined to repeat it." Edmund Burke, a British philosopher and statesman, made that statement in the 18th century, and you have probably heard something like it said in your history class or somewhere else. So, what's its relevance here? A little bit of the history of usability testing can help you see where the practice came from and how it's practiced today. Some people still think the traditional way is the only way it's done. If you want to take a quick peek at how it was practiced in the beginning and how it's practiced today, read on.

Traditional usability testing relies on the practices of experimental design

Usability testing, as it was commonly practiced from its beginnings until well into the 1990s, was a formal process, employing the methods of experimental design. As such, it was expensive, time consuming, and rigorous. Labs, where such tests were conducted, were managed by usability experts who typically had education and training as cognitive scientists, experimental psychologists, or human factors engineers. Because tests were viewed as research experiments, they typically required 30 to 50 "test subjects."

Who could afford to do it? Not many. So, not much usability testing was done.

However, in the early 1990s, some research studies showed that effective testing could be done with smaller numbers. Among those doing this research were Jakob Nielsen and his colleague Tom Landauer, both, by the way, human factors researchers who were well versed in the experimental design method for usability studies. However, they were seeking a quicker way to get results, and they found one.

"Discount" usability testing changed the way we think about testing

Nielsen and Landauer (both working as researchers at Bellcore at that time) determined that the maximum cost–benefit ratio, derived by weighing the costs of testing and the benefits gained, is achieved when you test with three to five participants, as shown in the classic "curve" (Figure 1.2).

For an explanation of the method used to establish the curve, see Nielsen's "Alertbox" column of March 19, 2000, at *www.useit. com/alertbox/20000319.html*

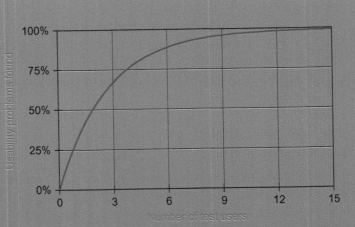

Figure 1.2 This curve shows why you only need to test with five users.

Here's what Nielsen says about the curve:

> The most striking truth of the curve is that **zero users give zero insights**.
>
> As soon as you collect data from a **single test user**, your insights shoot up and you have already learned almost a third of all there is to know about the usability of the design. The difference between zero and even a little bit of data is astounding.

The bold text is in the original.

According to Nielsen, you should stop after the fifth user because you are seeing the same things repeated, and you will have reached the optimal return of 85% of the findings to be uncovered.

Good ideas have a tendency to bubble up at the same time. Just so, other researchers were publishing similar findings from small usability tests.

Virzi, 1990 and 1992

Robert Virzi, a researcher at GTE Laboratories at that time, reported his findings from small studies in "Streamlining the Design Process: Running Fewer Subjects" and "Refining the Test Phase of Usability Evaluation: How Many Subjects Is Enough?" James

Lewis, 1994

Lewis, a researcher at IBM, published his findings in "Sample Sizes for Usability Studies: Additional Considerations." Virzi and Lewis each found that small studies uncover 80% of the findings from a particular test. Nielsen and Landauer said the number was 85%.

What these researchers gave us is evidence that small studies can be highly effective. Putting these research findings together, we can safely say that small studies can uncover 80–85% of the findings from a particular test. This result is not to be confused with uncovering 80–85% of usability findings for the *entire* product. That would take many, many studies. However, the findings from a particular study can frequently be applied to other parts of the product not tested.

There's more about doing this type of analysis in small studies in Chapter 8.

When compared to large studies, small usability studies give us the following advantages over large studies. They can be

- incorporated into the development of the product at little cost
- incorporated into the development of the product without adversely affecting the development timeline
- done early and often

These are the reasons why Nielsen called this approach "discount" usability testing. Nowadays we don't need to give it such a formal name. We call it usability testing.

Know when to conduct small studies

Today, the formal methodology of experimental design has largely given way to informal studies (although formal studies are still conducted and for good reasons).

These informal studies are in the category of "formative" usability testing. They are typically small in scope and often repeated during stages of product development. Their value comes from providing the development team with a list of findings to analyze and fix, then conducting another small study to see whether the fixes worked.

Formative studies also reveal what users like. These positive experiences are important to capture in a report or study notes so that they won't be lost as the product moves through development.

Formative studies are also a great tool for ending arguments. With a small study, developers can find out what works best for users, not what a vocal or powerful team member or manager thinks will work best.

Small studies, being small, don't provide metrics or statistics, but the list of findings that results from small studies provides great insights to developers that can be put into action right away.

Know how to conduct small studies

To get good results from small studies, you need to incorporate the following essential elements:

- define the user profile
- create task-based scenarios
- use a think-aloud process
- make changes and test again

Define the user profile

Most products are designed to serve the needs of a wide variety of users with different skill levels, domain knowledge, and a host of other factors. Even within a clearly defined user group, there can be significant variations. Wouldn't you like to know about all of these users and all of the variations among them? Of course. But the reality is that most budgets for testing are small, and whatever usability testing you can do must be done quickly so that your understanding of the users' experience can be added to the continuing development of the product.

When you are planning a small study with five or six participants, you need to pick *one* subgroup of the user population, create a profile of this user, and make this the basis for recruiting participants for your study. This is probably the most important part of planning so that you get good results.

When you are planning a larger study, you can increase the number of profiles you create and reduce the number of participants from each subgroup, as there will likely be some overlap in the findings from different subgroups. For instance, if you have a budget for a study with 10 participants, you can create three profiles for three groups of three with an extra person in one of the groups. More budget, more profiles.

Create task-based scenarios

For small studies to reap useful results, you need to give your participants specific tasks to perform. These tasks are embedded within scenarios, which are realistic descriptions framed around users' goals. When users are given a description of a goal, you can observe their methods for achieving the goal. Without a common set of scenarios, users will go their own way in an interface, which makes it difficult to see patterns of usage and recurrence of problems among and between users.

There's much more about creating user profiles and task-based scenarios in Chapter 5.

Use a think-aloud process

A *think-aloud* process is one in which you encourage the participant to share his or her thoughts with you while working with the product.

Why use a think-aloud process? Although thinking out loud is not "normal" for most people, the added dimension of having users share their thoughts, reactions, pleasure, pain, and so forth helps you understand so much more about their experience. Not only do you see the actions users take, but you also benefit from hearing *why* users are taking an action and *what* they think about the process—good and bad. When users think out loud, you don't have to guess what they're thinking. They tell you.

Chapter 7 goes into much more detail about how to establish a level of comfort for users when asking them to think out loud.

Make changes and test again

If you have budget and time for only one small usability study, then by all means, do it. However, small studies typically show you where the problems are, but not necessarily what the solutions are. A follow-up study can test the solutions to see if they work. Another small study can test the integration of aspects of the product as it moves through development. Because small studies are small in cost and small in time, follow-up studies can be added quickly and when needed without adversely affecting the overall development budget or delivery timeline.

This process of repetitive studies is called *iterative testing* (as shown in Figure 1.3). The essential advantage of iterative testing is that you can learn from users, make changes based on what you learned, then test again.

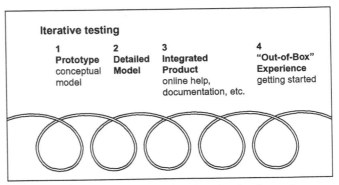

Figure 1.3 The iterative process shows testing throughout development.

Typically, in iterative testing, you will see the product improve. With fewer big issues surfacing that blocked users from progressing in earlier studies, the remaining problems now emerge because they have been set free from the "show stoppers" in an earlier test. Another benefit of iterative studies is that you can validate improvements to the user experience by showing improvements in responses from questionnaires you use in your studies.

Know when to conduct large studies

Most large studies are summative, with testing done when a product is fully developed. These studies require a large number of users because the results are generally used to produce metrics, such as success or failure on tasks, average time on task, completion rates, error rates, optimal navigation, search results, and other measures. These metrics may establish a baseline for future product development or to affirm that product requirements have been met. Summative studies can use the same set of tasks and scenarios from earlier formative studies, or they can focus on specific features or processes, now fully developed and integrated within the product, to validate a successful user experience.

Not all large studies are with finished products. In some cases, large studies are needed while a product is in development. Here are some reasons for conducting large studies for products in development:

- When you are testing large, complex systems, including large websites, and you want to understand the user experience for many different subgroups.

- When you are testing systems or features that require strong confirmation of high usability, such as those involving personal risk or injury if not properly used.
- When management will not be convinced by small studies.

Although everyone agrees that small studies can reap big results in many situations, some have questioned whether this approach works for big, complex websites. Because the original research on the validity of small studies is based on testing software, some people have challenged the validity of "the magic number 5" for studies of large websites with a large and diverse user base.

If your team or management feels that you need to understand a wide variety of users with many different goals and if you've been given the budget and the time to test with larger numbers, a formative study with a large number of participants addresses this need.

When the stakes are high, as would be true for systems where personal risk or injury is a potential outcome of poor usability, larger usability studies are needed to uncover more problems, even those that might happen only occasionally.

Finally, if management will not be convinced that a small study produces reliable results, you will probably be able to get support for conducting a larger study. I have found that if I can get management to observe these tests, they will want me to stop before I get to the end of the study because they have seen the same issues enough, after four or five users, to know they need to fix them. But if you cannot get management to observe, then a larger study will produce the stronger evidence management needs to believe the findings.

Large studies give you quantitative data that can be reported differently from small studies, which focus on qualitative findings.

Think of usability testing as hill climbing

Planning for usability testing is always influenced by the need to weigh the issues of time and money against the desired outcome of a usability study. If the desired outcome is to make progress by uncovering problems

See Rolf Molich's CUE (Comparative Usability Evaluation) studies at *www. dialogdesign.dk/cue.html*. Also see Spool and Schroeder, "Testing Web Sites: Five Users Is Nowhere Near Enough," 2001. For another view, see my counterargument at Barnum, "The 'Magic Number 5': Is It Enough for Web Testing?" 2002–2003.

Chapter 8 tells you all about working with the data from large studies, as well as small ones.

and fixing them—and the budget for testing is small—then the premise behind small studies holds true: better to test something than nothing.

If, however, your product is complex and your user base is large—and you have the time and budget to test with big numbers—then you will want to test with multiple users representing multiple goals.

See the sidebar, "Take a peek at a brief history of usability testing—then and now," for Lewis' contribution.

Hill climbing is actually a mathematical optimization technique, which is used to solve problems that have many potential solutions.

As you debate the issue of how many users you need for a usability test of a complex system, consider the view of James Lewis, one of the original proponents of small studies and a human factors engineer at IBM. Lewis reminds us that usability testing is like hill climbing: Every small study gets you farther up the hill. And there can be numerous paths up the hill. Even though different studies may take different routes up the hill and may discover different things along the way, Lewis says, "I can't think of any example from my experience when letting a usability test guide redesign led to a poorer design."

Summarizing Chapter 1

This chapter established the essentials for talking about usability, which include:

- a focus on users, not products—it's all about the user's experience, not the product's performance
- a grounding in the essential definitions of
  - usability, which encompasses:
    - the product's effectiveness and efficiency for users, as they work with the product
    - the elusive quality of user satisfaction, which is based on users' perceptions entirely
  - usability testing, which focuses on observing real users performing real tasks that are meaningful to them, and which can be classified into two types:
    - formative testing, done during product development to diagnose and fix problems
    - summative testing, done at the end of product development to confirm that the product meets requirements

- the key elements for conducting effective small studies, which include:
  - identifying a specific user profile for the study
  - creating scenarios that are task based and goal directed
  - encouraging users to think out loud as they work
  - testing again to confirm that the changes work for users
- the need for bigger studies
  - when the test is a summative evaluation and metrics are the goal, or
  - when more users are needed to see different user groups, or
  - when risk or personal safety is an issue, or
  - when management needs bigger numbers to be convinced that the results are representative of users
- the factors affecting the type of study you conduct, based on balancing your goals, management support, your budget, and your time
- the rationale for thinking of usability testing as hill climbing . . . pick your path and keep on climbing!

Testing here, there, everywhere

2

Do you need a lab to do usability testing? No.

Do you need to be with the user to do usability testing? No.

Do you need to be present at all to do usability testing? No.

If any of these answers surprise you, read on. If you haven't done usability testing yet because you thought you needed a lab or you needed to be present, you can start now without anything more than a pad and pen, the product, and the user.

These days, usability testing is easy and affordable because it doesn't require a fancy lab, expensive equipment, or even a dedicated room for testing. These days, you can do usability testing here, there, everywhere.

This chapter tells you how to do usability testing:

- in a lab with some
  - basic requirements
  - nice to have add-ons
  - specialized equipment for
    - eye tracking
    - testing smart phones and other mobile devices
    - testing interactive voice response (IVR) systems

Usability Testing Essentials. DOI: 10.1016/B978-0-12-375092-1.00002-7

- in any space, such as a conference room or office, that you can set up as an informal lab
- in the field
  - at a customer's site, in a conference room or office, or in customers' homes
  - in the "wild"—that is, wherever customers are—such as shopping malls, parks, driving or walking, and so forth
- remotely
  - with you observing in one location and the user in another location (called *moderated,* or *synchronous,* remote testing)
  - with the users working on their own without observation, but with equipment that tracks their transactions (called *unmoderated,* or *asynchronous,* remote testing)
  - with some new automated tools for quick feedback using small samples

There are many reasons to choose one technique over another, and certainly there are times when you will want to use a combination of techniques. To help you sort through the choices, I present each testing technique with its advantages and disadvantages.

Testing in a lab offers some benefits

Why would you want to test in a lab if you don't need one to do usability testing? Here are some reasons:

- It's there when you need it, saving the trouble of locating a space for testing, rounding up the equipment and supplies, and so forth.
- It demonstrates an organization's commitment to usability testing, which can be important for "selling" the value within a company.
- As a physical presence, it can be maintained and upgraded, particularly when a budget for the lab is authorized to support maintenance and improvements.
- It can be designed to create the ideal testing environment—one that's quiet, that provides space for observers, that provides the

basic requirements for testing, but also one that can accommodate any special requirements for testing your products, including requirements for testing with people with disabilities.

The bare essentials for testing in a lab

If you don't currently have a usability lab but you want to set one up, you need only a few things to get up and running. I call these the bare essentials:

- A *dedicated room* that can comfortably fit the user, the moderator, and perhaps one or two others as observers.
- A *desk or table and two (or more) chairs* for the participant, for the moderator, and for one or two observers.
- A *computer or laptop* (or whatever standard equipment is needed to support the product) and *Internet* access if you're testing a live website or web application.

Other equipment that's nice to have

Beyond the bare minimum, the choices you make about what you put into your lab will depend on how you plan to use it, what you plan to test in it, and how you plan to document the results. To go beyond the bare minimum, it's generally desirable to have these extras:

- A *camera* to record the session, which can be a webcam or a mounted camera. Recording the session can really help, especially when there is only one person conducting the session, since it gives you a way to revisit a particular problem that wasn't clear at the time of testing. Session recordings can also be used to make highlights to include in reports and presentations.
- A *microphone* that projects everything the participant says, as well as any sounds from the computer. This might not be needed if you are using a webcam with a built-in microphone. If you need an external mike, you might want one that sits on the desk or one that is portable and clips to the user's jacket or shirt.
- *More than one camera* to get different views from the session. If you have multiple cameras, you need a *mixing board.* If you're capturing what's on the computer screen, you need a *scan converter.* A typical setup is to make the computer screen the main image capture, with a small picture-in-picture of the participant in one corner.

- A *logging computer,* frequently a laptop, which can be used to take notes during the session. These notes can be created in Word, Excel, or other commonly used software.
- *Logging software,* such as Morae from TechSmith. With Morae and a small digital camera, you can record the session, log the findings, and make quick clips for reports and presentations.

In two-room labs, it's also nice to have

- *Headsets* in the control room that allow the team to hear the user while also being able to speak to each other at a low voice level. In situations where there is a lack of adequate soundproofing, this can be an important addition to the control room equipment.
- A *telephone or intercom* that the participant can use to call for help if he or she gets stuck. This might not be needed if the moderator sits with the participant, although it can provide a way for someone from the control room to call the moderator at the end of the session with questions from the team.
- A *white-noise generator in the participant's room* for noisy external environments or when soundproofing between the control room and the participant's room is not effective. Turning this device on before testing begins creates a background noise that is not distracting to the participant but that masks noises in the hallway or from the control room.

Specialized equipment you might need in certain situations

In addition to the basic equipment requirements and the nice-to-have add-ons for a usability lab, you might want to add specialized equipment to support testing of specific products. A complete list of specialized equipment is too long and varied to include here, but some commonly used types of specialized equipment include:

- eye-tracking equipment
- equipment for testing mobile devices
- equipment for testing IVR systems

Eye-tracking equipment shows you where users look

If you have the budget to expand your testing capabilities, you might want to purchase eye-tracking equipment. This type of equipment allows you to see exactly what users see and where they look by tracking their eye movements and the length of time they fixate on a certain part of a screen or a word, phrase, or object on the screen. A color-coded *heat map* of the page or screen shows the *hotspots*—those areas of the page that received the largest number of fixations and the longest time for fixations—for individual users and for all users in a study.

A sample results page (Figure 2.1) shows the heat map from a study of a corporate information page. The red color on the heat map shows the highest concentration for fixations, followed by yellow and then blue.

Nielsen, "F-Shaped Pattern for Reading Web Content," 2006

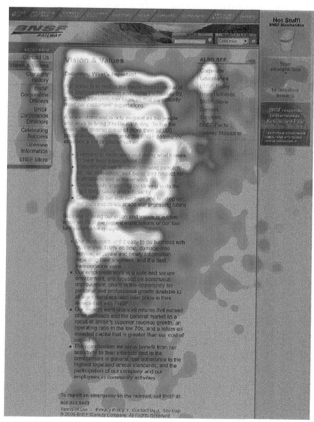

Figure 2.1 A heat map shows eye fixations on a website's corporate information page.

Web users scan content in an F-shaped reading pattern: two horizontal stripes followed by a vertical stripe:

For more on eye tracking, see Nielsen and Pernice, *EyeTracking Web Usability,* 2010. Also see *Usability News,* which reports research conducted by SURL, the Software Usability Research Laboratory at *www.surl.org/ usabilitynews*

- The first path of the eye is horizontally across the top of the web page.
- The second path is just below the top, again horizontally across the page.
- The third path is vertically down the left side of the page.

The days of putting users into uncomfortable headgear that required time-consuming calibrations are now behind us. Today's eye-tracking equipment works via a device within or attached to the participant's computer. An example of one eye-tracking setup is shown in Figure 2.2. The hardware is attached below the computer monitor. The software performs a quick calibration of the participant's eye-gaze movements, and the results of a study are presented in those handy heat maps, as well as a number of other reporting options you can choose.

Figure 2.2 EyeTech's eye-tracking device attached to the participant's monitor displays the results with a heat map.

Costs for equipment are coming down as the competition in this area increases. However, costs are still quite high and can run in the US$30,000 range. Weekly and monthly rental options have made the price and access to the equipment more affordable.

Equipment for testing mobile devices is helpful

Testing mobile and other handheld devices requires specialized equipment to hold the device in place or keep the device within the range of a camera so that you can capture everything in focus. Some labs have a camera mounted in the ceiling directly over the user's workspace, which can be used for testing mobile or other handheld devices.

You don't need a camera mounted in the ceiling, however, since specialized equipment is available to cradle the handheld device in a fixed position, or a camera mount can be attached to the device to allow the user to move more naturally.

If you happen to have a document camera already, like the one shown in Figure 2.3, you can use this for a mobile study. In this arrangement, the user gets to move naturally, but within a certain range, while working with the device. From the control room, you can see how the device is captured (Figure 2.4).

Figure 2.3 A participant holds a mobile device under the document camera.

Figure 2.4 The document camera captures what is on the screen. In this setup, the test facilitator uses a mixing board to select the document camera input as the main image and the inset image of the participant working with the device.

This solution is described in detail at *www.gotomobile.com/archives/ diy-gotomobiles-mobile-cam*

You can also build your own solution from off-the-shelf products at a local hardware, camera, and/or electronics store. Figure 2.5 shows one example.

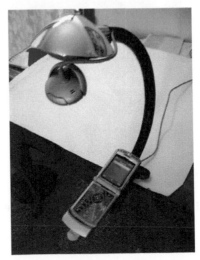

Figure 2.5 A do-it-yourself solution for testing a mobile device can be built using locally available parts.

Equipment for testing IVR systems lets you hear what the system says

When testing an IVR system, you need to be able to hear what the system says—for example, "Press or say 1 to find out your credit card balance"—as well as what the participant says. Without special equipment, you can use a telephone with a speakerphone so that the session records the system prompts and the participant's responses. But using a speakerphone makes voice recognition problematic, and it may not reflect typical user experience.

Equipment to test IVR systems, specifically, eliminates the need to put a phone on speaker. The example shown in Figure 2.6 takes signals from the phone and the IVR system and connects them to the logging and/or recording computer. Everyone can hear both sides of the communication and you can record the caller and the transaction. An Internet search for this type of device will bring up other product options.

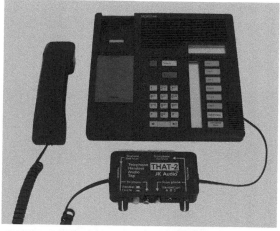

Figure 2.6 This device (*bottom center*) lets you connect the phone and the IVR system to your logging and/or recording computer.

If you don't have a permanent space for a lab, you can store any specialized equipment you need along with your standard equipment. The advantage of having a dedicated space is that all of your equipment can be up and running, so it's there when you need it.

If you don't yet have a permanent lab but you want to build or equip one, I next review some common lab configurations and options to give you a sense of what you can do with a small budget or a large one.

Formal labs can cost a lot, or not

Usability labs come in all shapes and sizes. They can cost a lot or not so much to build and equip. They can be one room, two rooms, or three rooms. Two-room labs have one room for the participant and another room, often called the *control room,* for the test team and observers. Three-room labs have a separate room for observers, often called the *executive viewing room.*

Back in 1994, when we opened our first lab at Southern Polytechnic, it was a two-room lab funded as part of an IBM Million Dollar Total Quality Management grant. The price tag to build the space and equip the room was US$100,000. I can't imagine that anyone spends that kind of money today. Comparable quotes today are in the US$25,000 range, based on what it costs if you contract with one of the lab-building companies.

Today, you can build or equip a lab yourself for far less. In 2009 we built a two-room lab for students (shown in Figure 2.7), and the equipment cost was US$6,600, as listed in the following table.

Figure 2.7 This two-room lab has a one-way mirror between the rooms. You're seeing the glass side from the control room.

Equipment	Vendor	Cost (US$)	Quantity	Total (US$)
Desktop computers	Sun Microsystems	934.72	2	1,869.44
RAM upgrade	Dell	64.90	4	259.60
20" Viewsonic VG2030WM	Dell	226.87	4	907.48
Watchport/V camera and TrackerPod	Eagletron	315.98	1	315.98
Four-camera package DM-STAR4i-PK1	DVRMaster.com	999.00	1	999.00
4' × 8' privacy glass and installation	Atlanta Glass Experts	710.00	1	710.00
Miscellaneous cables	Computer supply store	200.00	1	200.00
Logging software	Morae	1,400.00	1	1,400.00
Total				**$6,661.50**

One room provides a place for the participant to test the product. The other room is where the test administrator or team observes the participant and records the session. The glass wall in the space between the two rooms is called a *one-way mirror* because it's a mirror on the side where the participant sits and glass on the side where the administrator sits.

Figure 2.8 shows the schematic drawing of a three-room usability lab. The drawing provides the basic configuration for the lab shown in Figure 2.9. The participant room is the first room on the left, with the control room in the middle and the executive viewing room on the right. The executive viewing room has a clear glass opening in the wall that allows observers to see into the control room in the middle and then beyond to the participant room. Because all of the rooms are connected, people in the executive viewing room have direct line of sight to the participant.

When space considerations don't allow for this arrangement, the third room may be located somewhere else, typically close by but not directly connected to the lab. In this arrangement, observers watch and listen

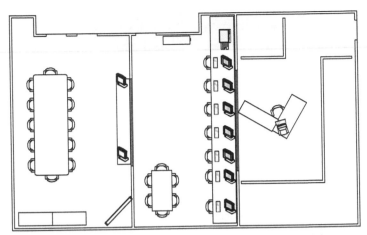

Figure 2.8 This schematic drawing of a three-room usability lab shows all three rooms connected.

Figure 2.9 The three-room usability lab at Southern Polytechnic, which is based on the schematic drawing in Figure 2.8, shows the view from the executive viewing room into the control room and beyond to the participant room.

to the participant via one or more flat-screen monitors in a conference room or theater-style arrangement.

Because the participant room is quite large and equipped with modular wall panels, this room can be configured to suit different testing situations. Figure 2.10 shows how we converted the room into a living room for a usability study of a digital self-install kit, in which a home cable subscriber/participant was asked to install the cable box.

Figure 2.10 This participant room is set up for a usability study of a digital cable box self-installation in a home environment. The author/moderator is in red.

Some labs also have a separate reception area, which provides a place to meet and greet the participants. When you can get it, this dedicated space can really help sort out how to handle the arrival of participants without having them inadvertently walk in on you during testing.

Informal labs can be set up anywhere at very little cost

An informal lab may be nothing more than a room you can use. Perhaps it's a multipurpose room that is used for meetings but can also be reserved for testing. If it already has a desk or a conference table in it, all you need to add is a laptop. Using software such as Morae, which captures and records the session with one or more small digital cameras, can reduce a great deal of the equipment cost to a very manageable size and budget.

You don't need the one-way mirror, mounted cameras, or any of the nice-to-have extras, so don't let the lack of space stop you from testing. You can do it anywhere.

If you don't have any space, you can rent space. Market research firms typically rent out their space, which already has the one-way mirror and two-room arrangement for the observers and the participants. In some cases a local usability lab will rent its space when it has some unscheduled days available. For very basic space, you can rent a meeting or conference room in a local hotel.

You can also take your test equipment on the road.

Field testing gets you into the world of your users

Up to this point, we've been looking at how and why you might want to test in a lab or in a multipurpose space at your office or nearby in rented space. Although a permanent lab offers the advantage of being set up and available when you need it and a multipurpose room gives you the ability to have what you need for testing in a handy stored location, you can also take your usability study on the road. When you do this, it's called *field testing*.

Field testing gets you out of the office and into the places where your users are. There's a lot of good that can come from seeing your users in their environments, as it helps fill in what's missing in the artificial setup of the lab.

You can get out into the field with nothing more than a laptop, or sometimes not even that. You can also get more elaborate with a portable lab, which can be packed into a suitcase and taken on a plane or put in the trunk of a car for easy transportation to the field. A portable lab can be purchased from one of a number of lab vendors or put together yourself with the elements you need, such as a webcam for recording the participant; software to log, record, and review the sessions; and whatever equipment the participant needs to do the tasks, such as a laptop or tablet PC. In some cases, you won't need to provide the equipment for the participants, because they will be using their own.

Figure 2.11 shows our portable lab, which was built in-house and packed into a suitcase fitted with padding to let us take it on a plane. When we get to our destination, we unpack and set up the lab in a few minutes, using whatever space is available (Figure 2.12).

Figure 2.11 Our portable lab packs into a suitcase.

Figure 2.12 In this portable lab setup, the author/moderator is sitting next to the participant. The logger on her laptop is using Morae to log and record the session.

Advantages of field testing

Here are some of the advantages of field testing over lab testing:

- Because you go to the user rather than having the user come to you, you get to see and learn about the actual context of use of your product in the following situations:
  - In an office or home context, which gives you an understanding of
    - The workspace, lighting conditions, access to documentation, type of computer used and whatever else is on it, Internet

connectivity, and other aspects that have a potential impact on the user's experience, as well as distractions and interruptions that the user faces.
- The artifacts that support users in their tasks, such as sticky notes on the user's monitor and personal job aids that help the user remember certain tasks or functions.
○ In "the wild" (the space that encompasses wherever the user goes), which gives you an understanding of
- The impact of noise and distractions such as other tasks the user is doing at the same time and interruptions for multiple reasons.
- The effect of conditions such as visibility in bright, natural light, or in the dark, and so forth. This is particularly helpful when testing the usability of handheld devices or kiosks in public spaces.
- If you do both lab testing and field testing, you get to compare the results of lab testing to field testing, using the same task-based scenarios and paying particular attention to any environmental differences in the results.

Disadvantages of field testing

Field testing has its limitations, though, which you need to consider when you are thinking of taking your testing on the road. Here are some of them:

- You cannot control the environment, so it is difficult to get reliable data on timed tasks.
- You cannot remove yourself from the environment as you can in lab testing in a two-room setup.
- You might not be able to hold the user's undivided attention, since the distractions of the workplace or home can interfere.
- You might not have the privacy to support think-aloud processes, or the participant might not feel comfortable thinking out loud when others are within hearing range.
- You typically cannot test the product with as many users, since the company you are visiting may be unwilling to allow for many disruptions among its employees, or you might have to travel from place to place within a city or between cities to get to your users.

- It costs more because of the additional time and expense required to be away from the office. And, when you make home visits, it generally requires that people go in pairs for safety and liability reasons.

- When field testing is a summative evaluation that takes place after the product has launched or just before launch, you cannot do much of anything with the findings except keep a log for the next upgrade or the next new product development cycle.

- When field testing is exploratory, in that you are gathering requirements for a new product or you are conducting early proto-type testing, you will have more data than you would normally get in lab testing, because you also need to analyze the environmental data you observed. The additional time required to do the post-testing analysis needs to be factored into the process.

The list of disadvantages is longer than the list of advantages, which could account for the fact that field testing is done less often than lab testing. However, there are huge gains to be gotten from field testing, not the least of which is the education of the team about the real world of your users, tasks, and environments. Clearly, the benefits can outweigh the costs when the need to get a deep understanding of the user's experience in the user's world is critical to product success.

But what do you do when you can't bring the user to you and you can't go to the user?

Remote testing extends your reach to your users

Remote testing provides options and opportunities to learn from users wherever they might be. Methods for remote testing are expanding rapidly, as are the terms people use when they talk about remote testing. However, it comes down to two main concepts:

For more on remote testing, see Bolt and Tulathimutte, *Remote Research: Real Users, Real Time, Real Research,* 2010.

- *Moderated testing* means having a moderator "present" when the testing takes place.

- *Unmoderated testing* means using a web-based application to conduct the testing.

Tools to support remote testing, whether moderated or unmoderated, are commercially available. As well, tools designed for other types of remote communication, such as for meetings, are also used. And, in some cases, companies have designed their own in-house tools.

Moderated remote testing is synchronous

Synchronous means that you and the participant are connected in real time.

Moderated, also called *synchronous,* remote testing is very much like lab testing. The significant difference is the spatial distance. In moderated remote testing, the moderator, test participant, and observers are not physically in the same space. In some cases, the observers may be in many different locations.

Advantages of moderated remote testing

Here are some reasons why moderated remote testing can be a good choice:

- You can't go to your users, either because you don't have the resources or the time, so you connect them to you.

- You can reach a diverse user population that is geographically (including internationally) dispersed.

- Your observers, maybe even your team members, aren't able to come to you, so you bring the participants to them.

- Your participants are unwilling to commit the time, even when they are local, to travel to your location, but they are willing to participate from their own locations. This is often the case when you are recruiting high-income or highly specialized participants.

- Even when your participants are local and willing to come to the lab, you want to learn how your product works in their environment, on their computer, with their browser, and so forth, but you are not able to arrange to go to them.

- Your testing schedule extends over a period of time (a week or more, perhaps) rather than in the compressed schedule of a day or two in the usability lab. This flexibility means that individual tests can be set up whenever users are available and within a broader timeframe.

Ethnio by Bolt/Peters (*http://ethnio.com*) is one of the recruiting companies that does this work using a web-based application.

- You can recruit at very little or no expense, and very quickly, by creating an online form, which you can set up to alert you as soon as someone completes it. If the respondent qualifies for the study and you are both available, you can conduct the study immediately. Or you can work with a company that does the recruiting for you.

- When you don't have a lab, moderated remote testing lets you get started quickly and at far less cost than establishing a lab.
- When you do have a lab but you're working with an out-of-town client or a widely distributed team, it can be cheaper to test remotely because of the cost savings for your client or team to stay where they are and the cost savings in the smaller stipend paid to participants, based on the convenience factor for them.

Disadvantages of moderated remote testing

So, what's not to like about the option of moderated remote testing? Several things:

- You can't see the participant and the application at the same time (in most cases). This is a significant drawback, since much can be gained from direct observation of the user while he or she is working. Even if you start off seeing the user via a webcam, when you switch to seeing the interface via the desktop-sharing feature, you typically lose the webcam view of the participant.
- Moderating a remote test is harder because you have to establish rapport without being able to see the participant. It's not a good way to start if you're new to moderating.

  For more on moderating usability tests, see Dumas and Loring, Moderating Usability Tests: Principles and Practices for Interacting, 2008.

- Getting the materials to the participant in advance has to be planned and managed. Instructions need to be included about when or how to open the documents. These instructions also need to explain how to access the session and/or download the appropriate plug-in.
- The setup time is longer and can be problematic. If the testing takes place on someone's computer at work, the company firewall could block access, or the company might not allow the participant to download the application. You might be able to address these issues in advance, which is why you need the extended setup time. But even when you address the setup issues, other problems can crop up, which you might not be able to fix. If you can't fix them, everyone leaves the session frustrated.
- You are at the mercy of the Internet. No matter how much planning and testing you do ahead of time, you will likely experience problems. Anecdotally, I have heard that 1 in 10 sessions will have some type of technical glitch. I've also heard that some systems bog down when there are too many observers. The state of the art isn't perfect, and there are many things beyond your control.

How to conduct a moderated remote test

If you decide that the advantages outweigh the disadvantages, you can conduct a moderated remote test using any of the popular online meeting tools, such as GoToMeeting or WebEx. With Voice over Internet Protocol (VoIP), these online meeting applications provide a sometimes free and generally easy way to moderate sessions from afar, using many of the same techniques that you would use in person.

That means you can ask the participant to think out loud while working through a scenario. You can see and record the participant's actions, either by having the participant share his or her screen with you or by sharing your desktop with the participant. You can record a video of the participant's activity within the application, along with the audio of the communication between the participant and moderator. The recording can be exported to a WMV file, which can be converted to another program for editing or played in Windows Media Player or similar applications without conversion. The session results can then be distributed broadly to anyone with an interest.

The technology to support moderated remote testing is getting better all the time, providing you with the capability to capture keystrokes, mouse clicks, and so forth, as well as providing built-in editing capabilities for video highlights. A quick Internet search will likely bring up a list of the companies and tools offering these products and services.

Unmoderated remote testing is asynchronous

Asynchronous means that you and the participant do not need to be present at the same time.

Unmoderated remote testing is also called *asynchronous* or *automated* testing. An application captures the screen, keystrokes, mouse clicks, navigation path, drop-off rates, and so forth and collates these data into a report. Commercial web-based applications include Keynote, User Zoom, and Relevant View. They share the capability to set up predefined questions at specific points in the user's activities or when a user takes a particular action.

Advantages of unmoderated remote testing

Numbers are impressive. Because of the quantity of responses that can be obtained, numbers *validate* questionnaire responses, errors, and so forth. Numbers *persuade* everyone involved that identified problems need to be fixed. So, when testing with 5 or 8 or 10 users is clearly not enough to convince management that changes need to be made, unmoderated remote testing can supply the convincing evidence.

Beyond the benefit of numbers, here are some other reasons for doing unmoderated remote testing:

For more on unmoderated remote testing, see Albert, Tullis, and Tedesco, *Beyond the Usability Lab: Conducting Large-Scale Online User Experience Studies,* 2010.

- You can do competitive analyses of your competitors' websites to see how your site stacks up against the competition.

- You can do benchmark testing to see whether target performance measures are being met.

- You can analyze participant comments by sorting and collating them thematically.

Disadvantages of unmoderated remote testing

Here's a list of reasons why you might not want to do unmoderated remote testing:

- You can't *see* the participants. This is the same problem shared by remote moderated testing.

- You can't *talk* to the participants. This is a problem unique to unmoderated remote testing, and it is a significant limitation of the method. Although you do get subjective feedback in the form of answers to the questions provided during and after the interaction, you can't ask any follow-up questions to pursue a deeper understanding of the issues.

- You can't confirm the *reasons* for participants' actions. You can learn that participants drop off at a certain point in the website or fail to use a particular feature, but you can't determine why. Again, the limitation is that you can't ask them.

- You can't ask complicated, multipart questions or provide complicated scenarios. Generally, the scenarios have to be straightforward and simple, as do the questions about the user's experience after the scenarios.

- It's expensive. You need a big enough budget to cover the testing and analysis for hundreds, even thousands, of tests.

New methods push the envelope on remote testing

The new kid on the block comes in the form of simplified remote tools, some that provide video feedback of the sessions and others that provide short survey responses to a burning question or two. These are either very cheap or available for a free trial.

Automated tools to watch people use your website

For Mac users, there's
Silverbackapp.com

In this category, there are several companies up and running, including UserTesting.com, OpenHallway.com, and Loop11.com. These are web-based, unmoderated testing services, but the twist is that the user's voice is recorded, along with the interface screens data. In some cases, participants are recruited from your screener. In other cases, you recruit the participants and give them the link to the session.

To take one—UserTesting.com—as an example, you complete a questionnaire that says what the demographics of your users are, how many users you want, what tasks you want them to perform, and a few other details. The participants are recruited as soon as you sign up and submit the information. They are instructed to think out loud as they work.

When they are finished, they complete a quick survey, and you get the survey responses and a recording of the session, including mouse clicks and keystrokes, in a 15-minute Flash video. You get results very fast, typically within an hour. The cost is very low. You'll have to check the website for current pricing for this one and the other companies offering this type of service.

How would you use this type of unmoderated remote testing service? Let's say your team has a design question and needs to know what works for users.

Set up a quick study.

The advantage of using one of these new tools is that you can get a very quick answer to your question for very little cost. The disadvantage is that the sessions are typically short, and you can't interview the participants to probe more deeply. However, used in conjunction with moderated remote or lab testing, these tools can increase your understanding of your users' experience so that you can build that knowledge into the product as it is developed.

Automated tools to get fast feedback in development

Another emerging set of web-based tools supports the need to get quick responses to issues of information architecture, website look and feel, and design. Two of these, developed by Optimal Workshop, are

- Chalkmark, which lets you do "micro" usability tests of a prototype to determine the "findability" of information. Participants are asked to perform a simple task. The combined results are displayed in the sample screen shown in Figure 2.13.

- Treejack, which provides feedback on the information architecture of a website. Participants are asked to perform a few tasks, which can be randomized from a database of tasks. Figure 2.14 shows a sample task with the results page indicating where people looked for the information on the screen.

Optimal Workshop is the development arm of a New Zealand-based usability consultancy, Optimal Usability.

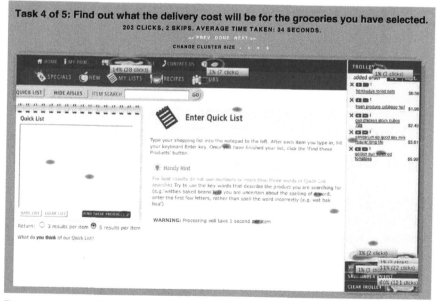

Figure 2.13 A question in Chalkmark asks participants to choose the path to find out how much the delivery costs will be for the groceries selected. The results show the average time on task and the places where people clicked.

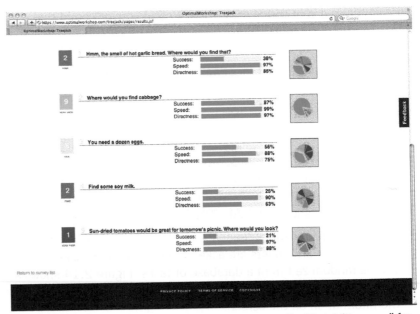

Figure 2.14 Treejack sample shopping task results give you the "findability scores" for the overall structure and for each task based on the three variables of success, speed, and directness.

For more tools you can use, a quick Internet search will likely produce a number of choices and options.

Choosing the right method is a balancing act

In the best of all possible worlds, you do not have to choose one usability testing method over another. Moderated, face-to-face testing is great for starters, but if you can't do this type of usability test and you have a website or web application to test, then one of the quick, inexpensive methods could get you under way. If you can include at least one other method, you can increase your confidence in the findings. Better still, include one of the larger automated testing options to get metrics.

All of these options depend, of course, on budget and support. But it's a great problem to have to choose from so many options, with more coming along all the time.

Summarizing Chapter 2

This chapter has given you options for testing and the advantages and disadvantages for choosing one option over another, as well as possibilities for combining options.

In case there was any doubt, I emphasized that there is no need to have a usability lab to do excellent usability testing. All you need is a pen and paper—or, more likely, a laptop computer—and you are ready to test. You can find a space at or near your company or client, or you can go on the road and set up in your client's or customer's office or in the homes or offices of your users.

If you want to set up a usability lab, the requirements include:

- the bare essentials of a dedicated room with a desk, two chairs, and the product
- nice-to-have add-ons, such as a webcam, multiple cameras, a microphone, and a logging computer
- for two-room setups, headsets for people in the control room, a telephone or intercom to communicate between the rooms, and a white-noise generator to drown out noises outside the participant's room

If your product or situation requires more equipment, a few additional types of specialized equipment could come in handy, such as

- eye-tracking equipment for data on where users look and for how long
- off-the-shelf or do-it-yourself equipment to test handheld devices
- equipment to support testing IVR systems

I also reviewed lab configurations and costs and covered these topics:

- Labs can cost a lot or a little to build.
- Options for room designs include one room, two rooms, or three rooms.
  - Two-room labs often have a one-way mirror between the participant room and the control/observation room.
  - Three-room labs have an executive viewing room, which can be directly connected to the other two rooms or nearby.

○ A dedicated reception area is also very nice, since it defines a place for participants to go on arrival for check-in.

Of course, you don't need a dedicated lab space—any space can be used for testing—and you don't even need a physical space, since you can go to your users. This is called field testing. Field testing options give you the advantage of

- going to the user rather than having the user come to you
- observing the user's actual environment to see what the user's world is like
- going "into the wild" with the user—out in the open where the user moves through the world

Field testing has its limitations:

- You cannot control the environment. Technical problems can, and do, happen more often than you would like. And there's little or nothing you can do about them.
- Distractions can disrupt or derail the participant, whether the testing takes place in the user's home or office or "in the wild."
- You generally cannot get to as many participants as you can in a lab setting.
- The cost of testing goes up because of travel time and expenses associated with reaching users in their locations.

However, there is a solution that addresses the limitations of field testing: remote testing, which is categorized in two ways:

- Moderated remote testing, which works pretty much like lab testing except that the user is not with you in your space and you can't see the user. But you can hear the user and talk to the user while the user is working, and you can record whatever the user is doing on his or her computer. This type of testing connects you to your users without the cost of travel and at your users' convenience.
- Unmoderated remote testing, which lets you test anytime without the need to be present. That's why it's also called *automated* testing. Companies that offer this service can set up the study and give you the results from hundreds or even thousands of participants.

Unmoderated studies are great for competitive analysis and bench-marking. They're expensive, so you need to be able to justify the added cost of using this method. Although you get a lot of data, you can't talk to the users yourself, so you can't follow up with them about questions you might have on the findings.

New tools are expanding our testing options and bringing down the costs in lots of interesting ways. Companies providing these services include web-based tools for

- recruiting and testing, with fast Flash video results
- information on "findability" issues, with results pages showing where users clicked and how often
- feedback on the information architecture of your website, showing navigation paths and success/failure rates

This sounds like a lot to take in. But consider this: You don't need *anything* to get started and to do excellent work. So, don't let anything stop you from testing.

Big U and little u usability

3

Up to this point, I've focused on the essentials of usability testing. To do that, I started with some definitions to give us a common vocabulary for talking about usability and usability testing. And I reviewed testing options, which include testing in a lab, testing wherever you can grab a space, and testing remotely, with or without you present.

Now it's time to fit usability testing into the big picture of user-centered design. This chapter opens up your toolkit to see where usability testing fits and what other tools you can use to support your understanding of your user's experience.

Introducing big U and little u usability

If you think of usability testing as "little u" usability, then you know it's the activity that focuses on observing and learning from your users who are working with your product to perform tasks that are real and meaningful to them. Even when it is done remotely, with or without you being present, this concept holds true.

Usability Testing Essentials. DOI: 10.1016/B978-0-12-375092-1.00003-9

So, what is "Big U" usability? This is the umbrella term that encompasses usability testing and a host of other tools that support your understanding of the user experience and the process of creating usable, useful, and desirable products.

Ginny Redish, a well-known usability consultant, put it this way in her keynote address at the 2004 conference of the Usability Professionals' Association: *Big U usability* is everything that goes into "creating a product that works for people. It encompasses the entire process and includes all the techniques in the usability specialist's toolkit. *Little u usability* is associated with usability testing."

This chapter focuses on Big U usability, the tools and techniques that you can use *before* development begins, *during* development, and *after* the product goes public.

After giving you a look inside your toolkit for the Big U tools you can use, I focus on one tool—*heuristic evaluation* (also called *expert review*)—not only because it is such a popular tool but also because it makes a great companion to usability testing.

If you are not currently using any of the tools in your UCD toolkit, or you are doing some usability work but want to expand your use of the tools, I end the chapter with some strategies you can use to justify the costs of applying Big U usability to improve your users' experience.

Using a user-centered design process

ISO 13407, Human-Centered Design Processes for Interactive Systems, provides a definition of the range of work that usability professionals do in support of user-centered design. This standard is being updated to focus on user experience and to align more closely with other usability standards. It will be renumbered ISO 9241-210.

The result of using the tools in your toolkit throughout development is a product that reflects user-centered design, or UCD.

As Figure 3.1 shows, the user-centered design process can be divided into three phases:

- analysis
- development
- post-release

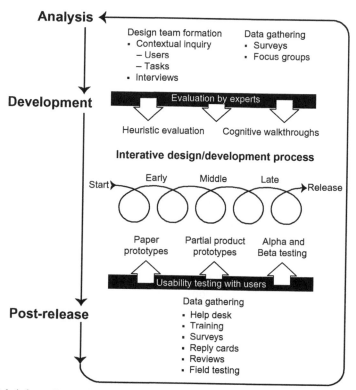

Figure 3.1 Information and user and expert feedback flow into product development with a user-centered design process.

At each phase, information by and about users is central to learning what to design, how to design it, and how to improve the next release in a cycle of continuous product improvement. Some evaluation techniques involve usability experts "inspecting" the product for usability issues. Other techniques involve gathering information that already exists within the organization. Some of these tasks begin before development begins; others after the product launches.

The arrows going around the outside of the illustration indicate that the process repeats as new products go into development. The looping spiral in the middle of the illustration, which was also shown in Chapter 1, indicates that the process is iterative, with input from experts and users feeding into the development cycle.

Opening your toolkit and seeing what's there

Your UCD toolkit is full of techniques you can use to learn about your users. Here's a brief description of some of these tools, organized by the place these tools are typically used in product development.

Analysis tools

Analysis tools are typically used before development begins. This is the stage in which you gather product requirements based on information you can obtain about users, tasks, and their environments. Some of this information may already be available from other parts of the organization. Your first step is to seek out this information from the relevant organizations. If it doesn't exist, you may want to generate the information yourself or in conjunction with the relevant organization. This information can come from the following sources:

- *Market research*—often conducted by your sales and marketing organization. Techniques commonly used for this phase include:
  - *Focus groups*—which are led by a facilitator who probes the group's participants for attitudes toward the company and its products, as well as their experience with competitor products. New features on the drawing board can be sounded out for potential acceptance or resistance.
  - *Surveys*—which can generate a large response from customers or potential customers. Web-based survey instruments, such as SurveyMonkey and Zoomerang, make surveys easy to create, distribute, and analyze.
  - *Blogs*—which can be used to solicit customer feedback on specific topics or potential new designs.
- *Internal information about users*—often available from one or more of the following sources:
  - *Technical support/customer support, also called the help desk*—which handles phone calls and Live Chat on your website. The people who respond to these calls and queries may have a system to track the types of problems users have. If they do not have a formal system, they will certainly know anecdotally where the users' "pain points" are.

○ *Training for internal users or for customers*—This group is charged with training, so the people in this group know what's hardest to teach others about the product and can also share what makes users most anxious about learning to use the product.

○ *Technical communicators*—This group is charged with writing the documentation, help, and embedded assistance, so the people in this group know what aspects of the product are hardest to document.

○ *Sales and field support*—This group hears what customers want when they are shopping for products, as well as what they like and don't like about your products and what the competition does better or worse.

• *Site visits/contextual inquiry*—getting out into the world where your users live or work, so that you can study your users' environment, gather requirements for new product development, learn what users are already using (including competitor products), and understand how your product can fit within their processes and their environment. Site visits can take many forms, but common practices for site visits include:

○ *Interviews*—which can be structured, with a planned set of questions, or semi-structured, with some core questions that can start the conversation.

○ *Shadowing a user for a day*—in which you follow the user around to understand a "day in the life" of the user.

○ *Critical-incident technique*—which is used in situations where you can't observe people doing their job because it involves privileged information or is dangerous or it doesn't happen very often. Instead, you ask them to describe the situation or show you how they do something in the situation.

○ *Scenarios and role-playing activities*—in which you ask your target user to step into a situation and walk through what happens. This technique can be used in place of, or along with, the critical-incident technique. In some cases, you may want to play the part of the customer in the role play.

Excellent resources for conducting site visits can be found in Courage and Baxter, *Understanding Your Users*, 2005; Kuniavsky, *Observing the User Experience*, 2003; Hackos and Redish, *User and Task Analysis for Interface Design*, 1998; and Beyer and Holtzblatt, *Contextual Design*, 1998.

Development tools

One or more of the following tools are typically used during development, although some of these tools can be used before development starts or after the product releases. These tools are used at various stages of development, and some are used iteratively throughout development.

Popular web applications for remote card sorting include WebSort (*www.websort.net*) and OptimalSort (*www. optimalworkshop.com*).

- *Card sorting*—a tool that is generally used early in development to learn your users' preferences for and understanding of the information architecture of your product, as well as their understanding of the terminology. This activity can be done in person or remotely, using a web-based application.

- *Participatory design*—a development strategy that involves potential users in the design process. In some cases, these users are asked to review a product in development and provide feedback; in other cases, they are actively involved in generating design concepts.

There's more about heuristic evaluation later in this chapter.

- *Heuristic evaluation*—an expert review, or inspection, of a product, using a specific set of guidelines or, in some cases, in a more loosely defined way.

- *Cognitive walkthrough*—another type of inspection, in which a team member, standing in for the user, walks through a prototype of the product to identify issues that affect ease of learning and related issues.

- *Usability testing*—the tool that is the focus of this book.

Post-release tools

These tools are typically used after the product has launched. They can be used to assess the effectiveness of the product in the user's environment of use, for requirements gathering for the next release, or for new product development. These tools include:

Chapter 2 has more about field testing.

- *On-site usability testing*—testing that is done after the product has been released, to validate the usability in the user's environment. This type of testing is called *field testing*.

- *Server log data analysis*—an automated tool that runs behind the scenes and around the clock. This tool provides an analysis of your website and can generate a lot of data, such as pages visited, customer drop-offs, fluctuations in the volume of traffic, and so forth. Google Analytics is a popular tool for this task, and it is free.

- *Longitudinal study*—usability testing that takes place over time through repeated contact with users. Such contact can start with test participants while a product is in development, or even before development begins, and continue after the product is in the user's environment. Or it can involve a smaller timeframe of a week or two. A popular type of longitudinal study is called a *diary study*. It is typically conducted remotely. Users are asked to keep a diary of their activities surrounding their use of the product. The artifacts from the study can be text, pictures, survey responses, audio recordings, and more. This tool is particularly effective for understanding usability "in the wild," such as with users and their mobile devices.

For a pictorial representation of these tools and many others in your toolkit, along with the documents that reflect the results of using these tools, see Figure 3.2. For more information on how to use these tools, here are two great resources:

- *Usability.gov*, the official U.S. Government website managed by the U.S. Department of Health and Human Services: *www.usability.gov/methods/index.html*
- The resources page on the website for UPA, the Usability Professionals' Association: *upassoc.org/usability_resources/guidelines_and_methods/index.html*

With all of these tools in your toolkit, you can see that you have plenty to choose from. Of course, all of these tools have their place and their usefulness, but one tool besides usability testing—heuristic evaluation—is picked above all others in the toolkit, so I want to tell you more about this tool and how to use it.

Choosing heuristic evaluation from the toolkit

When user experience professionals we surveyed to learn which tools they use most often, the table on page 61 summarizes what they said.

Although informal usability testing comes first in the list and was tied with heuristic/expert review for the top tool used in 2007, the surprising change from 2007 to 2009 is that informal testing dropped several places in 2009. However, if you combine the new category of remote, unmoderated usability testing in the 2009 survey with the categories for remote, moderated testing and formal lab testing, you

Figure 3.2 Here's a pictorial array of tools in your UCD toolkit.

Techniques used by usability professionals	Usage 2007	Usage 2009
Informal usability testing	77%	68%
Heuristic/expert review	77%	74%
User research, such as interviews and surveys	74%	75%
Interface/interaction design	73%	70%
Creating prototypes (wireframes or low-fidelity)	73%	69%
Personas and user profiles	66%	61%
Requirements gathering	63%	63%
Information architecture	63%	61%
Task analysis	60%	58%
Usability testing (in a lab)	54%	54%
Usability testing (remote, moderated)	42%	42%
Usability testing (remote, unmoderated)	NA	18%

Data from the *Usability Professionals' Association 2009 Salary Survey*, which includes questions on "Techniques" and compares the results from the 2007 survey with the results from the 2009 survey.

see that usability testing comes out as the technique of first choice for usability practitioners. But it is in close competition with heuristic evaluation. You may find yourself reaching for this tool as well, which is why I devote space here to tell you what you need to know about how to use it.

Conducting a heuristic evaluation

Heuristic evaluation is a review or "inspection" of a product by experts. Typically this means usability experts, but it can also mean double expertise: in both usability and the product domain. Heuristics are a set of principles, or "rules of thumb," used by the experts to inspect an interface in search of violations of the heuristics.

See Molich and Nielsen, "Improving a Human-Computer Dialogue," 1990. You can access Nielsen's revised heuristics at www.useit.com/papers/heuristic/heuristic_list.html

Jakob Nielsen and Rolf Molich devised the original set of heuristics, which Nielsen revised to include the following 10 guidelines, or rules of thumb, for usability:

1. Visibility of system status	The system should always keep users informed about what is going on through appropriate feedback within reasonable time.
2. Match between system and the real world	The system should speak the users language, with words, phrases, and concepts familiar to the user rather than system-oriented terms. Follow real-world conventions, making information appear in a natural and logical order.
3. User control and freedom	Users often choose system functions by mistake and will need a clearly marked "emergency exit" to leave the unwanted state without having to go through an extended dialogue. Support undo and redo.
4. Consistency and standards	Users should not have to wonder whether different words, situations, or actions mean the same thing. Follow platform conventions.
5. Error prevention	Even better than good error messages is a careful design which prevents a problem from occurring in the first place. Either eliminate error-prone conditions or check for them and present users with a confirmation option before they commit to the action.
6. Recognition rather than recall	Minimize the user's memory load by making objects, actions, and options visible. The user should not have to remember information from one part of the dialogue to another. Instructions for use of the system should be visible or easily retrievable whenever appropriate.
7. Flexibility and efficiency of use	Accelerators—unseen by the novice user—may often speed up the interaction for the expert user such that the system can cater to both inexperienced and experienced users. Allow users to tailor frequent actions.
8. Aesthetic and minimalist design	Dialogues should not contain information that is irrelevant or rarely needed. Every extra unit of information in a dialogue competes with the relevant units of information and diminishes their relative visibility.

9. Help users recognize, diagnose, and recover from errors	Error messages should be expressed in plain language (no codes), precisely indicate the problem, and constructively suggest a solution.
10. Help and documentation	Even though it is better if the system can be used without documentation, it may be necessary to provide help and documentation. Any such information should be easy to search, focused on the user's task, list concrete steps to be carried out, and not be too large.

Although these 10 heuristics were originally established for the inspection of software, they have been widely adopted, and adapted as needed, for any sort of product. There are now sets of heuristics for the web, for specific types of products, and for specialized user groups.

See, for instance, Chisnell, Redish, and Lee, "New Heuristics for Understanding Older Adults as Web Users," 2006. For other sets of heuristics, see *www.stcsig.org/ usability/topics/heuristic.html*

Conducting a formal evaluation

If you want to be formal about it, you will probably follow Nielsen's guidelines for conducting a heuristic evaluation. He recommends three to five evaluators for maximum cost–benefit, based on his findings that one evaluator discovers only 35% of usability problems, but that three to five evaluators produce a high degree of overlap in their findings. If the evaluators do not have domain knowledge for the product they are inspecting, a training session can be used to familiarize everyone with the product.

The evaluators agree on a description of the target user. In some cases, the evaluators are given a scenario of use or a set of tasks to guide their evaluation. These days, the evaluators often work with personas to help them walk in the shoes of their users as they inspect the interface.

There's much more about personas in Chapter 4.

Each evaluator independently reviews the product at least twice: once to become familiar with it and a second time to inspect the product against the set of heuristics. The results of each evaluator's inspection are then collected, often in a meeting where the issues are discussed among the evaluators.

Severity codes are assigned to the findings, based on their likely impact on the user experience. A typical code set might be:

- *catastrophe*—also called a "show-stopper"
- *major problem*—has significant potential impact on usability
- *minor problem*—low priority, but should be noted
- *cosmetic problem*—fix if there's time and it's easy

A report documents the usability problems with explanations of the principle violated by each one and the severity code assigned to it. Although Nielsen does not call for a list of recommendations as a standard deliverable from this inspection, recommendations are frequently an expected outcome in practice. Sometimes the recommendations are general, such as "Error messages need to be made clear and explicit." At other times, a more specific recommendation is offered, particularly when the solution seems clear to the evaluators. For example, inconsistent functionality of the Tab key to allow users to move through input fields can be identified as a high-priority issue to fix for consistency and user control and freedom.

Conducting an expert review

In formal practice, heuristic evaluation has a clearly defined methodology and generally a clearly defined set of heuristics for conducting the review. However, *heuristic* is not a word in everyone's vocabulary. So, to simplify the matter, some people prefer to call this process *expert review*. Others see a difference in the methodologies.

Depending on who you talk to, an expert review might mean:

- A single evaluator—the expert—inspecting the interface.
- A review that does not involve specific heuristics, because the evaluator has a high degree of experience with this evaluation method and uses this experience to identify issues in an interface based on a working knowledge of the principles behind the heuristics.
- The same as heuristic evaluation; just a more accessible term to use with nonexperts.

If you are asked to conduct an expert review, you probably want to clarify what the person asking for it wants. Then proceed from there.

Conducting an informal evaluation

Some people take a less rigorous approach to the process of heuristic evaluation or expert review by following a checklist.

Informal evaluations can be done with nothing more than the knowledge you have from experience. Perhaps one person on the team inspects the product and reports the findings informally in a memo or in a meeting. Perhaps several people conduct the inspection independently and then get together to share their findings informally. For a really informal but powerful way to do an expert review, see the sidebar, which was created by Whitney Quesenbery and Caroline Jarrett.

For a collection of 25 useful checklists for websites, see "Usability.Edu: 25 Incredibly Useful Usability Cheat Sheets & Checklists" at *http:// bestwebdesignschools.com/2009/ usabilityedu-25-incredibly-useful-usability-cheat-sheets-checklists/*

Five steps to a (user-centered) expert review

1. Don't look at it (yet)!
   You never get a second chance for your "first look."

2. Write a (short) story.
   - Who is using this product?
   - Why are they doing it?
   - How do they feel about it?
   - What do they expect to happen?
   - How are they different from us?

3. Try to use it (following the story).
   - Start from "Why are they using this product?"
   - What are they trying to do?
   - What questions do they have?
   - What else do they want to know?
   - Can they find the information they need?

4. Now look at it (now that you've had a chance to use it).
   Think about relationship, conversation, interaction, and appearance.

   ○ *Relationship*: How did user goals and business goals align?

   ○ *Conversation*: Were headings and text helpful and informative?

   ○ *Interaction*: Could the user find a good "first click" or know how to use an interactive feature?

   ○ *Appearance*: Did the visual design help or hinder?

5. Report

   ○ What are the problems you saw?

   ○ Find at least one positive point.

In the end, whatever approach you take to a product's inspection will provide you with a set of findings or issues that can affect usability. If you've never done an inspection before, it can help to start with a set of heuristics. Once you get comfortable with what you're looking for, guidelines tend to become internalized, and you can then do away with them.

Comparing the results from heuristic evaluation and usability testing

What if you have a small budget and you need to choose only one of these two top methods? First, you should try to persuade those making this request to let you do both by taking the budget you have and dividing it into two parts: a small heuristic evaluation (or expert review) and a small usability study.

See Nielsen and Mack, Eds., *Usability Inspection Methods,* 1994.

If you can't make the case for both and you have to choose, here's what the research tells us about the two methods:

- No inspection method predicts end-user problems as well as actual usability testing.

- Usability experts doing an inspection are better at identifying the most severe errors, compared to developers or nonexperts.

However, studies suggest that usability experts find twice as many minor problems as major problems. Even with experts doing the inspection, the results are likely to include "false alarms," meaning problems that have no effect on the users in testing.

- Usability experts are also better than developers and nonexperts at predicting users' reactions when they encounter an error; that is, they can more accurately judge what will really irritate users.

- Usability experts do a good job of identifying improvements that can be made to the interface.

- Usability testing and inspection methods do *not* have a high degree of overlapping findings.

This last point—that testing and inspection find different things—is an excellent selling point for doing both.

For more on a comparison of these methods, see the following sidebar.

What the CUE-4 study tells us about both methods

CUE, which stands for Comparative Usability Evaluation, refers to a number of studies organized by Rolf Molich, a Danish usability consultant.

CUE-4, the fourth study in the series, brought together 17 usability experts from around the world who each chose one method or the other to review the OneScreen reservation system at the Hotel Pennsylvania in New York City and write a report of findings. (I was part of CUE-4 and chose heuristic evaluation.)

In Chapter 1, I told you about CUE-2.

The findings from the reports submitted by the 17 participants indicate that expert reviews and usability tests produce roughly the same number of important problems and roughly the same small number of false alarms. The study authors base this conclusion both on their analysis of the reports and on the fact that all of the teams represented a high level of usability expertise. These findings may suggest that equal value comes from either method as long as the practitioners have experience in the method they use.

See Molich and Dumas, "Comparative Usability Evaluation (CUE-4)," 2008.

Putting both methods together: The 1–2 punch

The best of all possible worlds is not to have to choose between these two robust methods: heuristic evaluation and usability testing. Rather, put them together, since each brings value to the process of creating products that are useful, usable, and desirable. Here's what I recommend when you can use both:

1. *Do a heuristic evaluation (or expert review) first.* The results from this review can be used in two ways:
   - You can clean up the interface to get rid of those issues that can interfere with the user's experience. If there's time, this can be an extensive revision. If there isn't a lot of time, you can go for the "low-hanging fruit." Anything you can do to eliminate distractions will help your users focus on the experience of pursuing their goals with the product.
   - If you don't have time to make any changes to the product before testing, you can use the review to identify your goals for usability testing. Because you've inspected the product, you are now familiar with it and you have a good grasp of the problems you think users will experience.

2. *Do a usability study.* After your heuristic evaluation, you have either fixed the problems or identified a list of problems that you want to explore in a usability study:
   - If you have fixed the problems before testing, you can learn what additional problems emerge for users.
   - If you haven't fixed the problems before testing, you can learn whether the issues you identified in the review are, in fact, problems for users. When they are, you have increased the validity of your findings by combining your processes. When problems you've identified don't actually bother users, you can learn what doesn't need to be fixed.

3. *Use both methods at the same time.* When there's money in the budget to use both of these tools but insufficient time to do one and then the other, divide and conquer. Conduct an expert review and a usability study in the same timeframe, reporting the results separately, then combining the findings for your recommendations.

As you can see from this discussion of budget and its impact on your choice of the tools you can use, you may need to make the case for using one or more of these tools to support a user-centered design process. Making this case is often dependent on justifying the cost of testing in light of the potential cost savings in product acceptance and reductions in product support calls. This chapter ends with some strategies you can use to make the case.

Cost-justifying usability

When Randolph Bias and Deborah Mayhew published their collection of essays on cost-justifying usability, they ended the book by saying:

> Ten years ago, it was unusual for usability to be on equal footing with "product function" and "schedule" in the business decision equation. Ten years from now, this book will be unnecessary, except perhaps to help new usability professionals with their level of usability-justification efforts.

Cost-Justifying Usability, 1994

Turn the clock forward 10 years. The prediction had not come true. So, Bias and Mayhew co-edited a second edition of the book because, clearly, the need to cost-justify usability still exists, and the cases for how to do it needed to be updated for the Internet age.

Cost-Justifying Usability: An Update for an Internet Age, 2nd ed., 2005

If you find that your manager or organization does not need to be "sold" on the benefits of usability testing, then clearly, you work for a company that understands the value added by a user-centered design process. If, however, you meet resistance in your effort to start something or expand the use of the tools in your toolkit, you will need to make the case to justify the cost and the value of testing. You can begin by gathering metrics based on what is already known or available. Costs associated with products include:

- documentation
- technical support for customers
- internal support for employees
- training
- time on task (particularly when reducing the time on task can be documented in money saved, as is the case with customer support calls or internal applications, such as software and intranet usage)

- conversion rates from visitor to buyer
- increased traffic to your website, which can be tracked from server log data before and after the use of usability tools

If you can get current data for any of these measures before using any UCD tools, you can compare these numbers to the numbers after using UCD tools to make the case for UCD. The book's companion website has a case study showing how one company did just that, making a compelling case for the savings they got from usability testing.

www.mkp.com/testingessentials

No matter where you are in understanding your users' experience with your product, you can promote the use of more tools, or using the tools more often, or doing the work sooner in the development cycle.

Summarizing Chapter 3

This chapter took an aerial view of usability testing by placing it within a toolkit of techniques that support user-centered design. If you think of usability testing as "'little u" and the toolkit of strategies as "big U," you get the picture of how usability testing fits within the broad scope of methods to build usability into products.

Your toolkit is full of techniques, but a discussion of all of these is well beyond the scope of this book. So I gave you brief descriptions of the commonly used tools and pointed you to some valuable resources for more information.

However there's one tool in the kit—heuristic evaluation—that is used as often as usability testing, and sometimes more often, so I went into more depth for this tool.

Heuristic evaluation can be formal:

- The evaluation is based on a set of heuristics, which are rules or guidelines of usability.
- The evaluation is an "inspection" of the product in search of violations of these rules.
- Usability evaluators—usually two, three, or more—review the product independently, using the heuristics and a defined list of severity codes, to identify and rank the issues.

- A report presents the collated, ranked findings, often with recommendations for changes.

Heuristic evaluation/expert review can be informal:

- The review of the product does not use a specific set of heuristics.
- The review can be done by a single usability practitioner.
- The reporting process can be less formal, with the results presented in an informal report or a meeting.

The best process is one that combines the two most commonly used tools of heuristic evaluation/expert review and usability testing.

You get these advantages when you use both methods:

- Using heuristic evaluation before testing can give you exposure to the product and identify the tasks to test.
- Using heuristic evaluation at the same time as testing (or afterward) can identify a number of issues that might not arise in testing but that can and should be addressed to improve the product.
- The combined results provide a stronger confirmation of real problems for users.

This chapter also included a discussion of strategies to make the case for using any or a combination of the tools in your UCD toolkit. If you are using one method but want to add another, you may have to justify the request for additional resources by presenting the potential cost savings. Your case for cost-justifying the use of one or more tools in your UCD toolkit may be made on the basis of:

- a reduction in support calls, documentation, and training
- an increase in try-to-buy situations or increased sales from website visitors
- a savings in time on task, which can be particularly important in call centers as well as for internal employees using software or intranets

A multicultural team of students in a usability testing course at Southern Polytechnic was matched up with a sponsor: Karen Bennett, the Manager of User Experience for Intercontinental Hotels Group (the group that includes Holiday Inn). The student team comprised four Chinese students and two American students. Holiday Inn has a longstanding presence in China, but the Holiday Inn China website had never undergone usability testing.

One of the team's early tasks was to conduct a heuristic evaluation of the Holiday Inn China website. The goal of the evaluation was to uncover issues that would help the team plan the usability test. The following is an excerpt from the report of their findings. The book's companion website has the full report.

Heuristic Evaluation of

HolidayInn.com.cn

Holiday Inn Hotel Website
for Chinese-Speaking Users

Completed by Team CBR:

Yufei Duan
Yina Li
Ying Li
Qianying Liu
Niven Sellars
Michael Somer

February 7, 2008

Table of Contents

Heuristic Evaluation Overview for *www.holidayinn.com.cn*

Introduction

This heuristic evaluation of *www.holidayinn.com.cn* was completed on February 7, 2008, as a preliminary step in the preparation for a usability test of the website. From the information provided by the sponsor, the project team learned that the site's audience is mostly domestic Chinese (mainland) users. They book hotel rooms online for business and/or leisure purposes. Their ages span from the mid-20s to the 50s. Most of them are not comfortable using computers. The majority of them do not speak or read English.

To accomplish the users' goal of booking rooms on the website, the Holiday Inn (China) website must successfully guide users through the site.

Purpose

The purpose of this heuristic evaluation is to discover any potential usability weaknesses that might confuse users. The findings from the evaluation will be used to design appropriate scenarios for the usability test.

Methodology

The project team evaluated the website from a Chinese user's point of view. In our preliminary meeting, the team reviewed the overall structure and content of the site and determined our scenario, which is the process of booking or modifying a hotel room on the site. The site was evaluated based on Jakob Nielsen's 10 heuristics, which have been adapted for the web. First, the team completed individual heuristic evaluations. Then, in a follow-up meeting, the team compiled the individual evaluations.

Heuristic Evaluation Findings

Visibility of System Status

The system should always keep users informed about what is going on, through appropriate feedback within reasonable time.

A. URL filename mismatch

When the URL *www.holidayinn. com.cn* is opened, the URL at the top of the page changes into *http:// www.ichotelsgroup.com/h/d/hi/280/ zh/home*

This may confuse users, causing them to think this is not a legitimate site.

Suggestion:

- Do not redirect the URL to a different name; instead keep the address at *www.holidayinn.com.cn*

B. No obvious way to go back to Holiday Inn site from Priority Club site

Users may not understand the relationship among Holiday Inn, Priority Club, and other IHG hotels. In China, people are not familiar with the concept of one corporation owning multiple brands. If the users are directed to the Priority Club site, they can easily get lost. The only way they can go back to the Holiday Inn site is to hit the Back button or the Holiday Inn icon near the bottom of the screen.

Suggestion:

• Create an easily identifiable button that will take users to where they were before they were directed away from the Holiday Inn site.

Match between System and the Real World

The system should speak the user's language, with words, phrases, and concepts familiar to the user, rather than system-oriented terms. Follow real-world conventions, making information appear in a natural and logical order.

A. Unrecognizable logo

Users may not recognize the Holiday Inn logo because it is displayed in English. The only way users will know they are on a Holiday Inn website is if they look at the words displayed in the header.

Suggestions:

- Design a matching logo in Chinese.
- Have a brief description in Chinese underneath the logo.

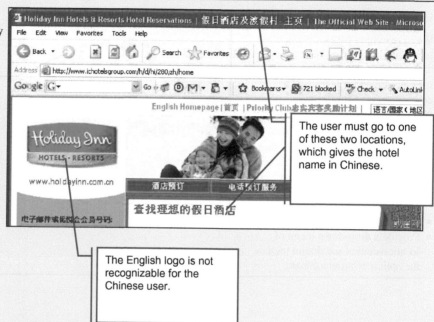

The user must go to one of these two locations, which gives the hotel name in Chinese.

The English logo is not recognizable for the Chinese user.

B. Awkward phrasing

This translation does not make sense. It is awkwardly phrased as "Receive Holiday Inn promoted sales (discount) activities."

Suggestion:

- Use localized language, not just direct translation. It should read, "Receive promotional sales discount information."

C. Awkward phrasing

When searching for hotels, users are sometimes requested to enter "State." "State" has a different meaning for Chinese users. The equivalent word for Chinese users is "Province."

Since the number of Holiday Inns is limited in China, it is easier for the user to simply select the city without being asked to select a province.

Suggestions:

- Use "Province" instead of "State."
- Provide a drop-down menu of locations/cities and do not include the option of province/state.

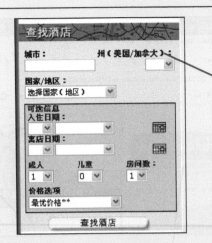

In this screen, instead of asking for "Province," it asks users to enter "State" (US/Canada). This may confuse Chinese users, since the word "State" refers to the government level between city and province in some provinces.

Findings and Conclusion

Key Findings

Our findings based on our evaluation of the website are prioritized into three categories: high, medium, and low priority.

High-Priority Issues

- *Localization.* Several problems within the website deal with translation issues that have not been properly localized. For example, the Chinese user will not understand the translation of "king size bed." There is no direct translation for this phrase; instead, the website calls it a "super large bed" (from the advanced search option). Similarly, when trying to communicate the idea of receiving information on the homepage, it has been translated as "receive promoted sales (discount) activities."

  On some pages, when trying to select a hotel location, the user is asked to enter a state instead of a province (customer service page). Another example of localized language problems is the sporadic use of either USD or CNY. This usage will potentially cause conversion or confusion problems for the user (search and result page/lowest Internet rate guarantee page).

On the homepage, a U.S. phone number is given: 1-888-Holiday. Chinese users will not understand how to numerically enter "Holiday" on their telephones, and they will not understand that they are making a call to the United States.

- *Error messages.* Some of the error messages do not specify what the error is. For example, one error message reads, "Could not find matching hotel, please change your options and try again." At this point, the user will not know what information he or she needs to modify to conduct a successful search. Some of the other error messages are displayed as codes that the user will not understand.

- *Layout design.* When the search results for hotels are displayed, the hotel's information is displayed with two different background colors. This may confuse the user into thinking that two hotels are being displayed.

- *Navigation.* When the user visits the Priority Club website, there is no clear option to return to the Holiday Inn website. This can potentially confuse users and leave them thinking they have arrived at a completely different website that is not affiliated with the Holiday Inn site. The branding and visual differences between the two sites can confuse users as to where they are. Aside from selecting the Back button on the browser (which should not be assumed that users will do), the only other option users have to return to the Holiday Inn site is at the bottom of the page, which cannot be seen on all computer displays without scrolling down.

- *Visual language.* Upon entering information to search for a hotel, the location overview page displays a map with cities and provinces where Holiday Inn hotels are located. Currently, the map displays gray icons that contain the province where a Holiday Inn is located. The visual language presented by the map leads users to believe that they can click on one of these icons to view more information about that specific Holiday Inn location.

- *Content.* When a user enters information in the data collection form on the homepage, a box appears where the user is required to enter a city name. Since Holiday Inns are not in all cities or even many cities in China, this will result in many errors for users. Currently, if a user enters the name of a city where a Holiday Inn is not present, it will tell the user that the search results were unsuccessful, without stating that there is no hotel in that city and without giving the user options to see where hotels are located.

Medium-Priority Issues

- *Localization.* On the homepage, "Priority Club" is written in English as well as in Chinese. Users who do not read English will not understand the English or know what it means.
- *Branding.* The homepage displays the Holiday Inn logo in English only. The audience may be confused by this.
- *Navigation.* There is inconsistency in the top navigation bar options on the Holiday Inn landing page and the subpages. When users click on a navigation option on the homepage, such as "Hotel Reservation," the navigation on the new page is completely different from the homepage.

  The homepage has the following options in the top navigation menu:

  - hotel reservation
  - phone services for hotel reservation
  - conferences
  - destination information

  Subpages list the following options in the top navigation menu, and share the same look as the homepage:

  - first time here
  - hotel reservation
  - special offers
  - phone services for hotel reservation
  - destination information

  To illustrate the problem, suppose that a user wants to view the contents of the Conferences button that was seen on the homepage. The user will not be able to click on it from a subpage because it is not in the top navigation bar where the user expects it to be. It can't be assumed that the user will know to return to the homepage to make this choice, because the navigation menus look similar but contain different information choices.

Low-Priority Issues

- *Localization.* When the user is required to put in confidential information during the hotel-booking process, an icon appears to indicate to the user that the site is trustworthy. The words on the icon are written in English. Chinese users will not recognize what this icon means without translation or because it is not from a local trust organization.

- *Online help*. There are very few options for help on the website. The closest example of online help is the FAQ link at the bottom of the "Lowest Internet Rate Guarantee" screen.

- *Layout design*. Users could be confused by the fact that the two pictures convey the same information. On the homepage, the exact same pictures are used in close proximity. Also on the homepage, the Chinese hotel locations are listed to the right of the international hotel locations, as opposed to being listed first.

- *Navigation*. The URL that the user enters in the web browser is not consistent with the URL that is displayed. The URL in the address bar on the homepage is *http://www.ichotelsgroup.com/h/d/hi/280/zh/home*, yet what is visible on the page is the address *www.holidayinn.com.cn* (located under the Holiday Inn logo). This difference in the URLs could lead users to believe that they might be at a scam site due to the mismatch of the web addresses.

- *Content*. The homepage navigation options have a redundancy issue. Currently, the first navigation choice reads "Book a Hotel Room" and the second choice reads "Book a Hotel Room by Calling." The distinction between these two links needs to be made clearer (or they need to be merged into a single link).

Conclusion

Our heuristic evaluation of the Holiday Inn China website revealed that there are a number of usability issues that our team can test with participants. The high-priority issues will be part of the scenarios used in the usability test. The project team looks forward to testing the above findings with actual users of *www.holidayinn.com.cn*.

Understanding users and their goals

4

By now, you should need no convincing that it's critical to know who your users are and what their goals are. Of course, you need to know about users and their goals for all aspects of user-centered design, but it's particularly important in planning for usability testing so that you can recruit the right participants and give them the appropriate tasks.

No need to reinvent the wheel. There's some excellent research that will give you a basic understanding of users and their goals. You can then apply this information to what you know about *your users* and *their goals* with your product.

This chapter is in two parts. The first part focuses on

- what we know about users in general
- what we know about web users in particular
- how generational differences can affect users' goals

The second part focuses on information you have or can get about your users and their goals so that you can create two important documents you will use in planning and preparing for usability testing:

- *Personas*—descriptions of your users, with details to bring them to life

Usability Testing Essentials. DOI: 10.1016/B978-0-12-375092-1.00004-0

- *Scenarios*—descriptions of the situations in which your personas would use your product to match their goals

When you combine these two types of research—what's already known about users and their goals and what you can gather about your specific users and their goals—you have everything you need to create relevant, meaningful personas and scenarios to shape the direction for your usability testing.

People are goal-oriented

Users are people with a goal, which your product needs to support.

That makes us all users. When we are faced with choices about new products, we approach our decision making by measuring the effort of learning the product against the potential outcome. As we grow up and older, we bring our experience with us, and this experience colors our perceptions about whether new products will be easy or hard to learn to use.

Despite our many differences, as adults we share the following characteristics:

- We want to act right away—to get going on the path of our goal.
- We need to know *why* we have to know something, particularly if it seems to get in the way of taking action.
- We learn best when the outcome is of immediate value.
- We develop *schemas*, or mental models, of how things are done, and we apply these when we learn how to use new products.

A *mental model* is a picture or map of a process or behavior that is created from a user's experience. For more on mental models, see Indi Young, *Mental Models: Aligning Design Strategy with Human Behavior,* 2008.

Our ability to use mental models can make us eager to accept new products or resistant to trying them, depending on what our prior experience has been. When we have a bad experience, we tend to avoid repeating it. We carry negative feelings about it with us. For instance, if we don't get an answer when we click on online help, we probably won't try it a second time. And this bad experience with online help with one or two products may create a mental model that help doesn't help with any product.

However, motivation plays an important role in our enthusiasm for learning something new. The more highly motivated we are, the more willing we are likely to be to persevere, even when the interface seems complicated or different. In other words, if we want to like the product, it affects our commitment to mastering it so that we *do* like the product. Often this motivation comes from a mental model that Brand X (fill in your favorite here) makes products I like. So, I know I am going to like this one.

Mental models also affect our web experience, as the research presented in the next part of this chapter shows.

When people use the web, they bring their experience and expectations

The web was not born yesterday. Today we can count on the fact that most of our target users have experience using the web, including some who have been using the web for 20 years or more and some who have been using it for their whole lives.

So, does this mean that we can assume that web users are now all experienced users? Yes—and no.

Jakob Nielsen did a study of web users to address the common lore that web users are now smarter. Here's what he found.

Experienced web users are

- better at physical movements, such as using the mouse and scrolling
- more confident at clicking and less afraid that they'll break something
- better at basic searching and use search frequently
- faster at doing things they do often on websites they use often

However, when these same users go to an unfamiliar website, they are often

- confused by the information architecture, not knowing how to navigate through the site or use the menu options

In fact, the web was "born" on Christmas Day of 1990. That was the day Tim Berners-Lee and a few colleagues set up the first successful communication between a web browser and the Internet.

"User Skills Improving, But Only Slightly," February 4, 2008

- overwhelmed by the volume of information and its unfamiliarity, especially when the site uses unfamiliar industry jargon
- baffled by the smallest usability problem

What this information tells us is that web users have gained some level of skill and confidence in moving around the Internet. But a *new site is a brand-new experience.*

People expect web objects to be in specific places

Experienced web users have a *schema*, or mental model, for where objects should be on a website. In a study to gauge user expectations, the participants were asked to choose from 25 squares on a grid for placing each web object. The placement of the web objects shown in Figure 4.1 represents the selection by the highest percentage of users:

Shaikh and Lenz, "Where's the Search? Re-examining User Expectations of Web Objects," 2006

- back to home in the upper-left corner of the page
- internal links on the left side of the page
- site search on the upper-right corner or near the upper-left corner
- advertisements either at the center top or right side of the page
- About Us in the footer or at the left side of the page

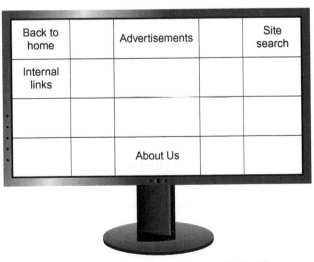

Figure 4.1 Users expect common web objects to be in specific locations on a website.

People don't want to read—they want to act

Because web users are in a hurry to reach their goal, they rarely *read* web pages until or unless they come to content that matches their goal. So, for instance, if their goal is to read the news of the day, they will do that, but only the news that interests them. If their goal is to get something done—to take some action—they don't want to read *about* it. They want to *do* it.

To accelerate their movement through a website, these users are looking for "trigger" words as they skim, scan, and skip over content. A *trigger word* is the one that matches their goal. When they see one they think is a match, they will click on the link as soon as they find it.

Effective web pages are designed to support this goal of fast action by users. As Ginny Redish, a well-known usability consultant, explains, good web writing:

Letting Go of the Words, 2007

- Is like a conversation—it starts with a question that a user has, such as:
  - How do I . . . ?
  - Where do I find out about . . . ?
  - May I . . . ?
- The website responds with answers:
  - by providing the specific information users want
  - by letting users grab the answer they want and then go on, until they reach the next question or point in the conversation

Since users read so little on the web, web content that is designed by letting go of the words matches their mental model for what they want to do and how they want to do it.

Make a good first impression—you might not get a second chance

First impressions are critical to users' perceptions of how easy or difficult their web experience will be. One study showed that 80% of web surfers spend only a few seconds on a website before deciding whether the site is worth exploring or they should move on.

Peracchio and Luna, "The Role of Thin-Slice Judgments in Consumer Psychology," 2006

*Consumer Reports' Webwatch
Research Report,* 2002

Part of creating a good first impression is establishing credibility, or trust. Users decide right away if a website can be trusted. Their decision about whether to stay or go is often based on this feeling of trust. But the qualities establishing credibility are in the eye of the beholder. Different things matter more to some people than to others, as we see in a large comparative study of health-related websites. This study compared subject matter experts and consumers using the same website, and here's what they found:

- Subject matter experts (SMEs) valued the reputation of the site and the authority of the content.

- Consumers were influenced by the visual appeal (professional look) of the design.

The following table shows the top-10 items the two groups chose for rating the website's credibility. Not only were the first items different for each group, but so were the last items:

- *SMEs put information accuracy at the bottom*—If the site is credible because of its reputation and the authority of the content creators, then information accuracy is not an issue.

- *Consumers put site functionality at the bottom*—They expect the site to work, but if it doesn't, because of a broken link or a page not loading properly, this causes a loss of credibility for them. Interestingly, this item did not make the top-10 list for SMEs.

To see a set of 10 guidelines on building trust on the web and the research that supports the guidelines, visit the Stanford Persuasive Technology Lab website at *http://credibility.stanford. edu/guidelines/index.html*

SMEs' ratings	Consumers' ratings
1. Name (recognition, reputation)	1. Design look
2. Information source (including citations)	2. Information design, structure, and focus
3. Company motive	3. Company motive
4. Information focus	4. Usefulness and accuracy of information
5. Advertising	5. Name recognition and reputation
6. Design look	6. Advertising
7. Information bias	7. Information bias
8. Information design	8. Writing tone
9. Writing tone	9. Identity of site sponsor
10. Information accuracy	10. Site functionality

What does this study tell us? The factors influencing users' perceptions of credibility can be very different. That's why knowing what matters most to users in general is important, but knowing what matters most to *your* users is essential.

Generational differences matter when it comes to the web

Research on generational differences tells us a lot about age-related attitudes and experiences when it comes to the web. The Pew Internet and American Life Project regularly studies Internet users to understand changes and trends among and between the generations. In its *Generations Online in 2009* study, it reported a lot of fascinating findings. Here's a glimpse:

Jones and Fox, *Generations Online in 2009*, 2009

> *Contrary to the image of Generation Y as the "Net Generation," internet users in their 20s do not dominate every aspect of online life. Generation X is the most likely group to bank, shop, and look for health information online. Boomers are just as likely as Generation Y to make travel reservations online. And even Silent Generation internet users are competitive when it comes to email (although teens might point out that this is proof that email is for old people).*

For a description of the generational categories used in the study, see Figure 4.2.

It might not surprise you that both the young and the old are on the Internet in large numbers. But what might surprise you is that the fastest-growing demographic is the 70–75 age group, which increased its presence on the Internet 26–45% of its total number since the prior study in 2005. Although the demographics for all groups are predicted to level out in time, it's important to understand that there are differences in usage among the age groups. So, let's take a closer look at these age groups to see their unique interests and capabilities.

What we know about older users

Let's start with what people mean when they say "older." First of all, there is no standard break point for older users. Some studies have included people in their 50s in this category. Others use 65 as the break point for defining "older." The Pew study categorizes older people in several age groups, even dividing baby boomers into younger and older boomers.

The AARP—a members-only nonprofit organization for "older" people—invites adults to join when they turn 50.

Generations Explained

Generation Name*	Birth Years, Ages in 2009	% of total adult population	% of internet-using population
Gen Y (Millennials)	Born 1977-1990, Ages 18-32	26%	30%
Gen X	Born 1965-1976, Ages 33-44	20%	23%
Younger Boomers	Born 1955-1964, Ages 45-54	20%	22%
Older Boomers	Born 1946-1954, Ages 55-63	13%	13%
Silent Generation	Born 1937-1945, Ages 64-72	9%	7%
G.I. Generation	Born -1936, Age 73+	9%	4%

Source: Pew Internet & American Life Project December 2008 survey. N = 2,253 total adults, and margin of error is ±2%. N = 1,650 total internet users, and margin of error is ±3%.

*All generation labels used in this report, with the exception of Younger - and Older - Boomers, are the names conventionalized by Howe and Strauss's book, *Generations*, Strauss, William, & Howe, Neil, *Generations: The History of America's Future, 1584 to 2069* (Perennial, 1992). As for Younger Boomers and Older Boomers, enough research has been done to suggest that the two decades of Baby Boomers are different enough to merit being divided into distinct generational groups.

 Pew **Internet**
Pew Internet & American Life Project

Figure 4.2 The generations are explained by name, birth years, percentage of the total adult population, and percentage of Internet usage.

Despite the different ways used to categorize "older" people, we know that they have a number of things in common. They generally have money to spend, and time, if they are retired, to determine how best to spend it. They use the Internet for many things, including information seeking, particularly about health-related issues, investments, and leisure-time activities. They also use the Internet to make and keep connections, especially with their families.

Studies of older users find that they tend to

- search less efficiently than younger users
- read more content but are easily distracted by movement and animation
- have difficulty reading small fonts (below 12 point), closely spaced text (kerning), and text with minimal white space between the lines (leading)

- have more difficulty than younger users in recalling previous moves and the location of previously viewed information, such as links previously visited

- may experience decreased contrast sensitivity (the ability to discern figure from ground), making it hard to see things on a screen

- may have difficulty using a mouse to click on an icon or using a cascading or mouseover menu

- may hear sounds less well

In addition to problems of decreasing vision, hearing, and motor skills that older users experience as normal aspects of aging, a certain percentage of the aging population suffers from disease, which can have a more significant impact on their computer capabilities. Medications they take for illness or disease can also affect their computer capabilities.

Tom Tullis, VP of Usability and User Insight, and his colleagues at Fidelity Investments have conducted studies with older users interested in tracking their investments online. Their studies have shown that older users engage in "cautious clicking," hovering over a link with their mouse pointer but hesitating to make the decision to click.

The team understood this to mean that these users weren't willing to take the chance of making a mistake. So they iterated their design, adding a tooltip that described what a link would do *before* the user actually clicked on it. Testing this change with 70 users of all ages showed that these tooltips significantly improved task performance for users over 65 and had no effect on users under 65. In other words, the improvement for older users didn't adversely affect younger users and may, in fact, have helped all users.

Whitney Quesenbery and Caroline Jarrett, two usability consultants who often work together on usability projects, came to similar conclusions regarding the impact of changes made to accommodate older users. In their revisions to the Open University website—a site that supports the large online student population of the university—they found that the changes made the website experience better not only for older users but also for users of all ages and literacy levels.

Quesenbery, "More Alike Than We Think," 2006

What we know about the Google generation

The study, *Information Behaviour of the Researcher of the Future*, was commissioned by the British Library and the Joint Information Systems Committee, 2008. A briefing paper is available at *www.jisc.ac.uk/media/documents/ programmes/reppres/gg_final_ keynote_11012008.pdf*

The Google generation is the group of people born after 1993 who grew up in a world dominated by the Internet and whose first stop for information is a search engine—most likely Google. Some naturally assume that these users are very skilled at searching and understanding the information they get. Not so, according to a study conducted by the CIBER unit of University College London. The study focused on the ways in which this age group retrieves and uses information.

Here's what the researchers found about the Google generation and their search patterns:

- The speed with which they search the web means that little time is spent evaluating information for relevance, accuracy, or authority.
- They have a poor understanding of their information needs; thus, they have difficulty developing effective search strategies.
- Their information literacy—the ability to know how to locate information and evaluate what they find—has not improved with widening access to technology.
- They exhibit a strong preference for natural language searches, rather than learning what keywords might be more effective.
- They don't assess a long list of results very effectively and often print off pages with barely more than a glance at them.
- They prefer a search engine like Google or Yahoo! over library-sponsored resources.
- Generation Y and older age groups are rapidly catching up to the Google generation in adopting similar information-seeking habits and expectations.

What we know about children

Nielsen, "Kids' Corner: Website Usability for Children," 2002

What do we know about kids? A usability study of 55 children, ages 6 to 12, in the United States and Israel observed children interacting with 24 sites designed for their age group and three mainstream sites designed for everyone.

The study found that:

- They often had the best success in task completion on the websites intended for adults—such as Amazon and Yahoo!—compared to sites intended for children, which were often complex and hard to navigate.

- Poor usability, combined with their impatience, resulted in many leaving sites quickly.

- Diverse design elements, including animation and multimedia effects, worked well.

- They rarely scrolled.

- They used "mine sweeping" to move the mouse over the screen to find any clickable areas, including ads.

- They clicked on ads, not being able to distinguish ads from content, particularly when the ads had appealing graphics.

What we know when we compare and contrast the generations

By now you know, if you didn't already, that the generations are different, particularly when it comes to Internet usage. Figure 4.3 documents some of these distinctions among and between the generations.

Pew Internet Research Report,
Generations Online in 2009

Rank	Gen Y	Gen X	Younger Boomers	Older Boomers	Silent Generation	G.I. Generation
1	Email	Email	Email	Email	Email	Email
2	Search	Search	Search	Search	Search	Search
3	Research product	Research product	Research product	Get health info	Research product	Get health info
4	Get news	Get health info	Get health info	Research product	Get health info	Make travel reservations
5	Watch video	Buy something	Get news	Buy something	Make travel reservations	Research product
6	Buy something	Get news	Make travel reservations	Get news	Visit gov't site	Buy something
7	Get health info	Make travel reservations	Buy something	Make travel reservations	Buy something	Get news
8	Visit SNS	Bank	Visit gov't site	Visit gov't site	Get news	Visit gov't site
9	Make travel reservations	Visit gov't site	Research for job	Bank	Bank	Get religious info
10	Get job info	Research for job	Bank	Research for job	Research for job	Bank
11	Create SNS profile	Watch video	Watch video	Get job info	Get religious info	IM
12	IM	Get job info	Get job info	Watch video	Rate product	Play games
13	Download music	Download music	Get religious info	Rate product	Play games	Rate product
14	Bank	IM	Rate product	Get religious info	IM	Read blog
15	Visit gov't site	Get religious info	IM	Play games	Watch video	Watch video
16	Research for job	Play games	Auction	Auction	Read blog	Download video
17	Play games	Visit SNS	Read blog	Read blog	Auction	Get job info
18	Read blog	Rate product	Play games	IM	Download music	Podcast
19	Download video	Read blog	Download music	Download music	Download video	Research for job
20	Rate product	Download video	Download video	Download video	Get job info	Auction
21	Get religious info	Auction	Visit SNS	Podcast	Visit SNS	Create blog
22	Auction	Create SNS profile	Podcast	Visit SNS	Podcast	Download music
23	Podcast	Podcast	Create SNS profile	Create SNS profile	Create blog	Visit SNS
24	Create blog	Create blog	Create blog	Create blog	Create SNS profile	Create SNS profile
25	Visit virtual world	Visit virtual world	Visit virtual world	Visit virtual world	Visit virtual world	Visit virtual world

Above this line, over 50% of internet users in the given generation engage in this online activity

Key: % of internet users in each generation who engages in this online activity

90-100%
80-89%
70-79%
60-69%
50-59%
40-49%
30-39%
20-29%
10-19%
(5-9%)

Figure 4.3 This activity grid shows online pursuits by generation.

With all of this background, you should be well prepared to apply this basic research to the information you will gather about your users. This combination of information sources will prepare you for two critical activities:

- creating personas of your users
- creating scenarios of their interests and goals for your product

Personas help you get to know your users

Alan Cooper, author of *The Inmates Are Running the Asylum*, 1999, is credited with inventing personas.

An early step in getting ready for usability testing—often an activity that is done on its own—involves creating personas of your users.

Personas are fictional representations of people that are created from real data about your users.

Since personas first came on the scene, they have been widely adopted as a common way to plan for a user-centered design process by keeping your users always in mind. Their strength lies in the focus they bring to design discussions. With personas, you reduce the tendency for designers to make false assumptions about what users will do with a product.

Tom Landauer has a name for this tendency of designers to falsely assume they know the users. He calls it the *egocentric intuition fallacy,* which is the misguided notion that developers can just intuit what users want by thinking about it. See "Behavioral Research Methods in Human-Computer Interaction," 1997.

With personas, everyone can talk about the users as specific people with particular needs, wants, desires, skill levels, and contexts of use. And when several personas are created, everyone can see the differences among them.

Personas are based on real information about real users

You've *thought* about your users. But you recognize that's not enough. You need to *know* about your users. Using the techniques described in your toolkit in Chapter 3, you know how to gather information about them, firsthand or secondhand. With this information, you are able to create personas for your users, based on a *compilation of behavior patterns* that align people into an *archetype,* or generic representation of a user group.

The essential characteristics of a persona include:

- *A name and a picture*—usually a representative name and a stock photo
- *Demographic information*—age, education, ethnicity, family status
- *Job title or main focus of activity*—could be homemaker, student, retired person
- *Goals*—product related and experience related
- *Environment*—context of use or relevant information about the environment
- *Technical or product domain expertise*—could also include attitude toward technology
- *A quote that sums up what matters most to the persona*—often taken from actual quotes from interviews or website visits

For more on personas, see Adlin and Pruitt, *The Essential Persona Lifecycle: Your Guide to Building and Using Personas,* 2010, and Mulder and Yaar, *The User Is Always Right: A Practical Guide to Creating and Using Personas for the Web,* 2006.

As an example of how this works, I've included the two personas created for the Holiday Inn China website study. The team prepared these personas to get to know their users for the heuristic evaluation and usability test of the website.

They began with information provided by Karen Bennett, User Experience Manager, InterContinental Hotels Group (IHG):

Key markets in China	Beijing, Shanghai, Guangzhou
Brand presence—the hotels represented in China	InterContinental, Crowne Plaza, Holiday Inn; Holiday Inn is the biggest IHG hotel in China (in terms of rooms booked) and was one of the first Western hotels in China
Target customers	Domestic and international travelers
Demographics of customers	Ages 24–55 Purchasing power—middle class to upper middle class
Type of travel	Business—well established Leisure market—growing

The team added to this information by reading articles about China's business and leisure traveler in U.S. magazines and conducting interviews with U.S.- and China-located friends and acquaintances. The two personas they created represent someone living in the United States and someone living in China:

- *Min He*—a U.S.-resident, Chinese-born mother and wife with limited computer skills. Although she works part time to support her husband's computer business, she uses the computer only for basic data entry associated with bookkeeping. She is a potential leisure traveler to China to visit family during the Beijing Summer Olympics (Figure 4.4).

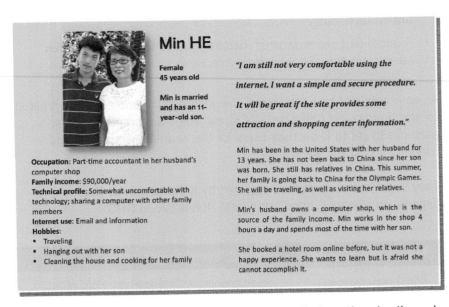

Min HE

Female
45 years old

Min is married and has an 11-year-old son.

"I am still not very comfortable using the internet. I want a simple and secure procedure. It will be great if the site provides some attraction and shopping center information."

Occupation: Part-time accountant in her husband's computer shop
Family income: $90,000/year
Technical profile: Somewhat uncomfortable with technology; sharing a computer with other family members
Internet use: Email and information
Hobbies:
- Traveling
- Hanging out with her son
- Cleaning the house and cooking for her family

Min has been in the United States with her husband for 13 years. She has not been back to China since her son was born. She still has relatives in China. This summer, her family is going back to China for the Olympic Games. She will be traveling, as well as visiting her relatives.

Min's husband owns a computer shop, which is the source of the family income. Min works in the shop 4 hours a day and spends most of the time with her son.

She booked a hotel room online before, but it was not a happy experience. She wants to learn but is afraid she cannot accomplish it.

Figure 4.4 Min He is a U.S. resident, originally from China. She is a wife and mother and helps her husband with his business.

Tony's profile is largely based on information from a cover story in *Time Magazine*, "China's Me Generation," by Simon Elegant, July 26, 2007, at *www.time.com/time/magazine/article/0,9171,1647228,00.html*

- *Tai "Tony" Chen*—a Chinese resident, a young professional, with strong computer skills and someone who travels as part of his job. He also travels to visit his parents in another city. Tony likes to be seen as "cool," so his choices in clothes, coffee, and where he stays when he travels are important to him. He especially likes Western brands. When he's with his friends, he goes by his Western name, Tony, which he adopted for use when British owners in his company's joint venture are in town (Figure 4.5).

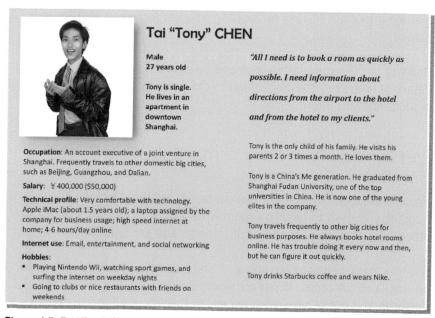

Tai "Tony" CHEN

Male
27 years old

Tony is single.
He lives in an
apartment in
downtown
Shanghai.

"All I need is to book a room as quickly as possible. I need information about directions from the airport to the hotel and from the hotel to my clients."

Occupation: An account executive of a joint venture in Shanghai. Frequently travels to other domestic big cities, such as Beijing, Guangzhou, and Dalian.

Salary: ¥ 400,000 ($50,000)

Technical profile: Very comfortable with technology. Apple iMac (about 1.5 years old); a laptop assigned by the company for business usage; high speed internet at home; 4-6 hours/day online

Internet use: Email, entertainment, and social networking

Hobbies:
- Playing Nintendo Wii, watching sport games, and surfing the internet on weekday nights
- Going to clubs or nice restaurants with friends on weekends

Tony is the only child of his family. He visits his parents 2 or 3 times a month. He loves them.

Tony is a China's Me generation. He graduated from Shanghai Fudan University, one of the top universities in China. He is now one of the young elites in the company.

Tony travels frequently to other big cities for business purposes. He always books hotel rooms online. He has trouble doing it every now and then, but he can figure it out quickly.

Tony drinks Starbucks coffee and wears Nike.

Figure 4.5 Tai "Tony" Chen is a young Chinese account executive in a British–Chinese joint venture company. He travels regularly as part of his job.

Personas are a creative activity, but don't get carried away

Personas are a great team-building activity because everyone on the team can contribute. No special technical expertise is required.

Persona development is also a great outlet for your creativity. But you have to be careful not to get carried away. Personas need to be anchored in real data. You use the data to personalize the characteristics of a composite user with details that are *relevant* to the product you are developing. If it's relevant to know what kind of car the person drives, include it. Otherwise leave it out. The same goes for any other personal detail.

Make decisions on what to include on the basis of whether the information helps you understand user motivation, fears, concerns, and goals as they relate to your product. The information about the persona of Tony, the young Chinese businessman who drinks Starbucks coffee and likes to wear Nikes, is relevant because it will reflect on the factors that are important to Tony in deciding whether to book a Holiday Inn hotel.

One way to curb your enthusiasm and control the inclusion of irrelevant details is to restrict the description of the persona to one or two pages of product-relevant information.

Personas should be a manageable number

Persona creation could go on forever, but to settle on a manageable number, you need to focus on your primary users. Then you can add other users that are secondary but important to get to know.

So, how many personas are enough? The number you create may depend on time and resources. If you are working with a team to create the personas and if you have ready access to the information you need to bring the personas to life, you can probably create 7 or 8 or more by dividing up the work. But if you have little time or resources, you may need to restrict the number to 2 or 3. A rule of thumb for the number of personas to create is more than 2 but less than 12.

Personas need to be visible

Once you've created your personas, you need to make sure you use them. If you store them out of sight, they could be easily forgotten. So, you need to display them in a way that makes them readily available to the team as they work. If the team is colocated, the simplest and most obvious way is to post them in the area where the team meets. Some teams even laminate them so that they will hold up over time. With your personas posted on the walls, the team can refer to them by name: What would John or Mario or Martha think about this feature? Would it help or get in the way of their goal(s)? If it helps one but gets in the way of another persona, how can we reconcile this problem?

Some companies get creative with the way in which they display their personas, using strategies such as:

- mugs, mousepads, or T-shirts with the personas on them
- stand-up, life-size cardboard cutouts of the personas

- a physical space built to show the environment that reflects where the persona lives or works—for example, in designing a new car, one company built personas of the target customer's bedroom or living room

When the team is not colocated, wikis and intranets can be used to share the personas with everyone on the team.

Scenarios tell the story of your users' goals

For each persona, you need to create a meaningful scenario that reflects your persona's goals within the world in which the persona lives. As was the case with information that might already be available to help you create your personas, you might find that you have information to help you get started in creating scenarios. For example, if the developers have created use cases, you can start from these.

A use case typically focuses on the interaction between the system and the user or how the agent/user uses the system to achieve a goal or task. It is task-specific. A scenario focuses on the *user* in pursuit of a goal. To create a scenario, you need to build it around your users—now fleshed out as personas—and their goals.

Start by knowing the difference between a task and a goal

To create good scenarios, you need to understand the difference between users' tasks and their goals:

- Tasks are things that users *do*—steps they must take, processes they must complete, acts they must perform—to achieve a goal.
- Goals are the *result,* or outcome, that users seek.

To put this distinction into an example: A task can be completing a registration form on a website. The task is required to get to the goal of accessing information or making a purchase. Users are interested in attaining their goal. The task is the necessary means to the end. If the user is sufficiently motivated to perform the task because the goal is in sight and worth the effort—that is, the user has identified something to purchase or has read an excerpt from a report and now wants to read the whole report—then the user completes the form. However, if the task of registration comes too soon—before the user is sufficiently motivated to comply—then the user becomes frustrated, perhaps seeing the barrier as too high. So, the user gives up.

Good scenarios focus on the users' goals.

Tell stories about your personas in a compelling way

For more about crafting stories, see Quesenbery and Brooks, *Storytelling for User Experience: Crafting Stories for Better Design*, 2010.

In creating good scenarios, think of the process as telling the story of your persona's experience. As Whitney Quesenbery says, "Stories set the personas in motion." Through the story, you are inviting your audience to enter the world of your persona and experience it from the inside.

These are the essential points for crafting the story in a compelling way:

- Make your persona the central character.
- Establish a problem or situation.
- Create a scene that is familiar, so that everyone in that persona group will say, yes, I know that situation or problem.
- Describe the main character's goal.
- Use the real data you have collected to ground the story in a composite presentation of the facts.
- Make the story memorable, with vivid (though relevant) details and quotes.

To give you an example of how this works, let's take the personas of Min and Tony and put them into scenarios that tell their stories.

What matters to Min when booking a hotel

Min and her family will be going to China this summer to visit relatives. Their son has never been to China, so Min is very excited about showing him her favorite places and introducing him to her family members who are still living there.

The family is planning to go to China when the Summer Olympics are being held in Beijing because their relatives have gotten tickets to some of the swimming events. Min knows this will be a wonderful experience for her son, Bai, because he is on the swim team at the Chinese Community Center and his coach thinks he has great potential as a competitive swimmer.

Min is the one who takes care of the family's shopping, cooking, and entertainment. So she will be the one to book the hotel and make the travel plans for the family. She's booked a hotel online before, but just for a trip to Washington, DC, and that trip was with a group from their church, so she didn't have to pick the hotel, just book the room.

This time she will have to find a hotel that lets children stay free in the room with their parents and that has a swimming pool. It would also be a plus if breakfast was included in the room rate. Min's goal is to find a room that fits these requirements and that costs no more than US$150 per night. For the location of the hotel, Min wants to find one near Wang Fu Jing, the biggest shopping street in Beijing, and near the subway, so they can take public transportation as they travel to the Olympic swimming events and to see family and friends.

Min uses the family computer at home and also keeps the books for her husband's business, using QuickBooks on her husband's computer at work. She sends e-mail to relatives, mostly to share pictures. But she doesn't do much more than that on the computer, and she never uses the computer for shopping.

Min's biggest concern in making the hotel reservations for their Beijing trip is that if she makes a mistake, she might not be able to fix it herself. She knows she will need to use the family credit card, so she is also concerned about security. She hopes that if she has a problem, there will be a phone number she can call.

What matters to Tony when booking a hotel

Tony travels regularly for his job in China, and he is very comfortable making the arrangements himself. In fact, he prefers doing this himself because he is very particular about the location of the hotel and its amenities. If the company books the hotel for him, they tend to go with the cheapest rate, but Tony knows what he is allowed to spend, and when he books his hotel room himself, he gets more of what's important to him.

For Tony, that means a big hotel that has a full restaurant, preferably one that serves Western/international food, and a bar or nightclub, if not in the hotel, then nearby. Tony does not want a hotel for tourists, so he looks for a hotel with a good business center. Of course, it goes without saying that Tony's room needs to have high-speed Internet access and a flat-screen TV with cable. It's a plus if the hotel has a shuttle to/from the airport.

Tony is comfortable using his credit card when he books a hotel, and he expects to be able to complete the booking process quickly and efficiently. He likes staying at name-brand hotels, particularly when they have a loyalty program that earns him room upgrades. So, he checks out his favorite hotel brand first to see what they have available. Because he often has to book a room at the last minute, he needs to know room availability right away.

There's more about how to use personas and scenarios to plan your usability test in Chapter 5.

The activity of creating personas and putting them into real-world scenarios brings your users to life and gives you a glimpse into their world. Not only do these personas and scenarios help you understand your users as people, but they also help you plan a usability test.

Summarizing Chapter 4

This chapter has given you the tools to understand your users and their goals. Research provides a starting point for learning about users, their tasks, and their goals. Here are some things we know from research:

- People are goal-oriented. Everything they want to do with your product is motivated by the pursuit of their goal.
- Web users bring their experiences and expectations to your website:
  - Over time, web users have gotten better at some things, but new websites often confuse, even baffle, users.
  - Users have expectations about where web objects should be located. These expectations come from "mental models" of use they create from their experience.
  - Users are impatient if they can't find the "trigger" words that will get them down the path of their goal. Content that doesn't contribute to their goal gets in their way.
  - First impressions really matter. Users don't stay long if they don't see what they want or like what they see.
  - Credibility is determined by what matters most to the particular user, but website credibility is important for all users.
  - Generational differences matter.
    - We know a lot about what matters to each generation, from Gen Y to the G.I. generation.
    - We know some specific things about the goals of older users and younger users:
      - Older users are using the web more often for more and different things.
      - Younger users are not adept at sorting through information to know what's good and what's not, or even to know what's an advertisement and what's not.
      - Children have the best success on sites designed for adults, but on sites designed for them, they get impatient with poor usability.

With this information about users in general and web users in particular, you can apply it to the information you have or can gather about your users and their goals. This combined information becomes the basis for two documents you will use as part of planning for usability testing:

- *Personas*—which put "flesh and blood" on the demographics of your users
- *Scenarios*—which put the personas into their own stories that reflect how they will want to use your product based on their needs, wants, and desires

Planning for usability testing

5

Whether you have the luxury of time or perhaps only a few days, you need to set aside time to plan for usability testing. The planning process can be divided into a number of steps, which begin with pulling together the people who will be part of the planning process and setting a time for the planning meeting. In the planning meeting, you and your team members will get as much done as you can in the time you have and then continue working on the test materials after the meeting and before testing.

This chapter provides essential test planning steps, including:

1. Scheduling the planning meeting, in which you:
   ○ establish test goals
   ○ determine how to test the product
   ○ agree on user subgroup(s)
   ○ determine participant incentive
   ○ draft the screener(s) for recruiting participants
   ○ create scenarios based on tasks that match test goals
   ○ determine quantitative and qualitative feedback methods
   ○ set dates for testing and deliverables
2. Writing the test plan
   ○ writing an informal test plan
   ○ writing a formal test plan

Usability Testing Essentials. DOI: 10.1016/B978-0-12-375092-1.00005-2

Scheduling the planning meeting

Planning a usability test begins with knowing who should be involved and what needs to be done. The process begins with scheduling the planning meeting and inviting the project's stakeholders to attend. If everyone is co-located, you can meet in person. If all or part of the team is distributed, you can set up a meeting with GoToMeeting or another online meeting collaboration tool or via conference call.

Once you've determined who should be invited to the meeting, you need an agenda so that the attendees can prepare and bring the appropriate information to make the meeting productive. An agenda can be crafted from the generic one shown in Figure 5.1. This one shows you not only

---

Planning Meeting Agenda

1. Establish test goals based on:
   a. How much money/budget you have for testing—this information affects many planning decisions, such as the size of the test (including whether this is a single study or part of an iterative testing cycle), the number of participants, the cost for recruiting participants, paying stipends to participants, and other costs, such as renting or allocating space, etc.
   b. Where the product is in development—this information affects the type of testing you will do.
   c. Who is sponsoring the test—this affects the focus of the study. Concerns of marketing will be different from concerns of technical support/user assistance, and so forth.

2. Determine how to test the product—this discussion may involve a review of the product and assessment of its status in development. The requirements for testing will be shaped not only by the status of the product being tested but also by the location of the participants: local, remote, or a combination.

3. Agree on the user subgroup(s)—depending on your budget for testing, this could mean settling on one subgroup or, with more money for testing, two or more subgroups.

4. Determine participant incentive—again, a budget issue, but this discussion often requires a review of options and agreement on what's appropriate in the situation.

5. Draft the screener(s) for recruiting participants—this critical part of planning is tied to the user subgroups for this test.

6. Create scenarios—based on selecting tasks that match test goals.

7. Determine quantitative and qualitative feedback methods—tied to your goals for the test.

8. Set dates for the following:
   a. Testing
   b. Drafts of test materials for review (beginning with the screener)
   c. Final test materials (for test plan)
   d. Product ready for test setup (walkthrough)
   e. Post-test deliverables—agree on what these are, when they will be delivered, and in what format (written, oral presentation, video highlights, combination)

Figure 5.1 This agenda for a planning meeting provides the topics with planning notes.

the items in a typical planning meeting but the rationale for including them in the discussion.

Unless you can set aside a half day or more for the planning meeting, you will probably not be able to produce all of the documents listed on the agenda, so you need to have a plan for assigning tasks to team members and sharing drafts of these documents for feedback and approval after the meeting.

This agenda can be daunting, since there are a lot of decisions that have to be made. That's why it's important to send out your agenda in advance, identifying specific items that need to be prepared in advance (and who should prepare them) and getting a block of time committed so that you can make significant headway in the meeting. If you can get only a few of the items on this list done in the meeting, make your top priority getting everyone to agree on the test goals, user groups, and key tasks. The outcome of a successful planning meeting is agreement on these key items for the usability test and a list of follow-up actions with due dates.

Establish test goals

As is frequently the case when you begin planning a usability test, your team or sponsor wants to learn *everything* about the usability of the product. As a result, the wish list can be quite lengthy. Yet the practicalities of time and budget—not to mention the stamina of participants in testing sessions—limit the scope of what you can do in any particular test. So, how do you choose what to test?

You begin by setting your test goals. This is your first agenda item and top priority for planning the test. Test goals focus on what you want to learn about your users' experience with the product at the point in development where you will be testing. If this is your first usability test, you need to decide what's most important to learn from your users. Maybe there's an issue that the team has debated, and you'd like to get user input to know which direction to take. Or you've gotten information from customer support that a certain feature of the product is causing problems for users, so you'd like to understand what the problem is from observing users working with the feature. Or, if it's a new product and you want to know whether users understand what it is and how to use it, you can focus on the new users' experience to understand whether their mental model for the product matches your design.

If you are planning for a follow-up study, you can set goals to learn whether earlier issues have been addressed in the redesign resulting from the prior study. Or you can set goals around new features you've added to the product.

www.wqusability.com
Also see Chapter 1 for a description of these usability dimensions.

If you're not sure how to identify your testing goals, you could use criteria such as Whitney Quesenbery's 5Es—Efficient, Effective, Engaging, Error tolerant, Easy to learn—to shape your discussion. Using the Es, your team can decide how to set goals for your study and how to measure whether these goals are met.

Here are some examples of goal setting using the 5Es:

- *Efficient*—Can users find the information they need to complete tasks without assistance? Can users perform a process within a predetermined timeframe?

- *Effective*—Can users successfully place an order or sign up for a service?

- *Engaging*—Do users rate their experience as satisfying or enjoyable? Do their comments (and body language) suggest that they are having a positive experience?

- *Error tolerant*—Do users experience errors? If so, how many? And when they experience errors, do they recover successfully? If they receive error messages, do they understand them?

- *Easy to learn*—Can users get started right away? Does their ability to do tasks improve as they become familiar with the system? Does the system architecture match their mental model for the way they expect the system to work?

These criteria and the relevant questions associated with each one not only shape the task list and the scenarios you will create, but also help you determine what you want to learn from observations and what you want to learn from post-task and post-test feedback methods.

Not included in this list of goals—but so important for understanding all of your users—is the goal of accessibility. Accessibility goals require special considerations and specialized recruiting for participants, so you may not be equipped to put this on your list for your first test. But, as you become experienced with the basic planning requirements for testing, you will likely want to understand the usability of your product for all users, and that means understanding the usability of your product for people with disabilities. The following sidebar gives you some useful information about accessibility goals and resources.

Accessibility goals are in everyone's interest

Is accessibility a goal? It certainly should be—if not for legal reasons, then for practical reasons. Knowing whether your product is accessible for people with disabilities or limitations imposed for other reasons—such as diminished eyesight or mobility brought on by age or infirmity—helps you understand how to reach a part of your user population that you may not be currently reaching. Yet accessibility is often viewed as a nice-to-have goal if time and resources allow.

Legal reasons to address accessibility

The Web Content Accessibility Guidelines (WCAG) are a recommendation of the World Wide Web Consortium (W3C). W3C is a web standards organization that launched the Web Accessibility Initiative (WAI) in 1997 to ensure that W3C guidelines support access for all people. Europe and part of Asia have similar initiatives.

In the United States, Section 508 (a 1998 amendment to the Rehabilitation Act of 1973) sets standards for accessibility of information technology. It applies to all electronic and information technology products that are developed, purchased, or maintained by the federal government, which gives it a broad reach into private industry. State governments often use 508 as the baseline for their own state standards.

The Americans with Disabilities Act (ADA) affects private business as well, extending protection to all people with disabilities to provide them with equal access.

What does this alphabet soup of rules, regulations, and organizations mean for your product? It means there is plenty of information available on how and why to address accessibility, with lots of help on how to do it. These guidelines codify the requirements into a series of rules, but there's no substitute for knowing your users.

Making the business case for testing for accessibility

There's an excellent business case to be made for addressing accessibility. When improvements are made for people with disabilities, studies have shown that the user experience also improves for people *without* disabilities.

Accessibility benefits people without disabilities, including:

W3C WAI has an extensive literature review of web accessibility for older users at *www.w3.org/WAI/intro/ wai-age-literature.php*

- older people
- people with low literacy
- people without native language fluency
- people with low bandwidth connections or older technology
- people with low web literacy skills

In other words, all boats rise when you address accessibility.

Some major corporations, including Microsoft, IBM, and Fujitsu, have championed accessibility, publishing guidelines for universal access. Fidelity.com has made accessibility a core part of its planning and testing methodology.

For more on making the business case, see "Additional Benefits from a Business Perspective" in Shawn Lawton Henry's introduction to her book, *Just Ask: Integrating Accessibility Throughout Design*, 2007 (*www.uiAccess. com/JustAsk*). The book and website are an excellent resource. Also see Henry and Arch, "Developing a Web Accessibility Business Case for Your Organization" at *www. w3.org/WAI/bcase/Overview. html*

Others have been made aware of the need to address accessibility the hard way. Take Target as a high-profile example. The big-box discount retailer assumed that the Americans with Disabilities Act did not extend to websites, particularly when the company provides access through its brick-and-mortar stores. That all changed when the National Federation of the Blind brought suit against Target and won. Similar lawsuits or structured settlements have been settled against hotels, travel sites, and banks.

If you find yourself needing to make the business case for addressing accessibility, a number of resources on the Internet can give you ammunition.

Determine how to test the product

This agenda item has several parts. In determining how to test the product, you need to decide:

- *What to test*—based on where the product is in development
- *Where to conduct the test*—based on choices for lab testing, field testing, testing remotely, some combination, or another option
- *How to test*—based on resources, timing, and your goals

What to test—Product

Your discussion about what to test will focus on where the product will be in development when you want to conduct the usability test.

Ideally, you will be testing iteratively throughout product development. If, however, this is your company's first usability test, it is likely that management or the test sponsor will want to wait to test the product until it's nearly complete. This type of testing is called *summative* evaluation because it assesses the usability of the product at the end of development. It's useful and valuable to do summative testing when you want to confirm that requirements have been met for the product.

But if this is your first test, you should work to persuade the decision makers to test earlier in development so that the findings from testing can lead to more user-centered development of the product. This type of testing is called *formative* evaluation, and it can be used to test very early paper prototypes or partially developed products, the information architecture of the product, or a particular feature by itself.

There's more about summative and formative evaluation and the merits of both in Chapter 1.

Where to test—Location

Once you have decided where the product will be in development when you do the usability test and what your goals are for the test, you need to decide where you will conduct the test:

- *In a lab*—by testing in your own lab or one that you will rent
- *In a conference room*—by reserving a room for the test
- *In the field*—by going to the users in their environment
- *At a distance*—by testing remotely

There's more information about types of testing and the requirements for each in Chapter 2.

If you have a lab, you'll probably want to use it, especially if this is your first test of the product. Of course, you don't need a lab to conduct testing. Reserving a conference room or renting a local facility works just fine.

If you've done lab testing of the product already, you may want to get out into the field so that you can see how the product works in the users' environment. A combination of lab testing in one study and field testing in another study gives you a fuller picture of your users' experience because it combines controlled and natural testing environments.

You can also do remote testing, which gives you the reach to your users wherever they are and in their own environments. You can decide that you want to use remote testing for all of your test sessions, or you can decide to combine some remote and some lab testing in a single study.

How to test—Design

As you've moved through your agenda, you've made some important decisions about the goals for your usability test and the status of the product you'll be testing. Now you need to discuss the type of test design you would like to set up. Some methods for structuring the test design include these:

- *"Typical" test of the product*—when you present users with a number of tasks within scenarios, which gives you similar feedback on their experience with your product. Usually formative for products in development.
- *Benchmarking*—when you test your product with users to establish metrics, or benchmarks, for the product, as well as requirements for new product development. Usually summative for completed products.
- *Comparison of designs*—when you present users with two or more designs so that you can see whether a preference emerges.
- *Competitive evaluation*—when you present users with tasks to complete in your product and one or more competitor products to learn their preferences or to measure your product against the competition.

Later in this chapter, I provide some guidelines for comparative and competitive testing.

The decision on the type of test design you want affects the scenarios you will create and the post-task and post-test feedback mechanisms you will use. In addition to making this decision, you will also need to decide how much time you want for each test session. If you are using the "typical" approach, you will probably set up scenarios that can fit into sessions of an hour to 1½ hours. Longer sessions than this can tax the concentration of participants and the team, so if you need to test in a longer session, you probably want to build in a break in the middle.

Using the one-hour session as an example, a typical test day will have setup time of an hour, followed by participant sessions of an hour each, with short breaks in between and time for lunch in the middle. In a day, you will likely get to see five or six participants. If you run your findings meeting at the end of the day, you can add a couple of hours to the length of the day. This test schedule makes for a long but productive day.

But what happens if you don't have even a day for testing? What if you don't have the budget for testing in the usual way? What if your development cycle is so tight that the team can't wait for results before moving on? All of these questions are realistic and frequently asked. The answers come in the form of some fast and effective testing methods that speed up the process of testing and delivering results. In the world of ever-tightening schedules—made more so for those companies using an agile development methodology—these faster testing techniques keep usability in the picture. The following sidebar gives you some of these techniques.

Testing faster, cheaper

Agile programming requires agile usability testing methods

In a waterfall development methodology, each phase of development is clearly defined on a timeline with milestones to mark progress in distinct phases. Planning for usability testing is a matter of scheduling testing at specific points along the development timeline.

Nowadays, a growing number of companies have switched to the agile development process, which is making it more challenging to insert usability testing.

If you are not familiar with the agile method, here's how it works in a nutshell: Design teams work in very short development cycles, called *sprints*, of one week to one month, typically several weeks. In each sprint, the goal is to get a feature or a group of features designed and coded. The overall goal is to deliver working software early and frequently.

For an excellent explanation of how one company has done this, see Sy, "Adapting Usability Investigations for Agile User-Centered Design," 2007.

How does usability testing fit into this pace of activity? As some user experience teams have found, the solution lies in the adoption of some fast and agile testing methods. Building user experience methods into the agile development process works particularly well when the user experience team works in parallel with the development team so that UCD practices can be a separate but coordinated part of product development.

The RITE method is well suited to agile and other rapid development processes

For a full explanation of the way the process works, see Medlock Wixon, McGee, and Welsh, "The Rapid Iterative Test and Evaluation Method: Better Products in Less Time," 2006.

RITE stands for Rapid Iterative Testing and Evaluation, a great name that says it all. Developed by the user testing team at Microsoft's Games Studios, RITE addresses the business need to make fast changes to a design as soon as a problem is identified. RITE is quick, and it is agile. Using the RITE method, you can schedule a few participants during a sprint or just after it and fix whatever problems you see before having a few more users work with the product to confirm that the fixes work.

Making RITE work requires full team commitment, including key decision makers who are both knowledgeable of the product design and able to approve changes. The methodology works like this:

- Key decision makers observe the participants in testing.
- The findings are analyzed immediately after a test session concludes or, in some cases, at the end of the day.

- As soon as there is agreement that a problem exists and the solution is known, the change is made immediately. If the team isn't sure they're seeing a real problem, testing proceeds until the problem and solution become clearer.
- The changed interface is retested with the next participant.

Unlike traditional usability testing—in which you wait until you have seen all of the users, then analyze what you saw, then recommend changes, then make the changes—the RITE method focuses on redesigning to fix problems and then confirming that the solution works with users.

Other testing techniques provide fast feedback

In addition to the RITE method, other techniques may suit the needs of your product, your schedule, and your goals. Among the growing number that are being used are these:

- *Weekly testing*—Participants are recruited and scheduled every week so you can test whatever you have ready. Since participant recruiting has the longest lead time in planning for testing, this technique takes the delay out of the picture. If your company has several development teams working on different products, this weekly testing schedule can be managed with a sign-up sheet for testing on a first-come, first-served basis. If you don't have an internal usability group to do this recruiting and scheduling for you, you can set it up yourself.

- *Quick testing at a conference*—You can plan for testing at a conference or trade show, which gives you access to lots of potential users. This works particularly well when your users are hard to recruit. Using your company's exhibit booth to catch interested participants for a short, informal usability session, you can get a fast response to new features and functions that you are trying out in development.

- *Five-second tests*—This technique can be done with a paper prototype at a place where your users gather, such as a shopping

For more on using RITE and integrating best usability practices in agile development cycles, see the first-quarter issue of UPA's *User Experience Magazine*, 2010, which has several articles on this topic.

See Pawson and Greenberg, "Extremely Rapid Usability Testing," 2009.

mall or park, or you can use a free web tool available at *www. fivesecondtest.com*. Using the web tool, you upload a screen you want users to review for five seconds, then take some action. With this technique, you get feedback on first impressions and other aspects of your design, such as where users first click and what they remember about your website after only five seconds.

The point about all of these techniques is that there are many clever options to choose from, no matter how little time or budget you have. In your planning meeting, you can keep the focus on choosing the right method, knowing that there will be one that best fits your situation.

Agree on user subgroups

At this point in your planning, you have determined the goals for your study and the type of test you will conduct. You now need to agree on the user subgroups for your study.

Chapter 1 gives you the background on why we often use a small number of participants.

As you know, you can conduct a study with 5 users and get excellent results as long as the users are all from the same subgroup. If you have time and budget to test with 10 participants, you can identify two subgroups, or possibly even three. The more participants you plan to recruit, the more subgroups you can draw from.

Whether you have budget or time for only one day of testing or for several days, you need to decide on the subgroup or subgroups you want represented in your study. This decision can be difficult to make, because your team or your sponsor often wants to know about the user experience for many different groups of users. In your planning meeting, you need to get buy-in on who your users will be for this study.

There's more on personas in Chapter 4.

If you have developed personas, this makes the task a bit easier because it gives you a starting point to discuss which personas you want to include. However, a persona represents a *type* of user, and there could be a number of subgroups within a single persona. Also, personas do not typically include the specific characteristics you will be seeking to match for your study.

So, you need to come up with a list of characteristics for each subgroup. Let's call this list of characteristics for a particular subgroup a *user profile*. You will need a separate user profile for each subgroup. In your planning meeting, you may have time to generate only the list of characteristics for each subgroup. After the meeting, you can convert these subgroup characteristics into the screener, then circulate it for feedback and approval by the team and any other stakeholders before recruiting begins. If you need to start recruiting right away, this is the first deliverable you need to finalize during or after the meeting.

Define the characteristics of a subgroup

A single, definitive list of characteristics for each subgroup would not be possible to create, but here are some characteristics that typically generate differences among subgroups, using the examples of software and websites/web applications.

For software:

- familiarity with the type of product you are testing
- familiarity with your product—current or earlier version
- domain knowledge as it relates to your product
- technical skills as they relate to use of your product
- computer skills
  - computer usage
  - device usage
  - Internet usage
- software skills
  - applications
  - usage
- job category
  - job title and type of work relevant to your product
  - could include other categories such as:
    - student
    - retiree
    - stay-at-home parent

For websites and web applications:

- familiarity with the web, based on types of usage/activities and amount of time per week/month
- familiarity with websites/applications that are competitors or that share the same space as your website or application

You notice that I did not organize the characteristics by "novice" versus "expert." These terms are extremely difficult to define. And asking people to categorize themselves rarely works, since they will interpret the meaning of the terms in widely different and generally inconsistent ways.

To better place users in categories of expertise, it helps to focus on their experience with the tasks or tools you will use during testing. Once you've established some minimum and maximum ranges, you can group potential participants into experts, intermediates, or novices. You can then decide whether you want to see users in all three of these categories or only one or two.

For example, one study may focus on new user experience with novices. Another may focus on new user experience with people who have used relevant, related products, but not your product. Another study may focus on experienced users of your product who are being introduced to a design change or new features. Or, if you can recruit from several subgroups representing these users, you can combine them in your study.

Focus on user motivation

For all subgroups, matching user motivation to study goals is the most important factor in deciding who to recruit. For instance, if you are testing a website that provides information about cars to allow users to make a purchasing decision, all subgroups of users must share the common goal of being interested in this information because they are planning a new car purchase. Perhaps you set a limit of intent to purchase in the next six months. Without this real motivation, participants in the study are likely to treat the tasks as exercises that have no real meaning for them.

Mix some characteristics within a subgroup

Now that you've established the subgroups of users you want to use, you can mix in a number of characteristics within a subgroup while still maintaining consistency among the critical factors you've identified regarding motivation, skill level, and experience. Depending on the goals of your study and the variety of users within subgroups, you can get a healthy mix from the following characteristics:

- *Age*—The range can cover the entire user population, or you can set a smaller range, such as 18- to 30-year-olds.

- *Gender*—Typically, you want a 50/50 mix or close to it, unless your users are mostly (or all) male or female.

- *Education*—If all levels of education are represented in your users, the range can be from a high school education (or less) to a Ph.D. However, you may want to narrow the range. For instance, if you are seeking only low-literacy users, then defining the education level is a critical factor (although there can be other reasons for low literacy).

- *Language*—Sometimes it's appropriate to have second-language users, which does not necessarily mean low-literacy users.

- *Ethnicity*—You may want to have a mix of ethnicities if the product's users include these ethnicities. If there is a dominant ethnicity, this becomes a critical factor.

- *Disabilities*—People with disabilities can be a subgroup of its own, which would move it to a separate category, or you may want to include people with disabilities. This can be determined by either seeking people with disabilities or not ruling out people with disabilities if you identify them in screening.

- *Economic factors*—Household or individual income can be helpful in understanding purchasing power, market differentiation, and other factors. If a minimum economic requirement is established, you can solicit information by learning whether respondents:
  - own or rent a residence
  - own or lease a car or truck—one or more, brand, model, year
  - own products like the one you'll be testing—how many, what brands

Or if specific income brackets are required for your study, a question about household or individual income can be used.

Combine characteristics in a user profile

It won't be necessary to include all of the characteristics you listed in your user profiles. But it will be necessary to decide what's most relevant to your study, based on your goals. Some examples from different types of studies will show you how to choose what to include and what to leave out.

Example: File Transfer Protocol (FTP) software

Two subgroups were identified by the team as novices and advanced users on the basis of these characteristics.

Novice user:

- complete beginner in the domain—no prior experience or even concept for FTP
- must have home computer with network connection
- minimum one year Internet experience
- minimum ½ hour/day Internet use (or four hours per week)
  - surf Internet for information, shopping
  - download information from Internet
  - use e-mail, use attachments
- optional technical abilities can include use of digital camera, or MP3s or downloaded music
- no network concept understanding (terms such as *host* and *IP address* are likely to have no meaning)
- must *not* have had experience designing or building a website (except, perhaps, using a wizard to create a web space at a portal site such as Yahoo!)
- must have interest in creating a website or using a host site to share or post files (for example, eBay)
- must *not* have had experience loading files to an FTP server
- must be native/fluent English speakers (no English-as-a-second-language [ESL] speakers)
- age not an issue—no restrictions, no need for age distribution

Advanced user (based on team-generated persona for technical and power Internet user):

- job title/description: Webmaster, IT manager, or IT professional

- goal: seeking to gain productivity
- current FTP user, but not a current or recent customer (may select users with prior experience with software, earlier version)
- FTP experience with one or more other FTP products:
  - list of products here
  - other (for any product not included in the list)

Questions to ask potential participants:

- How long and how often have you used FTP products (for each of the preceding)?
- How would you make a second simultaneous connection?
- Do you manage encrypted files? If so, how?

Example: Website for information about distance learning courses and programs throughout a public state university system

- ten participants in two groups
  - current undergraduate students
    - traditional ages 18–21
    - nontraditional ages 22–35
  - graduate students
    - current
    - prospective
- must have interest or experience in taking distance learning (online) course or program
- must not have visited the website being studied
- priority for those who are interested in or currently seeking an education degree, especially in math and science
- must use computer a minimum of three hours per week (not including e-mail) for a variety of things, which could include school-related research, other information seeking, shopping, social networking, bill paying
- equal number of men and women
- some second-language speakers
- diverse ethnicity

Example: Self-installation of a digital cable box

- must have cable/satellite TV now or indicate that they are thinking of getting it
- must indicate preference (among choices) for attempting the self-installation versus paying a fee for a professional installation
- for those who are current cable subscribers:
  - must not have done the cable installation for their current TV themselves
  - must have some other equipment connected to the TV, such as VCR, DVD, stereo
- must have some comfort level/experience using or performing at least one of the following:
  - using computer/Internet—at least three hours per week
  - installing hardware—printer or fax—to their computer
  - adding or upgrading a component to a computer, such as a memory card
- equal number of men and women
- variety of
  - ages between 18 and 55
  - household incomes
  - ethnicities
  - education levels from less than high school diploma to college degree
- seek some ESL speakers, especially Spanish as first-language speakers

Determine participant incentive

Because you are asking people to take time out of their busy lives to help you understand their experience with your product, you need to compensate them for their effort. This is a tricky subject, though, because you want to make the incentive feel like a thank-you gift and not a bribe. In other words, you don't want the incentive to influence the remarks they will make as they work with the product and complete questionnaires. You also want to avoid recruiting "career participants" who do this sort of thing strictly for the incentive.

More about recruiting is covered in Chapter 6.

What's an appropriate incentive?

When it comes to determining the appropriate incentive, as with most things associated with usability testing, "It depends." The amount will vary according to the general cost of living for your city and the convenience of getting to your testing location. The amount could be US$50–60, particularly if it's easy to get to your testing location. In Atlanta, with our awful traffic congestion, we find it difficult to recruit for less than US$75 in participant incentive. This dollar amount is based on a typical study of about an hour, but it factors in the commute time as well as our request that participants check in 15 minutes early to complete paperwork.

If you are going to recruit from more than one subgroup of your user population, the incentive may not be the same for every subgroup. For instance, some of your users may be nonprofessionals, such as students, who can be recruited for less incentive than professionals in high-income salary ranges. Or you may be recruiting from a large pool of potential participants who are readily available. In this case, the incentive can be less than when you are recruiting hard-to-find or hard-to-get participants. For these hard-to-get participants, such as IT network managers, you will need to increase the incentive to US$150–200 or more.

Besides cash, common incentives include gift cards or debit cards. The face value of the card would match the appropriate cash incentive. It's best to make the gift card or debit card generic enough to allow the participant to use it in many places or for many things. Amazon.com cards work for this, as one example. Another approach is to offer a variety of product-specific gift card options from which participants can choose. This works well when you are planning for a number of studies, because you can buy the various cards in advance and have them on hand.

What do you do when you don't have money for incentives?

The participant incentive is part of the cost of doing a usability study, so the amount you can offer participants may be determined by the budget for testing. If your budget does not include money for incentives, there are ways to recruit without providing an incentive. Friends and family are one source for potential participants who will not likely need an incentive. If you find yourself with no choice but to recruit friends and family, you want to strive to get *as close as possible to your real users* in the subgroups you are interested in for this study.

Carolyn Snyder, a usability consultant, offers this advice when you're responsible for getting the participants' incentives from an ATM: "Make the amount match the way in which ATMs provide cash." Since U.S. ATMs don't typically dispense $5 bills, Carolyn suggests making the incentive some figure in multiples of $20s or $50s.

If your target participants are internal users, you may not have to provide an incentive. In this case, refreshments can be an appropriate incentive. If a small incentive is appropriate, it can be something like movie passes or a meal ticket for the company cafeteria or a coffee card from the local coffee shop.

In some cases, such as employees at the U.S. federal level and at some state agencies, participants cannot accept an incentive. When participants cannot accept an incentive, they may still have sufficient motivation to want to participate in the study.

Whatever incentive or motivation you can use to recruit participants, you need to decide what it is so that you can include it in the screener.

Draft the screener for recruiting participants

As I said earlier, the screener is usually the first document that has to get done, because you can't begin recruiting until you have the screener. That's why I've included this task in this chapter. In the next chapter, you'll see how to use the screener for recruiting.

As you move through your agenda, the hard work of determining your subgroup or subgroups of users is now done. If this is all you get done in the planning meeting, that's a significant part for an effective study.

You still need to draft the *screener*, which is the document that will be used to recruit participants.

Unless you have set aside a big block of time for the meeting, you probably won't get the screener drafted during the meeting. Instead, you may need a separate meeting for this, or agreement for someone to take the lead on drafting and circulating the screener(s) for feedback and approval from interested team members. Whether you do the recruiting yourself or use a recruiting agency, you will want to get buy-in on the specifics of the screener so that whoever does the screening is working from an approved document.

If you've never drafted a screener before, you will benefit from getting feedback from everyone. Once you get comfortable with the process, you can ask those with an interest to opt in to the review process.

Figure 5.2 is an example of a screener for the usability study of the digital cable box self-installation, which you can use to help you prepare your screener.

Digital Cable Box Self-Installation Study

Study Dates: May 12–14, 20xx

Study Times: 8:30 AM to 5:30 PM

Recruiting Goal: 21 participants, plus backups

Special Notes for Recruiters:
- Equal gender distribution
- Some English-as-a-second-language speakers, preference for Spanish
- Representative age distribution (18 to 55 yrs)
- Representative education mix of no college / some college / college degree

Candidate

Name: _____

Recruited by: _____

Qualifies?
☐ Yes ☐ No
Maybe, depends on:
_____
_____

(Although we are seeking some candidates with English as a second language, all respondents must be able to communicate clearly in English. If you have doubt as to their ability to communicate clearly, terminate.)

Candidate speaks in clear, understandable voice?   ☐ Yes (continue)   ☐ No *(Terminate)*

Recruiter Introduction

Hello, my name is _____from The Usability Center at Southern Polytechnic State University in Marietta, Georgia. We are conducting a study about how people learn to connect home entertainment products to their cable service, and would like to ask you a few questions. If you qualify for this study, we would like you to participate in a single one-hour session at our facility. You would be compensated $75.00 for your time.

If selected, will you allow us to videotape you?   ☐ Yes (continue)   ☐ No *(Terminate)*

Screener Questions

Because this study involves connecting home entertainment products to cable, we're looking for people who own a TV and perhaps also some other equipment, such as a DVD, VCR, or stereo. Perhaps you already have cable or satellite service to support your use of this equipment. Or, you're thinking of getting service in the near future.

Does this sound like you?   ☐ Yes (continue)   ☐ No *(Terminate)*

What type of television(s) do you have? (brand, size, etc.) **(If none, *terminate*)**

_____
_____

Are any of your televisions connected to any recording or playback equipment, such as a DVD, VCR, or stereo? If so, what is the equipment? (brand, type, function, etc.)

_____
_____

For your TV reception, what type of service do you currently have? Who is the provider? (Cable/Comcast, satellite/DISH Network). Other? **(If none, *terminate*)**

_____
_____

Figure 5.2 This screener is for the digital cable box self-installation study.

Who installed it?

Company installation_____   Friend or relative_____

Hired a consultant/contractor_____   Self-install_____(**Terminate**)

Before answering the next question, please consider the following statement: It costs $41.95 for a professional installation of a digital entertainment package. If you do it yourself, the same package is only $9.95. However, if you are not able to perform the installation successfully and the vendor has to send a technician to assist, you may be charged an additional $35.00 for the help provided. Now, given the choice between a professional installation and a self-install, which would you choose?

☐ I would choose to do it myself for $9.95 because I am confident about my chances for success

— OR —

☐ I would choose to do it myself for $9.95 and I would be OK with paying $35.00 for help if I needed it

— OR —

☐ I would **not** choose to do it myself and would pay $41.95 for a professional installation. (**Terminate**)

Questions About Computer Use and Experience

Do you own a computer?   Yes ☐   No ☐

If no, do you use a computer?   If yes, ask where: (**If they do not use a computer,** *terminate*)

☐ At work   ☐ Library
☐ School   ☐ Other

What do you typically use the computer for? _____
_____

When thinking about the time you spend using a computer **in an average week**, how many hours do you spend using it? Would you say you spend: (**Read list**)

Less than three hours per week	1
Between three and five hours per week	2
Between six and nine hours per week	3
Between 10 and 20 hours per week	4
More than 20 hours per week	5

Have you **personally** ever installed an add-on or upgrade component to a computer, like memory or a graphics card?   ☐ Yes   ☐ No

(If yes) What was it? _____

Have you ever installed hardware, such as a printer or a fax to a computer?   ☐ Yes   ☐ No

(If yes) What was it? _____

Demographic/Other Questions:

Record gender from voice:

Male	1
Female	2

Figure 5.2 This screener is for the digital cable box self-installation study. (*Continued*)

We want to recruit candidates from a **variety of age groups**. Please tell me in **which category your age is.**

- ☐ Less than 18 years *(Terminate)*   ☐ 40–45 years
- ☐ 18–23 years   ☐ 46–50 years
- ☐ 24–29 years   ☐ 50–55 years
- ☐ 30–35 years   ☐ 56 or older *(Terminate)*
- ☐ 36–39 years

Which of the following categories best describes your race or ethnic background? *(Read list)*

American Indian or Alaskan Native	1
Asian	2
Black or African American (not of Hispanic origin)	3
Hispanic or Latino	4
Native Hawaiian or other Pacific Islander	5
White or Caucasian (not of Hispanic origin)	6
Other	7

Do you work?   ☐ Yes   ☐ No

(If yes) What type of work do you do? _____

　　　And is that full-time or part-time? (Circle one)

What is your highest education level?

- ☐ Completed high school
- ☐ Some college
- ☐ Completed college. Degree in? _____

Which of the following categories includes your **household** income? *(Read list)*

Under $50,000	1
$50,000 to $75,000	2
$75,001 to $100,000	3
$100,001 to $125,000	4
$125,001 to $150,000	5
More than $150,000	6
Prefer not to say	7

Thank you! This concludes our questionnaire.

If you are selected for this usability study, you will receive $75.00 for your participation. When you come to our Usability Center 15 minutes before your session starts, we will ask you to sign a release form that allows us to videotape your activity for research purposes.

If you are selected for this study, what's the best way to reach you to schedule your session?

Cell: _____

E-mail: _____

Daytime number: _____

Evening number: _____

To be completed later:

Scheduled session day: _____

Scheduled session time: _____

Figure 5.2 (*Continued*)

Create scenarios based on tasks that match test goals

The next item on your agenda is determining the tasks you want your users to do with the product. Now that you know who the users are for this study, you can match the tasks to their goals for the product and your goals for the study.

To decide on the tasks, which will be crafted into scenarios, think about the questions you want your users to answer. Figure 5.3 shows you how to move from a question about navigation on a website to a task to a scenario.

Create "real" scenarios

Scenarios need to feel real to all of your participants. Here are some of the elements that you need to address in writing realistic scenarios:

- Use the language of the user, not the product.
- Put the tasks into a context of use that matches the user's world.
- Give the user a goal, not a list of steps to accomplish the task and reach the goal.
- Say as little as possible to present the goal. You don't want to write a short story or overload the user with unnecessary details. And you don't want to give away more information than the user would be expected to have to perform the task.
- In situations for which the system requires personal information from a user, provide this type of information to reduce unnecessary exposure of a user's personal details. You may need to create a unique set of data for each participant, starting with a specific user name and password, which the system you are testing will recognize.
- In some cases, you may want users to use their own information to make the tasks more realistic and meaningful. In these situations, you need to review this requirement during screening to make sure participants will be comfortable and can bring the information they need. Be prepared to have a fake set of data available for use if some change their mind about using their actual personal information.

Question:

Will users look at the top navigation bar to start their search for information?

Task:

Seeking information about online programs for military personnel. Correct choice is *Featured Degrees* in top navigation bar. Users can also find a link to programs for military personnel in the description of featured programs in the center of the homepage, but it may be below the fold on their computer screen.

Scenario:

You have a friend in the military who wants to enroll in college courses while serving. You want to see if there are any online programs your friend could apply for. How would you go about doing this on this website?

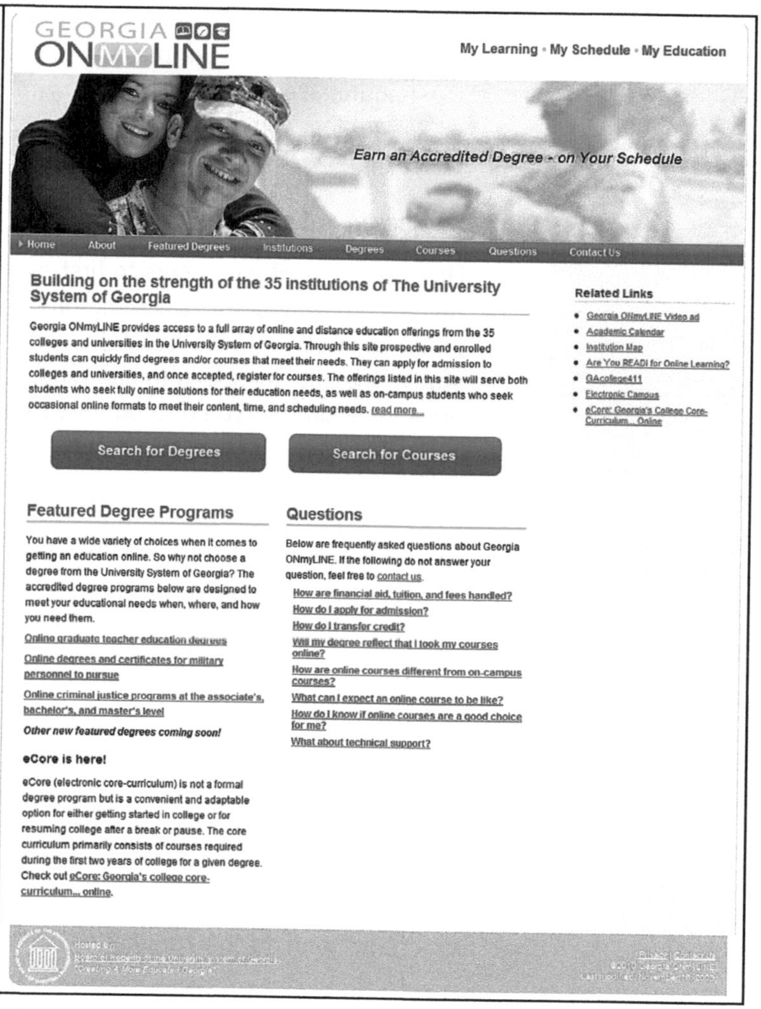

Figure 5.3 This example shows how to create a scenario by starting with a question, which is crafted into a task, which leads to a scenario that contains the task.

- To support scenarios that ask users to respond to certain situations, provide a description to help users, such as:
  - Information to enter into a text box or to put in a text message. For example, you can tell them that when prompted for the reason for their inquiry, they will respond that they are reporting a service outage. Or you can tell them that they need to send a text message to a friend to say that they're going to be 15 minutes late.

○ Any other information to standardize users' responses in a scenario. For example, you can specify how many of something to purchase, for whom, and how much to spend (with the credit card number you provide).

Decide on your first scenario

How do you want your users to first experience your product? What's the best starting point? Deciding on your first scenario should be based on the answers to these questions, which are tied to your goals for the study. Specific questions to help shape the first scenario will also be dependent on the type of product you are testing.

For a website:

- Are you interested in how they find it?
- Or do you want them to start from the homepage?
- If they are current visitors, do you want them to start with a new feature or service?

For software:

- How does the user get started?
    - ○ Is there an application they should install?
    - ○ Or do you want to install the application and have them start by clicking on the application?
- If you're focusing on a new feature, will they already know the basic features?
- If you're focusing on instructions or tutorials, do you want them to
    - ○ Start by taking the guided tour to learn the software?
    - ○ Or start with a specific task to see what instructions or help they need?

For hardware:

- Are you interested in the out-of-box experience?
- Are you focusing on the documentation for setting up the product?
- Are you interested in learning what users can do without documentation?

Your first scenario is often designed to capture initial impressions

At whatever point you start the test, it's often a goal to capture users' first impressions, especially when the study is formative. A typical first scenario that I frequently recommend is called the "look and feel" scenario because it asks participants to look around the homepage or the first screen or page view of the product and share first impressions by responding to these sorts of prompts:

- What type of site or application is this?
- What do you think you can do here?
- Look over the tabs or links and share what you think these mean and what you think will happen if you click on them.
- What would be the first action you would take?
- Are there any words or labels that you don't understand?
- What's your general impression of the site from the homepage or first screen?

Your first scenario should be short

Planning a short first scenario has several advantages:

- It allows participants to see how this process is going to work and, if they have any initial anxiety about it, to get comfortable.
- It allows you to correct any unforeseen technical problems and other logistical issues.
- It gives you a natural stopping place to reinforce the importance of having the participant think out loud. Having this natural break to remind the participant about this is especially important if the moderator is not sitting with the participant.

Chapter 7 tells you more about options for the location of the moderator.

Other scenarios come from your task list

After deciding how you want to start the test, you next need to decide how many other scenarios you want to create, using the technique that was shown in Figure 5.3. You probably have more tasks (and questions) than you have time, so you will need to set priorities for the scenarios you create and assign some estimates of the time for each scenario. You can also create some optional scenarios to use if there's time remaining in some sessions.

Your scenarios could be organized in a number of ways, such as the ones that follow:

- a sequence of tasks that has to be performed in a particular order
- most frequently performed tasks
- tasks getting the most calls to the help desk
- the most critical tasks (which may not be tasks that are performed most frequently)
- new tasks/new features
- tasks or task flows that are the subject of internal debate (the user can show the team what works, what doesn't)
- comparative tasks using alternate designs of your product or your product and a competitor's product

See the sidebar for more about how to set up comparative/ competitive testing.

Comparative/competitive testing requires special considerations

Comparative testing lets you try out different designs to learn user preferences. *Competitive testing* lets you assess your product against a competitor's product or assess competitor products against each other. These types of tests can produce valuable insights in both formative and summative testing, but they require special handling to set up scenarios that provide balance and fairness.

If you have never done a usability test before, I wouldn't recommend that you start with this type of testing. I also wouldn't recommend testing more than two options until you get comfortable with handling the data, because the data analysis gets more complex with each additional product you include.

However, if you've done some basic testing before and the team's goal for this study is to compare alternate versions of a design or certain tasks in your product with similar tasks in a competitor's product, or to do a competitive evaluation of products currently on the market, then you will want to set up this type of test.

Here are some of the questions you will need to discuss. The answers will shape the way you set up your scenarios and design your study.

- *Will the same users test both products?* This type of testing is called *within-subjects* design. With the same participants using both products, you want to set up an A–B, B–A comparison. That means that half the participants will begin with the A product and half with the B product. Within the tasks, you may want to vary the order again, such that half the participants are exposed to task A first, with the other half exposed to task B first. This assumes that the tasks do not need to be performed in sequence. The within-subjects approach takes more time, clearly, because participants are performing the same tasks twice. However, the same participant tests both products.

- *Will half the users test one product and the other half test the competitor product or alternate design?* This type of testing is called *between-subjects* design. Because you have reduced the number of participants by half for testing each product, you will typically need more participants to get a clear picture of your users' preferences. However, the testing session takes less time than the within-subjects design because participants are working with only one product. Using this approach means that you have to screen participants very carefully to match the characteristics of the users for either product.

As you can see, there are advantages and disadvantages to each of these approaches. So, the team needs to decide which approach is a better match for the study's goals, time, and budget for testing. Once the approach is chosen, you can craft the scenarios to fit the situation.

Decide how scenarios will end

Your participants need to know when they have completed a task and you need to know when they think they are done. To get this feedback, you will want to write the ending into your scenarios. Typically, this includes a request that they tell you when they are done. An example is something like this: "When you have completed this transaction, let us know that you are done."

It's important to hear this from the participant, since it is a common finding in usability studies that the participant thinks the task is complete when, in fact, it is not. It is also sometimes the case that you observe the participant complete the task, but then you see that he or she continues beyond the completion point to confirm that it is done correctly.

Knowing when the participant thinks the task is finished can be critical to understanding whether users can complete a transaction successfully on their own and whether they feel confident that they have done it correctly. If you hear participants say, "I *think* I did that right," you very likely have a problem you need to address.

Decide how to provide the scenarios to the participant

How will you distribute the scenarios to the participants? Consider these two approaches:

- Give the participant the first scenario. Ask the participant to tell you when he or she is done so that you can then give the participant the next scenario, or the post-task questionnaire and then the next scenario. Do this for each scenario.

- Give the participant all of the scenarios, and tell the participant to continue with the next scenario when he or she has completed each one.

When you vary the order of the scenarios, you want to avoid numbering the scenarios so that participants don't get the impression that they are being asked to do some but not others. Instead of using a number for each scenario, use a descriptive heading to help you keep up with them.

The advantage to the one-at-a-time approach for providing scenarios is that you can interact with the participant between scenarios and you can control the number and order of the scenarios you give the participant. This method works well if you are on a tight schedule or are varying the order of the scenarios for different users.

The advantage to providing all of the scenarios at once is efficiency, in that the participant can move through the scenarios, along with any post-task questionnaires embedded at the end of each scenario, without interruption. This method works well if your goal is to see participants do all of the scenarios, regardless of the time it takes. It also works well as a strategy if the scenarios are linked, so that the participant finishes one and then naturally moves to the next one.

However, if the participant doesn't complete one task successfully, you may have to interrupt the flow of the scenarios to help the participant get to the next level. Using this approach means you will need to schedule sufficient time between participants to provide the flexibility to let the session run until all of the scenarios are completed (or decide to stop at whatever point the session needs to end).

Use these scenario examples for ideas

The following examples of scenarios build on the earlier examples in this chapter of the characteristics of subgroups. The scenarios are crafted to match the tasks with participants' goals for the product and your goals for understanding their experience with the product.

Example: Website for students interested in distance learning

Scenario 1: Take a look at the website

Open up this website (minimized on the tray at the bottom of your screen) and tell us:

- your first impressions
- what you think the site is about
- what you think you might want to do here
- without actually clicking on anything yet, what you think you might want to click on first
- what result you think you would get by following that link

Scenario 2: Is distance learning right for you?

You are thinking about the advantages of taking courses online, but you're not sure if distance learning is right for you.

See if there is information on this site to help you determine whether you are a good fit for distance learning.

Note: The scenario does not use "e-learning," which is the terminology on the website.

Scenario 3: Finding a degree or course of interest

Part A. Finding degree or course

You have decided you want to find a degree or course that you can take online. According to your questionnaire, you are interested in [*field of study*]. See if you can find a school that is offering something online that you want to take.

Note: The task is unstructured to allow participants to pursue a real goal and/or interest. They were screened to match their motivation to the website's purpose.

Part B. Costs and signing up

Now that you have found something online that suits your needs, do the following:

- Find out how much it costs.
- See if you can sign up for this course or degree.

Example: Digital cable box self-installation

Sometimes, as in the case of the following instructions, the task is a process that fits into a single scenario. In this study, the focus is on the documentation for the self-installation process. The goal of the study is to learn whether the documentation succeeds in providing the support users need to successfully install the digital cable box. An additional goal is to understand when users need to call customer support and, in such cases, whether they are able to complete the self-install after receiving help from someone.

Instructions to participant

Use the documentation to help with the installation, even if you would not normally do this. Remember, we are testing the documentation, not you.

Set up your entertainment system so that the digital cable box, the TV, the DVD player, and the stereo are all connected.

If at any time you feel you need help, call our help desk.

When you are done or ready to stop, give us a call.

Determine quantitative and qualitative feedback methods

Depending on whether you are conducting a formative or summative evaluation and what your goals are for the study, you may want to focus on one type of data collection or another. However, a combination of both quantitative and qualitative collection methods can give you a fuller understanding of the user experience.

If your product is fairly robust, it can be useful and important to set metrics for the study. Management likes metrics because metrics can be used to support the business goals for the product. User experience practitioners like metrics because they can help make a case for product improvements based on usability testing and for more usability testing.

But metrics don't tell the whole story of your users' experience. And if your product is at a very early stage of development, metrics may not be appropriate at all. However, when the product is sufficiently developed to take measurements as well as listen and learn from the participants, it's highly effective to combine metrics with your observations, comments from participants, and their responses to open-ended questions.

For planning purposes, you want to decide which types of data collection you will use. In this chapter, I give you the basics to discuss your options. A few definitions should help shape the discussion.

There's much more about analyzing both quantitative and qualitative data in Chapter 8.

Performance and preference data are quantitative

Performance and preference data are primarily *quantitative*. In other words, the findings can be counted and measured against benchmarks established to determine success or failure.

- *Performance data* are based on measurements of users' actions, such as time on task; number of errors; recovery from errors; success or failure at task completion; use of help, documentation, or embedded assistance; and so forth. When you set specific performance metrics, you need to base each metric on data. If you arbitrarily set a metric that users must complete the install process within five minutes, their "success" in doing this task in this timeframe may not have any correlation to their perception of ease of use or satisfaction with the process. If you don't have good metrics before you start testing, you can establish them from your analysis following the first study and then use them as a baseline for future studies.

- *Preference data* are based on users' responses to questions on post-task and post-test questionnaires. These responses provide quantitative data when they can be measured, using participants' ratings on tasks (for example, with a five-point scale from very easy to very difficult).

Chapter 6 gives you information on how to create your own or use available questionnaires.

In the planning meeting, you will decide the types of performance and preference data you want to collect. For collecting preference data, you may want to create your own questionnaires, or you may want to use one of the standard questionnaires.

Observations and user comments provide qualitative feedback

Observations of your participants yield rich *qualitative* feedback. Qualitative feedback is gathered by noticing what participants do while they are engaged with the product. You may want to note nonverbal feedback, such as users' facial expressions, body language, and nonverbal utterances, including laughing, sighing, moaning, and even, occasionally, screaming (not to mention cursing!). Don't underestimate the importance of gathering this feedback: It will tell you a great deal about your users' experience.

Chapter 8 gives you information about how to analyze the feedback you get from test sessions.

Qualitative feedback also comes from noting participants' comments as they are thinking out loud while they work and participants' responses to open-ended questions in a questionnaire or interview after they have completed scenarios and at the end of the testing session. Their candid comments can provide rich insights into their experience, both positive and negative.

Set dates for testing and deliverables

Now that you have discussed the goals for your usability study, identified your user subgroup(s), and decided on the tasks to put into scenarios, you have one item left: setting dates for testing and project deliverables.

You may already know the test dates. But it's often the case that you have a timeframe for conducting testing, but you haven't set dates yet. Setting the dates for testing may depend on the availability of the core team members, the availability of the lab or space you'll use for testing, and the discussion you have had in this meeting about the status of the product you want to test.

In addition to setting the dates for testing, you need to decide on the schedule you will use for each testing day. Typical testing takes place during normal business hours, but there could be good reasons to test after hours and on weekends, since you need to match the test schedule to the availability of the users.

Another consideration is how to schedule participants from more than one subgroup. If you are doing two days of testing, and if the participants will be easy to recruit, and if you have more than one subgroup, you might want to schedule one subgroup on one day and another subgroup on the other day. This makes the end-of-day analysis a bit easier. But if you don't have much time and you need as much flexibility as possible, you will probably want to leave participant scheduling up to the recruiter (which could be you!).

Chapter 6 tells you about recruiting and scheduling participants.

Finally, you need to consider the stamina of the moderator in setting your schedule. If you are planning to test with four to six people per day in one-hour sessions, a single moderator should be able to take the schedule in stride. But if you're planning a longer daily test schedule with more participants, you should consider using more than one moderator. The following sidebar—which is based on feedback from experienced practitioners—provides food for thought on the optimal number of participants a moderator and others on the team can handle per day.

Chapter 7 tells you how to test with two or more moderators.

How many one-hour sessions are optimal for a day?

This is actually a two-part question. The answer to the first part—How many sessions are you good for in a day?—affects the second part— How long does it take to do the analysis? Cliff Anderson, a veteran of usability studies, posed these questions to a professional, private Internet discussion group. His results, based on 30 responses, are shown in the table that follows.

Question	Mean	Median	Mode	Low	High
How many one-hour sessions are you good for in a day?	4.87	4.75	4	3.5	6.5
How long does it take to analyze 10 one-hour sessions and write up the results?	39.8 hours	40 hours	40 hours	6 hours	80 hours
How many years have you been doing user testing?	13	14		2	29

The message to take away from these results is that testing can be quite taxing to the moderator and the team if you try to schedule a lot of participants in a day. But analysis, which comes after testing, is where the time commitment is much greater and the timeframe in which to deliver the results may be much shorter.

Preparing a test schedule

You may not get the actual schedule done in your planning meeting, but you need to decide the general outline of the schedule so that recruiting can get underway.

What's in a typical test day? There may be no such thing as a "typical" test day because, as with so much associated with usability testing, "It depends." If you're planning to do a walkthrough and/or pilot in advance or on the first day of testing, if you're planning to do analysis during the day at several break points or at the end of the day, if you're using the RITE method or another rapid response/redesign approach . . . all of these variables affect your test schedule.

However, a test day, in general terms, has some common characteristics. You've always got sessions and (if you're sane) breaks in between. You've always got participants, usually one at a time. You may or may not include time for analysis, prototype changes, or debriefing at the end of the day. But if these activities don't occur during your test day, they will typically occur as soon as possible afterward.

The *ideal* test schedule is one that builds in flexibility so that delays can be made up quickly. The *reality* of a typical test day is that the first delay can cause a ripple effect throughout the day, made worse by a schedule of back-to-back sessions.

Setting up the schedule that suits your situation

Your schedule needs to accommodate the timeframe for each session, the breaks between sessions, and the time for setup at the beginning and debriefing at the end. If you're starting with a pilot test, you need to schedule time to make changes afterward. To give you an idea of how to set up your schedule, take a look at this table, which shows you several schedule options for a one-day study of one-hour sessions.

	Option 1: Debrief at end of day	Option 2: Debrief during the day	Option 3: Pilot plus testing and debrief
8:00–9:00 A.M.	Setup/preparation	Setup/preparation	Setup/preparation
9:00–10:00 A.M.	Participant 1	Participant 1	Pilot test
10:15–11:15 A.M.	Participant 2	Participant 2	Pilot debrief/revision
11:30–12:30 P.M.	Participant 3	Debrief	Participant 1
12:30–1:30 P.M.	Lunch brought in	Lunch brought in	Lunch brought in
1:30–2:30 P.M.	Participant 4	Participant 3	Participant 2
2:45–3:45 P.M.	Participant 5	Participant 4	Participant 3
4:00–5:00 P.M.	Debrief	Participant 5	Participant 4
5:00–6:00 P.M.	Debrief	Debrief	Participant 5*
6:00–7:00 P.M. or later	Wrap up or prepare for next day	Wrap up or prepare for next day	Debrief or wrap up/prepare for next day
*Start time is 5:15; debrief begins at 6:30.			

This schedule shows 15 minutes between participant sessions. You could expand it to give yourself more time between sessions, but it's not a good idea to compress it, since you really need the flexibility of at least 15 minutes between sessions to allow for any resetting you need to do, such as reassembling the paper prototype, clearing the cache on a website or application, or deleting the account you had the user create.

Another variation to this schedule is that you could start earlier or later and go into the evening, particularly if you need to schedule evening sessions when your participants are available.

You could also set the debrief for another day, so that you can maximize your testing time with participants and see one or two more per day. If you are paying for a lab rental and you want your observers to see as many participants as possible, this could be an important consideration.

If you conduct the debriefing/analysis session at the end of the day, it can be more than an hour or two, although it's good to set a time limit on this activity (with the option to continue another day or in different medium).

Setting dates for deliverables

The next item related to setting dates is determining when the draft deliverables will be circulated for review and when the final deliverables will be completed. In addition, you need to decide who will take the lead on each of these deliverables. As I said earlier, if testing is going to be soon, the first deliverable needs to be the screener, since screening for the right participants has the longest lead time.

The due date for the deliverables will be determined by your plan to test the test. If the product and the testing facility and the team are available before full testing begins, you will need the deliverables for a walkthrough or pilot. If it's not feasible to test the test in advance, then the deadline for the deliverables may be the day before testing starts.

Chapter 9 is all about the ways in which you can report your findings.

Finally, you want to agree on the post-test deliverables so that everyone understands when results will be available and in what form.

Writing the test plan

No matter how much buy-in you get for everything you have planned for your usability study, you still need to document it. Whether informal or formal, the test plan is the record of the decisions made about what to test, how to test, who to recruit for testing, and so forth. Without this document, individual memories may vary, decisions may become blurred, and the outcome from testing could be challenged.

The test plan puts everything in writing. If the planning meeting gave you the time you needed to produce drafts for all of the materials to be used in the test, then the test plan can be written immediately after the meeting. More common, however, is to continue working on materials for the test after the meeting. In this situation, you should think of the test plan as a living document that evolves as the materials get fleshed out.

It's best to determine a freeze date for the test plan, though, so that everyone can agree to work with the same plan, based on the last revisions allowed.

The test plan can be informal or formal, depending on the needs of the recipients of the plan. The type of test plan people expect should be decided in the planning meeting.

Writing an informal test plan

An informal test plan can be nothing more than the notes or minutes from the planning meeting. The three pages of Figure 5.4 show the notes from a meeting to plan the usability study of FTP software. I have used parts of the planning process for this study as an example in this chapter.

Planning Meeting Notes

New version, release xxx
Two user groups—novice and advanced
Meeting participants: (*list*)

Date of meeting: January 6, 20xx
Meeting time: 1:00–5:00 P.M.

Product goals:

- increased conversion rate following product release
- reduced support calls

Test goals:

- confirm whether the install is simplified for new users
- learn what new users do when error occurs
- learn new users' expectations from name, download, install experience
- learn advanced users' perceptions of new product (compared to other products)
- learn advanced users' perceptions of new features (e.g., PGP)
- understand the experience for the new user in the purchasing model of try/buy

Status of product for test/issues:

New version of current product: mature product; not done formal testing before; many features added to product over time; lesser-skilled users are now using the product. Testing will take place at two points in development so that changes resulting from first test can be tested in a follow-up study.

Issues in current product, to be studied and improved in new release:

- initial screen is confusing
- product doesn't have modern look and feel
- confusion over two interface options in the product; which to choose?
- problems with file transfer manager opening in new window

Figure 5.4 These notes from the planning meeting document the decisions made for testing the FTP software.

New product features include:

- multiple interfaces (MDI type model); goal is to be more flexible
- file transfer manager embedded in the interface (not separate window)
- log-in embedded in interface
- Internet Explorer embedded as a choice for interface design

User profiles [these were developed from the characteristics of the user subgroups]:

Two user groups: novice and advanced (screening questionnaires to be drafted by assigned team member)

Novice user:

- must have home computer with network connection
- minimum one year Internet experience
    - minimum ½ hour per day Internet use (or 4 hours per week)
    - surf Internet for information, shopping
    - use e-mail, attachments
- must have downloaded information from Internet
- technical abilities can include use of scanner, digital camera, MP3, or downloaded music
- no network concept understanding (terms such as host and IP address are likely to have no meaning)
- must not have had experience building a website (except, perhaps, using a wizard to create a web space at a portal site like Yahoo!)
- must have interest in creating a website or using a host site to share or post files (example, eBay)
- must not have had experience loading files to an FTP server
- age not an issue
- must be native/fluent English speaker (no ESL speakers)

Advanced user:

- current FTP user, but not a current or recent customer (may select users whose experience with product is at least two versions earlier)
- likely to be Webmaster, IT manager, or IT professional
- looking to gain productivity
- has had FTP experience with one or more other FTP products: (list to follow)

Questions to ask potential participants:

- How long and how often have you used FTP products (for each of the products on the list)?
- How would you make a second simultaneous connection?
- Do you manage encrypted files? If so, how?

Tasks for Scenarios (to be drafted by assigned team member):

Novice user:

1. Initial impressions—install (five screens). After installation wizard is completed, ask user for impressions of process, product, name of product, etc. Also find out perceptions of options and functions.
2. eBay or similar site. Connect to the site. Upload a file. Add another file.
3. Download file(s) from public site like NASA (Mars photos).

Figure 5.4 These notes from the planning meeting document the decisions made for testing the FTP software. (*Continued*)

Advanced user:

1. Launch product. Upload all files to one server.

2. Create connection to second server. Add sites.

3. From local server, upload files to two other servers. If they do this in version A, ask them to find another way to do it (to discover the differences with Version B).

4. Your company has just made a policy that all files shared on servers must be encrypted using PGP. Encrypt your local files; provide access for four people.

Performance measurements:

- help (use and types)
- errors and recovery
- time on tasks
- satisfaction
- learnability
- ease of use

For advanced users: Comparison with other FTP products

For both user groups:

- Would you purchase the product?
- How much would you be willing to pay for it?

Dates for deliverables and testing:

- screening questionnaires completed by Jan. 9; recruitment begins
- product prototype to team members for scenarios; freeze date on prototype for the test Jan. 13
- all materials for walkthrough must be reviewed by team and completed by Jan. 14
- walkthrough (two versions of scenarios for two user groups), Jan. 15, 11:00 A.M. to noon; 1:00 P.M. to 2:00 P.M. (lunch provided; revisions made over lunch and after second user, as needed)
- revision to materials as needed; finalized by Jan. 16
- pilot Jan. 19, 1:00 P.M. to 3:30 P.M. (two users—novice and advanced—back to back)
- revision to materials as needed, same day
- testing dates (specific schedule for recruiting, sent separately)
  - day 1, Jan. 20, 8:00 A.M.–4:30 P.M. (setup, five participants)
  - day 2, Jan. 21, 8:00 A.M.–7:00 P.M. (setup, four participants + replacement, if needed; debrief)

Figure 5.4 (*Continued*)

Writing a formal test plan

A formal test plan is produced when full reporting is required or expected. Even when not required, a formal test plan can be helpful when key stakeholders are not present at the planning meeting.

A formal test plan typically contains the following sections:

- *Title Page*—identifies the document as the test plan for a particular product/group/company/date(s). The plan is directed to the sponsor (or key decision maker) for the study and identifies who the plan is from, either the team lead or the group or external consultancy.

- *Table of Contents*—reflects the first- and second-level headings in the test plan, with corresponding page numbers.

- *Purpose/Executive Summary*—a purpose statement provides an overview of the test plan and the purpose of the test. An executive summary is more explicit, providing management with a succinct but clear description of the critical elements of the test plan. This is usually a one-page summary that executives and managers can read quickly and know the essential elements of the plan.

- *Problem Statement and Test Objectives*—establishes the issues to be addressed in the test, framed as goals.

- *Methodology*—describes the type of test and the method to be used.

- *User Profiles*—describes the users for this test. If the test will address two or more subgroups of users, then each profile provides the specific characteristics.

- *Participant Incentive*—defines the amount or type of incentive to be used in recruiting participants.

- *Screeners*—created for each user profile. Can be included in the report or in the appendix.

- *Task List*—describes the tasks that will be included in the test, sometimes with the objective of each set of tasks included to show how these tasks match the study's goals.

- *Scenarios*—presents the tasks within realistic, goal-directed descriptions. The tasks and goals can be included at the top of each scenario. Can be included in the report or in the appendix.

- *Evaluation Methods*—describes the data collection methods, including the types of data that will be collected (quantitative and qualitative). If questionnaires have been developed or identified at this point, they are included.

- *Test Environment and Equipment*—describes the equipment in the facility if it is not known to the report's readers. Also, if the testing environment needs to be configured in a certain way or requires additional equipment, that information is documented here.

- *Deliverables*—describes the reports that will be delivered following testing. Also describes the method and type of delivery—formal or informal, paper or electronic document; oral presentation/meeting; video highlights tape—and dates for delivery.

Summarizing Chapter 5

This chapter presented the steps you need to take to plan your usability test. Those steps become the agenda for the planning meeting you will have with the key stakeholders to decide on the elements of your usability test. The agenda items for the meeting include:

- setting test goals by deciding what's most important to learn from users in this study
- determining how to test the product by discussing what to test, where to test, and how to set up the test
- agreeing on the user subgroup(s) you will use by defining the characteristics of each subgroup and putting these characteristics together in user profiles
- determining the appropriate incentive for each subgroup
- drafting the screeners based on the characteristics of the user subgroups
- selecting the tasks to put into scenarios by matching your goals with your users' goals and crafting scenarios that feel "real" to your users
- determining the quantitative and qualitative feedback methods you'll use to capture metrics and observations
- setting dates for testing and deliverables for the test and the test results

With all of these decisions made in the planning meeting, and with deliverable dates set for completing the elements for the usability test, you now want to document your decisions. That's what the test plan does.

Chapter 6 covers information on how to create these questionnaires.

The test plan for the Holiday Inn China website usability study was presented in a formal report because it was going to the sponsor/client, the User Experience manager at Intercontinental Hotels Group, for review by the manager and others. The plan contains several appendixes, which include questionnaires to be used in testing sessions. Because every part of the test had to be approved by the sponsor, these parts are included in the test plan.

Part of the test plan is included here. To see the complete test plan, visit the book's companion website at *www.mkp.com/testingessentials*

Usability Test Plan for
HolidayInn.com.cn

Holiday Inn Hotel Website for Chinese-Speaking Users

Prepared for: Karen Bennett, Project Sponsor,
User Experience Manager at IHG

Cc: Dr. Carol Barnum, Project Advisor

Completed by: **Team CBR**
Yufei Duan
Yina Li
Ying Li
Qianying Liu
Niven Sellars
Michael Somer

Date: March 02, 2008

Purpose

The purpose of the *holidayinn.com.cn* usability test is to collect feedback about how users use the Chinese Holiday Inn website, what problems they may encounter using the site, and what improvements they would like to see to make it easier to book a hotel room.

Ms. Karen Bennett, the User Experience Manager of InterContinental Hotels Group, is the project sponsor. She would like to learn about users' experiences on the Chinese website compared to their experiences with a competitor website: *www.elong.com*. If time permits, she would also like to know how their experiences compare with *www.holiday.com*, the U.S. website.

This test plan describes:

- problem statement and test objectives
- user profile to recruit for testing
- testing methodology and tasks/scenarios
- test setup in the usability center
- plans for data collection and reporting
- project deliverables
- questionnaires and other materials to be used in testing, in appendices:
  - Appendix A: Participant screening questionnaire
  - Appendix B: Pre-test questionnaire
  - Appendix C: Post-task questionnaires
  - Appendix D: Post-test questionnaire

For the appendices mentioned here, see the complete study on the companion website.

Problem Statement and Test Objectives

This usability test of the Chinese Holiday Inn website will provide qualitative and quantitative data addressing IHG's interest in understanding Chinese users' experience. We will assess the users' experience with booking a room as well as their satisfaction with the site. Tasks for testing *www.holidayinn.com.cn* include:

- *The general feeling/layout of the site:* Does the layout suggest the route first-time users will take to book a hotel?

- *The procedure for booking a hotel online:*
  - *Basic search:* Is it easy to use?
  - *Advanced search:* Can users accomplish their goals on the advanced search screen?
  - *Entering personal information:* Does the website require reasonable and suitable information for Chinese users? Do users understand all information requirements?
- *Language:* Do users understand all the wording on the website? Are there any translation mistakes or misunderstandings?
- *Information in confirmation e-mail:* How quickly can users receive the confirmation e-mail after booking a hotel online? Does the confirmation e-mail contain enough information to suit users' needs?
- *Perceived reliability of the site:* Do users trust the website? Do they fill out the personal information readily?
- *Navigation:* Can users find the most efficient navigation when they book a hotel or browse the website?
- *Satisfaction:* Which aspects do users like and which aspects do they dislike?

These questions were devised using information supplied by our sponsor and our assessment of potential usability problems resulting from our heuristic evaluation of the site (submitted previously).

This usability study will be designed to allow us to obtain mostly qualitative data. The focus of the study will be task-oriented and directed toward how the user subjectively responds to the issues listed above. Participants will be given a pre-test questionnaire to get information about their hotel booking experience and expectations, followed by scenarios that direct them to perform specific tasks. Post-task questionnaires after each scenario, as well as a post-test questionnaire, are designed to obtain detailed and specific feedback about *www.holidayinn.com.cn* features.

Users will be scheduled in one-hour sessions to include pre-test and post-test questionnaires. Users will be given 40 minutes to complete five scenarios. If participants complete the scenarios in less than 40 minutes, we have designed an extra scenario to obtain additional feedback.

The test will be conducted in a full-scale usability lab at Southern Polytechnic. Logging and recording of sessions will be done using Morae, with backup recordings on DVD. The participant computer will have Microsoft's Chinese character-based language installed.

User Profile for U.S.-Based Participants

To recruit prospective test participants who represent the site's actual users, the project team identified two primary users groups and created two descriptions of those users. Personas for these two user profiles were submitted previously.

Since the situation is that of testing the Chinese website within the United States, we will use only one of the user groups/personas, which will allow us to recruit these users to participate in the study in the Usability Center.

The characteristics of the U.S.-based user group, along with other questions about prior experience, behaviors, and other criteria, will make up the screening questionnaire (Appendix A) for identifying suitable test participants.

A general description of the user characteristics is as follows:

- must be able to speak and read Chinese as well as English
- first language must be Chinese
- travel purpose is either business or pleasure
- age must be between 24 and 55
- need a mix of female and male
- must have experience booking a hotel room online
- must use the Internet at least five hours per week
- must not have any prior experience with the Chinese Holiday Inn website

Methodology and Tasks/Scenarios

This section describes the testing methodology and scenarios we will use with six participants in one-hour sessions.

Number of Participants

We plan to test a total of six participants: three who travel for business and three for pleasure. To ensure an adequate number of participants, we plan to recruit eight users based on our screener; two out of the eight are backup participants.

Length of Sessions

The total length of each session will be an hour; including:

- *Welcome and pre-test questionnaire:* 10 minutes
- *Task scenarios:* 40 minutes
- *Post-test questionnaire:* 10 minutes

The estimated time for each scenario is noted below.

Test Procedure

The test will begin with an overview briefing, followed by the scenarios described below, post-task questionnaires, and a post-test questionnaire.

Participants will not be allowed to use any resources that are not available on the Holiday Inn website (that is, no use of Google or other outside sources). This restriction will not be stated in the moderator's introduction to avoid influencing the participants' actions. However, if participants want to use external resources, the moderator will notify them that such action is not allowed for testing purposes.

Overview/Briefing (10 minutes)

The moderator will welcome the participant and have him/her sign the video consent form. Next, the moderator will explain the facilities and ask the participant to think out loud. Also, the moderator will provide the participant with the pre-test questionnaire (Appendix B).

Scenario 1 (5 minutes)

You and your spouse are thinking of going back to China for the Summer Olympics. You heard that the Holiday Inn has several locations in Beijing.

You will visit the Chinese Holiday Inn website. (This will be minimized on the desktop.) Take a moment to look at the homepage without clicking on anything. After you have familiarized yourself with the homepage, tell us: What do you think you would do on the site to book a hotel room?

Scenario 2 (15 minutes)

You are going to book a hotel room for your stay in China. You want to reserve one hotel room with one bed for two people in Beijing. You will stay from July 20 to July 25. Here is the information you need to book the room:

- *First name:* Jing
- *Last name:* Li
- Reserve for you and your spouse
- *Location:* Beijing
- *Check-in date:* July 20, 2008
- *Check-out date:* July 25, 2008
- *Credit card type:* Visa
- *Credit card number:* 1234 2345 3456 4567
- *Credit card security code:* 990
- *Credit card expiration date:* 10/2010
- *E-mail:* holiday@gmail.com

Scenario 3 (5 minutes)

You just answered a phone call from your relative who lives in Beijing. She wants you and your spouse to stay at her house during the visit. You accept the invitation, so you must now cancel your Holiday Inn reservation.

Scenario 4 (5 minutes)

You have some relatives in Changchun, Jilin Province. You want to visit them during your trip to China. See if there is a Holiday Inn available in Changchun from July 26–30.

Scenario 5 (10 minutes)

Go to the competitor site *www.elong.com*. See if a hotel room is available for you and your spouse between July 21 and 25 in Beijing. (*Note:* You are not going to actually book a hotel room on this website.) Look at the search results page and tell us:

- What do you think of this site?
- What do you like about it?
- What do you dislike about it?

Scenario 6 (optional; 5 minutes)

- Go to the Holiday Inn U.S. website (*www.holiday.inn.com*).
- Take a moment to look at the homepage without clicking on anything.
- Tell us what you think of this website compared to the Holiday Inn China and eLong websites.

Closing (5–10 minutes)

Moderator will ask the participant to complete the post-test questionnaire (Appendix D).

Preparing for usability testing

6

In your planning meeting, you began your preparations for testing. You created or assigned due dates to complete the screener and the scenarios. You also determined the feedback mechanisms you will use to gather qualitative and quantitative feedback.

This chapter is about the other activities you will need to do or assign as you prepare for testing. These activities include:

- recruiting participants
  - how to do the recruiting yourself
  - how to recruit through an agency
  - how to plan for no-shows
- assigning team roles and responsibilities
  - developing team checklists
  - writing the moderator's script
- preparing or using other forms
  - preparing a video consent form
  - preparing a special consent form when testing with a minor
  - using a non-disclosure agreement
  - preparing an observer form

It's somewhat of an arbitrary distinction to break planning and preparing into two phases and two chapters in this book, but I did it this way because the agenda items covered in Chapter 5 result in decisions that shape your preparations for testing. One of these decisions—the criteria for the screener—has to be done before recruiting can begin.

Usability Testing Essentials. DOI: 10.1016/B978-0-12-375092-1.00006-4

- creating questionnaires
  - creating a pre-test questionnaire
  - creating post-task questionnaires
  - creating a post-test questionnaire
- using standard post-test questionnaires
  - using the SUS
  - using the CSUQ
- creating or using qualitative feedback methods
  - using product reaction cards
  - ending with an interview
- testing the test
  - conducting the walkthrough
  - conducting the pilot

Recruiting participants

Recruiting takes time. If you do the recruiting yourself, you can expect to spend a great deal of time screening potential participants and scheduling them and then following up with phone calls or e-mails to keep them informed (and motivated) to attend at their scheduled time.

If you hire an agency, you need to give the agency enough lead time to do the recruiting. They often want one or two weeks for this task.

How to do the recruiting yourself

If you are doing the recruiting yourself, you can draw from your current customers or prospective customers, assuming you have access to them. Your company may have a database of prequalified or current customers. If you do not have a database to draw from, you can solicit participants from your company's website or a blog that reaches current or potential customers. Even better, if you have some lead time or plan to do testing on a regular basis, you can start recruiting now for potential participants who fit your user profiles. Once you have specific test dates and a screener, you can contact the ones that match your user profile(s) for your study to see if they are available.

When you don't have a current, active list of potential participants to use for recruiting, you can recruit through professional groups or organizations in your area or through your network of friends and connections. Putting out a request through friends, family, business associates, and community connections often leads to qualified applicants for screening.

If these connections are not likely to yield results, particularly when you need to recruit quickly, Craigslist can provide the means to spread the net broadly in your area or in other cities if you are recruiting in more than one location. Craigslist has a presence all over the United States as well as cities throughout Canada and in a number of other countries. Craigslist is free if you are not posting a classified job opening. You can post to "community" or "services" or "gigs," with the latter two having a subsection for computers, if your usability study is computer- or web-related. However, for a small fee (currently US$25), you can post to the classified jobs section, using the "et cetera" category at the end of the list.

www.craigslist.com

Using a public source such as Craigslist for recruiting means that you need to screen even more carefully than usual to reduce or eliminate "professional participants," those people who respond to these study queries on a regular basis. One way to guard against the professional participant is to include a link to a survey in SurveyMonkey or one of the other online survey instruments. The responses to the survey will help you narrow down the applicants to those most likely to qualify as participants.

As part of screening the potential participants, you need to confirm their availability during your testing dates. You can schedule them as soon as you see that they qualify for the study, or you can get all the times they are available so that you can evaluate all the eligible participants to see which combination gives you the best representation for your study requirements. For instance, you may need to balance age, gender, and education. That means you will need to work out a schedule based on the participant pool and their availability for timeslots during the testing period.

Then you have to contact them again to let them know that you are confirming their participation for a specific date and time. Then you need to hear back from them to be sure they are still available and interested in participating. Then you need to contact other qualified applicants to confirm their willingness to be backups in case of cancellations.

When you have confirmed everyone's participation, you need to send them directions to the testing location, a visitor parking pass (if required), and a phone number they can call before their session if they need assistance or are running late. If you're conducting remote testing, you need to send them instructions on the preparation process.

For those people you do not choose for this study, you should send them an e-mail or call them to thank them for their interest and to ask whether they would like to be contacted again if you have another study.

How to recruit through an agency

If you are not doing the recruiting yourself, you can work with a market research firm or temporary employment agency. Market research firms tend to have a database of potential participants who can be screened by the relevant fields to match your user profiles. These participants are likely to be comfortable with the requirements of sharing their thoughts about products and with the need to be videotaped. Temporary employment agencies can be effective when you are looking for participants with specific business or computer skills, since agencies typically have this information for their applicants.

If you have not worked with the agency before, you will need to review the screener criteria with them and maybe review some or all of the pool of participants to confirm that they are a good fit for your study. In addition, you need to understand how the agency handles no-shows and cancellations. Some agencies recruit and bill you for backups, for instance, even if all of your participants show up. Another issue to be clear about is who pays the incentive. If the agency is paying the incentive, the amount and the method of payment to the participants should be specified in the contract.

To standardize the communication between the recruiters from the outside agency and potential participants, you will want to produce a script for the recruiters to read or approve one that they produce. Using a script for recruiting minimizes possible bias that could be introduced by the agency and increases the likelihood that participants aren't misinformed about what they'll be doing. A script also works well for your own recruiting, particularly when there is more than one person involved in screening participants. I learned the necessity of providing a script the hard way when one of the participants in a study shared with me that she had been told she would be the "guinea pig" for our study.

How to plan for no-shows

Even with your best efforts or the efforts of a recruiting agency, you can anticipate, typically, at least 10% no-shows.

When you're conducting small studies with five or six participants, you really want all of them to participate, because fewer may not be enough. And if your study is only one day, you may not have much flexibility to add a person at the end of an already long day. In larger studies, you can afford to lose one or two participants without adversely affecting the results.

But whenever it's critical to see a specific number of users in a specific timeframe, you will need a backup plan for the no-shows. Here are some options:

- *Have a backup participant ready.* If possible, recruit a backup participant who can be available all day and who is able to get to your location in a short time. If a scheduled participant doesn't show up, you can call the backup person and hope that the person can arrive quickly to participate. Because you are asking the backup participant to be available all day, you may need to pay that person more incentive, unless it's not an inconvenience for the person to be on standby. If you are recruiting more than one subgroup of users, you will need a backup for each subgroup.

- *Schedule an extra person or two.* To prepare for the likelihood that you may have a no-show or cancellation at the last minute, schedule an extra person at the end of the day. If you have more than one subgroup in your study, you will need to schedule an extra participant for each subgroup. If everyone shows up, you can either cancel your backups (but compensate them for being willing to participate) or, if there's time, go ahead and use them.

- *Schedule an extra person from your company.* If you are testing in a lab or conference room at your company, you can recruit a backup person from someone who is already on site. This should be a last resort, however, because a person from your company is not going to be your real user unless, of course, your real users work at your company. However, it may be possible to recruit someone who is not familiar with the product and who matches your user profile in some respects. Although this person will not be your "real user," it may turn out that this person confirms findings you are seeing from other users, thereby strengthening the findings. Recruiting an extra person from your company typically means that this person can come right over, if needed, keeping you on schedule.

Assigning team roles and responsibilities

There's no requirement that you have a team to conduct a usability test. But it sure helps to have at least one other person, and more is even better. With a team, you can spread the workload, provide more eyes and ears as observers and analysts, and build support for the test and test results. Although team size can vary, a core team has several roles, which can be shared or combined, as appropriate.

Remote moderated testing benefits from having a team adopting these same roles, with some modifications to suit the remote testing situation.

Here are the typical roles, which are determined, in part, by the room or lab arrangement for the study:

- *Moderator* (also called *facilitator*). This person has direct interaction with the participant, so this should be the most people-oriented member of the team. This is the most challenging role on the team because the moderator must avoid biasing the participant during his or her interaction with the participant. This is also, arguably, the most tiring role, since the moderator must always be "on," and that means being as personable with the last participant as with the first.

- *Logger/note takers*. If the team has logging software, such as Morae, to log observations, the logger should be the fastest typist on the team. It helps if the logger is knowledgeable about the product so that he or she can accurately log what happens.

There's more about creating an observer form coming up.

If the team sits in the same room with the participant, the logging function may be shared by several team members, using an observer form to standardize the logging process. One person may be assigned to time the tasks using a stopwatch.

- *Observers.* Others on the team may not have official functions, but they can take unofficial notes or just sit back and watch.

- *Technician.* If you're testing in a lab with multiple cameras and picture-in-picture capabilities, you might want one team member to be responsible for setting up the cameras and selecting the picture-in-picture features for the study. In studies where the participant moves around to do certain tasks, it may be necessary to switch cameras.

  If you are recording to DVD, this person may need to start the recording at the beginning of the study and stop it at the end. If the testing situation requires special technical support, someone with the appropriate skills may need to be brought in to serve in this role. This extra help is often needed in remote testing for those times when the setup doesn't work properly.

- *Help desk.* If you want to make technical or customer support available as part of your study, you will need a person to serve as the help desk operator. This person should be knowledgeable about the product (frequently the product manager fits this role well), so that when the participant calls or asks for help, the person serving as help desk operator knows exactly what the problem is. If the team is short-handed, this role can be combined with one of the other support roles.

There's more about these team roles in Chapter 7.

Developing team checklists

Checklists are the "to-do" lists for each of the active members on the core team. They remind each person what his or her responsibilities are before, during, and after each test session. They will be used in the walkthrough, then modified as needed for testing.

Even seasoned user experience practitioners rely on checklists that can be modified or adjusted to suit the specifics of the testing situation. In the rush to get ready for each test session, using checklists can help everyone stay on task. Sample checklists for the moderator (Figure 6.1), the logger (Figure 6.2), and the technician (Figure 6.3) will give you some sense of how to create the specific checklist that you need for your role on the test team.

These checklists are also available for download from the companion website at *www.mkp. com/testingessentials*

Moderator's Checklist

Before participant arrives

☐ Make sure product is loaded properly and ready for first scenario

☐ Make sure phone and microphone are properly positioned

☐ Make sure pen is on the desk for questionnaire completion

Welcome

☐ Introduce yourself, thank participant for having an interest in participating

☐ Offer refreshment

☐ Escort participant to evaluation room

☐ Ask participant to sit at the desk

☐ Sit beside the participant

Consent form, pre-test questionnaire, instructions

☐ Show participant the location of cameras, phone, microphone

☐ Explain the purpose of the test

☐ Go over consent form, allow time to read and sign; if this has been done already, ask participant if he/she is comfortable with being recorded

☐ Explain that there are observers who are very interested in learning from the participant about his/her experience

☐ Ask for questions, concerns

☐ Give pre-test questionnaire

Instructions

☐ Explain process of using scenarios, one at a time, while participant thinks out loud

☐ Review how think-out-loud process works, with examples

☐ Demonstrate how to use the phone to call the help desk or to indicate completion of a scenario

☐ Explain that after each scenario, there will be a quick questionnaire to complete, then the next scenario

After each scenario, post-task questionnaire

☐ Offer plenty of reassurance, especially when tasks prove difficult

☐ Give feedback on the quality of the think-out-loud procedure; if necessary, encourage more feedback from participant by reviewing the process again, with examples

☐ Ask participant to clarify any thoughts or actions as requested by team members

☐ Give post-task questionnaire to participant

☐ Set up product at starting point for next scenario, if needed

After completion, post-test questionnaire

☐ Give post-test questionnaire (or whatever feedback mechanisms are being used)

☐ If appropriate, introduce participant to team; generously thank for experience

☐ Provide stipend for participation (or direct participant to office for payment)

Figure 6.1 Here's a sample checklist for the moderator.

Logger's Checklist

Before the test

☐ Turn on logging computer

☐ Review logging codes in logging software

☐ Enter new test information into logging software

☐ Check headphones and microphones for logger and team

☐ Test logging software

☐ Check logger's monitor

☐ Change monitor views as necessary

☐ Do a test print from logging software; troubleshoot any problems:

    ☐ Check cable from logging computer to printer

    ☐ Check paper and ink in printer

☐ Do a test copy in copier; troubleshoot any problems:

    ☐ Check paper in copier

    ☐ Check toner cartridge

After each participant

☐ Print log file

☐ Copy log file for team members

☐ Distribute copies to team members

☐ Place original in participant's folder

☐ Set up logging software for next participant (if any)

At end of day

☐ Back up logging software data files

☐ Set logging software for next day (if appropriate)

☐ Turn off computer

☐ Turn off printer

☐ Turn off copier

Figure 6.2 Here's a sample checklist for the logger.

Technician's Checklist

Before each test participant arrives

☐ Turn on equipment

☐ Adjust cameras to proper settings for recording

☐ Select picture-in-picture setting for recording

☐ Check sound coming into and out of the control room

☐ Label DVD for the session

☐ Load DVD

During each test session

☐ Synchronize starting times with the logger/data recorder

☐ Adjust audio in control room and headsets as needed

☐ Change picture-in-picture settings as needed

After the test participant leaves

☐ Finalize DVD recording

☐ Eject DVD and put in labeled case

☐ Prepare for next participant (if appropriate)

☐ Turn off equipment (at end of last session)

Figure 6.3 Here's a sample checklist for the technician.

If you have a usability lab that is available to different groups in your company and you want to make one checklist for anyone to use to set up the lab for a study, you can standardize the setup procedures in a single list. The sidebar that follows shows you a pre-flight checklist for our lab associates so that whoever gets to the lab first can run through what needs to be done.

Lab Associates' Preflight Checklist

Study Name: _____

Date: _____

Equipment

☐ Check Control Room monitors, cameras, and headsets; sound check for room audio and headset audio

☐ Set up video mixing board with PIP

☐ Verify Morae Recorder and Morae Manager programs are working

☐ Align document camera and Morae camera for recording

☐ DVD—make test recording

☐ Check phone to and from Participant Room

☐ Copier turned on and working

☐ Executive Viewing Room—turn on LCD projector and check screen setup

☐ Check audio from Participant Room

Supplies

☐ Paper: Check Control Room copier and printer and Participant Room printer

☐ Confirm: Stapler, staples, pens out and available

☐ Confirm DVD (+RW) disks, labels out and available

Notes:

_____

_____

_____

Writing the moderator's script

In addition to the moderator's checklist, the moderator needs a script. The script is used throughout the testing session—whenever the moderator interacts with the participant—to ensure that the moderator says the same thing to each participant.

Seasoned veterans in this role as moderator may feel confident enough to dispense with the script, using a detailed checklist instead. However, writing out an informal script, even for experienced moderators, helps moderators prepare for a smooth delivery.

Some moderators may feel peculiar reading from a script, believing perhaps that it makes them look unprepared or unprofessional. But if

A sample script for the Holiday Inn China website usability study is included at the end of this chapter.

the moderator says, "I'm reading from the script to be sure that I say the same thing to each person and to be sure that I cover everything," this explanation can ease the feeling of awkwardness for the moderator. Naturally, this statement is written into the script.

The moderator's checklist can be used as a guide to create the script, which typically covers the following topics:

In Atlanta, I usually talk about the traffic and ask if the participant had any problems getting to the lab. Commenting on the weather always makes a good ice breaker.

- *Welcome the participant.* Thank the person for coming; engage in small talk to put the participant at ease. Offer something to drink, such as water, coffee, or a soft drink.

- *State the purpose of the study.* This part of the script is helpful in clarifying why the participant is here. It also gives you the chance to emphasize that you are interested in everything the participant thinks and does—positive thoughts and negative thoughts—while working with the product. If you are not the developer, you can emphasize that you are completely open to anything the participant might want to share to help improve his or her experience, particularly since you are not the developer. Even if you are the developer or on the development team, you can stress that you really want to learn from the participant about what works well and what does not. That's why you're doing this usability test of the product.

- *Provide forms required for participation*, unless these have been completed in advance. If a video consent form has already been signed, restate what you will do with the recording of the session and ask the participant if he or she is comfortable with this arrangement. If the participant seems to hesitate before replying, you can probe to see what's making him or her uncomfortable and then reaffirm that the recording is strictly for a specific purpose, as stated on the video release. Then you want to recheck to see if the participant is OK with being recorded. If the product is in development and the company requires a non-disclosure agreement (NDA), remind the participant that the study is for a product in development, which is why you are asking the participant to agree not to discuss it with anyone.

- *Describe the participant room.* Show the participant the cameras, the microphone, the one-way mirror, and anything else that the participant should know about the room setup. If observers are in the room with you, explain what they will be doing. If your team is observing from the control room on the other side of the one-way mirror, tell the participant this. The same disclosure should be made about observers in another room, such as the executive viewing room or a remote location. This information may make the participant a bit uncomfortable, but it's your job as the moderator to inform the participant of what is happening and to set the participant at ease about why people are observing. I tend to keep this information somewhat vague—I don't say how many people are observing.

I have found that when I offer to let the participants meet the team *after* the study so that the team can thank them for everything, this appeals to the participants and eases any concerns they may have about who is observing.

- *Explain the testing process*. Tell the participant that you will be asking him or her to perform some tasks with the product, which you will provide in the form of scenarios. Explain where you will be when the participant is working with the scenarios. If you will be sitting beside the participant, explain why and what your role is. If you will leave the participant to work alone, explain how the participant should tell you when he or she is finished. If you want the participant to use the phone during the session (either to call for help or tell you when the task is completed), explain what will happen when the participant calls. For example, I say, "When you call to tell us that you are done, I will come back in with a short questionnaire to get feedback on your experience with that scenario, then give you the next scenario."

  If you're providing help via a help desk or customer support person (a team member serving in that role), explain that if the participant calls the help desk, it won't work just like a real help desk. I tell the participant, "Rather than directly answer your question, which is what you would expect under normal circumstances, the help desk person is more likely to explore the problem with you, seeking to understand your concerns."

- *Describe thinking out loud*. Because the think-out-loud protocol is so important in most formative usability studies, you want to help the participant understand how it works and why it's important. I explain to the participant, "I realize it's not 'normal' to think out loud while working, but doing so will help the team get insight into your experience when you share your thoughts this way." I also give them examples of what I mean by sharing their thoughts, such as "I like this because . . . This is not at all what I expected to see when I clicked on that link . . . I have no idea what this word means . . . I sure wish this product would let me do X here. . . ." If I'm sitting with the participant during the session, I say, " I may ask questions or remind you to share your thoughts if you fall silent."

- *Ask the participant to share any questions or concerns*. Soliciting questions or concerns from the participant at this point gives you a chance to clarify any confusion the participant may have and to confirm that the participant is comfortable. Remind the participant that he or she can stop at any time. Thank the person again for participating. Ask if the participant is ready to get started.

I find that when I ask participants to read the scenario out loud, it seems to help them transition to thinking out loud more easily.

- *Start the study.* Hand the participant the first scenario. You can sit with them while they read the scenario and then ask them to restate what they are supposed to do, or you can read the scenario to them and then ask them if they have any questions about the scenario.

Preparing or using other forms

The moderator's script mentioned some forms, such as a video consent form and a non-disclosure form. If you have these forms already, you just need to be sure they are available for your test. If you don't have them, you need to prepare or acquire them. In addition, if you are expecting observers, you may want to prepare an observer form for them to use.

Preparing a video consent form

Participants will need to sign a consent form giving you permission to record them for the test. Some organizations have strict requirements for obtaining this consent. Universities typically require approval for studies by an institutional review board (IRB). Your organization may have a standard consent form that it uses. If it does not, you need to create one.

The consent form needs to stipulate the purpose of the study and the ways in which the recorded material will be shared and used. It needs to explain how the participant will be identified. Some organizations allow first names; others require that participants be identified by numbers only (Participants 1, 2, 3, etc.). The form needs to make clear that the participant is free to stop at any time and to deny consent at any time. Figure 6.4 shows a basic consent form.

It is common practice to request that this consent be given before testing begins. Some practitioners suggest that the participant be asked to confirm consent again after the study concludes. In our screening, we tell potential participants that they will be asked to give their consent to be videotaped, and we ask them to let us know whether they are

---

Usability Center Video Permission Form

I hereby give my permission to be videotaped as part of my participation in the _____
Usability test conducted _____ [date] at the Usability Center at Southern Polytechnic.

Only my first name may be reported in association with the session results.

I understand and consent to the use and release of the video recording to the Usability Center and to the client. I further understand that the video recording and any highlights extracted from it may be used for review by the client and by the Usability Center. Representative video excerpts may also be used within presentations to the client, at professional meetings, and as part of research.

I give up any rights to the video recording and understand that the recording may be used for the purposes described in this release form without further permission.

I understand that if for any reason I do not want to continue I can leave at any time during this recording session. I can also deny consent at any time.

_____   _____

Printed Name   Date

_____

Signature

Figure 6.4 Here's a sample video consent form.

comfortable with this request. We then repeat the question in our script/ orientation, even after they have signed the consent form.

Preparing a special consent form for testing with minors

Any time you are testing with minors—participants under 18 years of age—you need to get consent from a parent or guardian. We add the following statement to our standard video consent form:

Consent of parent or legal guardian, if individual participating is a minor

I consent and agree, individually and as a parent or legal guardian of the minor named above, to the foregoing terms and provisions.

Signature _____ Relationship _____

Using a non-disclosure agreement

Whenever you are working on a product in development, you are likely to need a non-disclosure agreement (NDA).

Most companies have non-disclosure agreements in place. They often are lengthy, densely worded documents prepared by lawyers to cover every conceivable situation. For instance, they may deal with the handling of proprietary documents, which are not typically given to usability test participants. In usability testing, the main concern is to have people not talk about what they saw in the session. Ask your legal team if they can prepare a suitably stripped-down NDA for usability testing.

Although participants should be given the opportunity to read the NDA before signing it, experience indicates that most participants sign it without bothering to read it. If, however, you want to avoid the possibility that someone may want to take the time to read the NDA before starting the study, you can send it out in advance.

If you are also an "outsider," as is the case if you are a usability consultant, you, too, will need to sign an NDA, generally before you can discuss or see the product.

Non-disclosure agreements are not generally used when the product is already on the market.

Preparing an observer form

If you have observers who will be contributing to the discussion of the findings, you can create an observer form to standardize the method they use to take notes. This form makes it easier to collect the findings at the end of each session.

The form can be open-ended, such as the one shown in Figure 6.5.

Customized observer forms can be created to assign specific types of observation to different observers. For instance, one observer may note all of the issues associated with screen labels and nomenclature; another may note the starting and stopping points for tasks and success or failure for each task. If you're using logging codes, you can include these on the observer form.

Participant number/name:	Date/time of session:	
Scenario/task	Issue/problem	Observer's name and comment

Figure 6.5 Here's an example of an open-ended form for observers to use during testing sessions.

Creating questionnaires

The number of questionnaires you will need to create depends on the format of your study. If your study is being conducted very early in product development, such as at the paper prototyping stage, you may not need to create any questionnaires. If, however, you want to get structured feedback from participants before, during, and at the end of the test, you will want to create questionnaires. The types of questionnaires you will want to consider developing include:

- pre-test questionnaire
- post-task questionnaire
- post-test questionnaire

You may not want to use all three types of questionnaires in every study, but some studies work very well with all three types because each one provides a different kind of information to help you understand your user and your user's experience with your product. Administering one or more of these questionnaires takes away time from the user's engagement with your product, so you need to weigh the pros and cons of using one or more of them in your study.

I typically use all three of these questionnaire types since they don't take long to administer and they produce quantitative, as well as qualitative, feedback that can clarify or enhance our understanding of the user's experience.

Creating a pre-test questionnaire

Let's assume that everyone who is scheduled for the study has met the criteria specified in the screener. Still, there are differences among the participants that can be useful to know. A pre-test questionnaire provides a way to get additional relevant information about each participant.

Here's an example of how this type of questionnaire works. For a study of a website for a private liberal arts college for women, we recruited the target population for this type of college (tenth-grade, high-achieving girls with an interest in attending a small liberal arts college). In addition to the information we received to qualify them for the study, we wanted to know more about the ways in which they were using college websites to help them determine their interest in a college. Figure 6.6 uses a number of open-ended questions to learn more about their search strategies and criteria for narrowing their search.

You can ask the participant to fill out the pre-test questionnaire on arrival or as part of the orientation. Or, if you are using a recruiting agency, you can ask the agency to get this information after selecting the participants for the study. That way, you will have it in advance of testing. However, if you have observers, it works well to read the questions to the participant so that everyone can hear the responses.

The benefit of using a pre-test questionnaire is that it can shed light on a participant's specific actions and responses during the test. For instance, if you learn that a participant is particularly interested in the college library and likes to see what information is provided about the library on the websites she visits, this information will help you understand why she looks for a link to the library on the homepage.

Sometimes the pre-test questionnaire is in the form of a semi-structured interview using some questions to get the conversation going with the participant. For instance, in the study of the digital cable self-installation kit, I asked participants to tell us how they like to set up new equipment. I probed about how they use the information that comes with the equipment, such as the Getting Started Guide or related documentation. I asked them to share what they typically did if they got stuck while doing an installation. Then I explained that the study was focusing on the documentation for a self-install kit. I expressed appreciation for understanding what their normal process was but asked them to use the documentation in our study, even if this wasn't their normal process, so that we could see how the documentation worked for them.

I could have screened for participants who stated a preference for using the documentation, but doing so would have made it harder to find participants. Instead, our team decided that it would be helpful to know participants' preferences but ask them to begin with the documentation.

Pre-test Questionnaire

1. As a student considering college, what information do you look for about a college?

2. What are your top criteria in choosing a college? Please list at least three items.

   (1)

   (2)

   (3)

3. Which colleges are you considering? For each college you list, please explain what appeals most to you about it.

College	**Most appealing aspect**
•	
•	
•	
•	

4. Which majors or subjects are you interested in studying in college?

   •

   •

   •

   •

5. Which college websites have you visited? Name at least three.

   (1)

   (2)

   (3)

Figure 6.6 Here's a sample pre-test questionnaire that was used for a website study for a private women's college.

Our thinking was that if the documentation helped even those who wouldn't normally use it, it would help those who did use documentation as well as those participants who used it only when they got stuck.

By using a pre-test interview questionnaire, the team was able to learn valuable information about the participants' preferred method of setting up new equipment and then relate that to the way in which they used or abandoned the documentation during the test.

Creating post-task questionnaires

See the "Writing good questions" sidebar (see page 179) for advice and examples on how to write good questions or statements for your questionnaires.

If you have organized your study around separate scenarios, you may want to get immediate feedback from participants after the completion of each scenario. Waiting to get feedback until they have finished all of the tasks or scenarios reduces participants' ability to recall their experience after each one. Creating brief post-task questionnaires—even a single statement or question—gives you this feedback right away and doesn't take up much time.

The question or questions can be the same for each scenario and can be as generic as:

- Rate the ease or difficulty of performing this task (using a range of responses from very easy to very difficult).
- Rate the time it took to complete this task (using a range of responses from less time to more time than expected).
- Rate the likelihood that you would use this feature/task (using a range of responses from very likely to not likely at all).

Or the questions could be targeted to the specific scenarios, as shown in the post-task questionnaire in Figure 6.7. This questionnaire was used in the study of the website for information on distance learning courses and programs in a public university system.

Creating a post-test questionnaire

As the term suggests, the post-test questionnaire comes after the participant has completed all of the scenarios. This questionnaire is generally designed to allow the user to rate the overall experience. The

---

Post-task Questionnaire

Circle a number in response to the following questions

1. When thinking about taking courses online, how would you rate the information you discovered in this website?

    Not helpful   1   2   3   4   5   Very helpful

    Explain your rating:

2. How would you rate the **quality** of the information you found about your ability to be an effective distance learning student?

    Not helpful   1   2   3   4   5   Very helpful

    Explain your rating:

3. How would you rate the **usefulness** of the information you found in helping you determine whether you are a good candidate for distance learning?

    Not helpful   1   2   3   4   5   Very helpful

    Explain your rating:

Figure 6.7 This post-task questionnaire follows a task to find a tool on the website to help users understand whether distance learning is a good choice for them.

questions typically map to the goals of the study. The questions can be closed-ended or open-ended questions or a combination of both. An example of the post-test questionnaire for the File Transfer Protocol (FTP) software study (for advanced users) is shown in Figure 6.8.

Post-test Questionnaire

1. Overall, please rate how easy or difficult it was to use this program.

   ☐ 1—very difficult

   ☐ 2—somewhat difficult

   ☐ 3—neither difficult nor easy

   ☐ 4—somewhat easy

   ☐ 5—very easy

2. How easy or difficult was it to figure out the correct menu choices and procedures?

   ☐ 1—very difficult

   ☐ 2—somewhat difficult

   ☐ 3—neither difficult nor easy

   ☐ 4—somewhat easy

   ☐ 5—very easy

3. How much time do you think you would need before you felt proficient using this software to perform tasks you normally perform?

   ☐ 10 to 30 minutes

   ☐ 1 to 2 hours

   ☐ 3 hours or more

   Explain your response:

4. Please rate your overall satisfaction with this program.

   ☐ 1—very dissatisfied

   ☐ 2—somewhat dissatisfied

   ☐ 3—neither dissatisfied nor satisfied

   ☐ 4—somewhat satisfied

   ☐ 5—very satisfied

5. If a less technically knowledgeable colleague asked you to recommend an FTP program, would you recommend that your colleague try this one?

   ☐ 1—No [Go to question 6]

   ☐ 2—Yes [Go to question 7]

6. If you answered No to the previous question, please explain why.

Figure 6.8 Here's the post-test questionnaire for the FTP software study.

7. Do you think you would want to download a free, 30-day version of this program to evaluate?

   ☐ 1—No [Go to question 8]

   ☐ 2—Yes [Go to question 9]

8. If you answered No to the previous question, please explain why.

9. If you answered Yes to question 7, what do you think would most influence your decision about whether to purchase this program at the end of the evaluation period?

10. What do you think would be a reasonable price for this program? [This question was requested by marketing.]

Figure 6.8 (*Continued*)

As you can see, this questionnaire is longer than the typical post-task questionnaire because it seeks to get participants' feedback on their total experience. Some studies put significant emphasis on this part of the session, apportioning as much as half the test time period for the post-test questionnaire process. When this much time is allotted, the format is often more open-ended questions, including any questions from the team that result from their observations of the user during the test.

There's more on this topic coming up in the section on interviewing at the end of a test.

Writing good questions

It takes practice to create questions that don't bias the responses you hope to get. Although it is beyond the scope of this book to give you a tutorial on survey creation, you should read up on this topic before creating your own questionnaires, since it is so easy to inadvertently inject bias into your questions unless you know how to avoid it. After you've drafted your questionnaire, you should test it with several people to see whether the questions are clear for your targeted user.

Two good sources on creating effective questionnaires are Salant and Dillman, *How to Conduct Your Own Survey*, 1994, and Fink, *How to Conduct Surveys: A Step-by-Step Guide*, 2008.

The sample statements and questions here can guide you in the basics for creating effective questionnaires. Many of the statements in the samples use a Likert scale, which asks participants to register their level of agreement or disagreement with the statement. Here's an example:

The terminology was easy to understand

1	2	3	4	5
Strongly agree	Agree	Neither agree nor disagree	Disagree	Strongly disagree

To avoid bias and the tendency for people to give a similar response to a series of statements, you should vary the statements, as this next one does:

Using this product was difficult

1	2	3	4	5
Strongly agree	Agree	Neither agree nor disagree	Disagree	Strongly disagree

Another approach to creating questions is to use a positive/negative format, which presents both ends of a continuum and asks that the participants select the appropriate response, as in the following example:

How easy or difficult was it to use the online help?

1	2	3	4	5
Very easy	Somewhat easy	Neither easy nor difficult	Somewhat difficult	Very difficult

Still another approach is to avoid using any value words, such as "easy" or "difficult," so as to make the statement neutral. Here's an example:

Using the online help was . . .

1	2	3	4	5
Very easy	Somewhat easy	Neither easy nor difficult	Somewhat difficult	Very difficult

You might also want to include some open-ended, but structured, questions or statements, such as these:

Question 1: What was the best part of this experience?
   or

Statement 1: The best part of this experience was . . .

Question 2: What was the most frustrating part of this experience?
   or

Statement 2: The most frustrating part of this experience was . . .

Using standard post-test questionnaires

Rather than creating your own post-test questionnaire, you may prefer to use one of the standard ones. A number of usability post-test questionnaires are widely used and readily available. Two of the most popular are

- *SUS*—System Usability Scale. Developed by John Brooke at Digital Equipment Corporation, uses 10 Likert-type statements with responses based on a 5-point scale.
- *CSUQ*—Computer System Usability Questionnaire—developed by James Lewis at IBM, uses 19 questions on a 7-point scale.

For an excellent comparison of these questionnaires and others, see Tullis and Stetson, 2004. In their comparative evaluation of two websites using five questionnaires to determine user preference, they found that SUS and CSUQ produced the most consistent results with varying sample sizes.

Using the SUS

The SUS has been in use for quite some time, having been developed in 1986. The 10-item questionnaire is short, and free, as long as you acknowledge the source. A SUS score is best presented as a single number—ranging from 0 to 100—representing a composite measure of the overall usability of the system being studied.

Figure 6.9 shows the 10 items in SUS. The even-numbered items are positive statements, and the odd-numbered items are negative statements. This alternation is done to balance the responses. As you can see, the statements use the word *system*, which reflects its original use for software evaluation. It is common practice to substitute *website, product*, or *interface* for *system* without affecting the results.

See Finstad, 2006.

See Lewis and Sauro, 2009.

In addition, some tweaking of the language of the questions is acceptable. For example, one study showed that non-native speakers in particular have difficulty with the word *cumbersome* in item 8. You can change it to *awkward* or to *cumbersome/awkward* without any impact on results. If you want to rate "usability" separately from "learnability," you can pull out items 4 and 10 and score these separately. However, you can't tweak it too much or it stops being the SUS. In order to be widely useful, the SUS is necessarily general. If you want to get more specific about aspects of your product, you can add questions at the end. Just be aware that you shouldn't include these in the SUS score.

If you are using Morae for logging, the software includes the SUS questionnaire and calculates the score for you. If you don't use Morae and need to calculate the score yourself, here's how the inventor, John Brooke, explains how to do it:

> First sum the score contributions from each item. Each item's score contribution will range from 0 to 4. For items 1, 3, 5, 7, and 9, the score contribution is the scale position minus 1. For items 2, 4, 6, 8, and 10, the contribution is 5 minus the scale position. Multiply the sum of the scores by 2.5 to obtain the overall value of SUS.

I realize that this sounds a bit tricky to do, but the sample in Figure 6.9 shows you how to calculate the score.

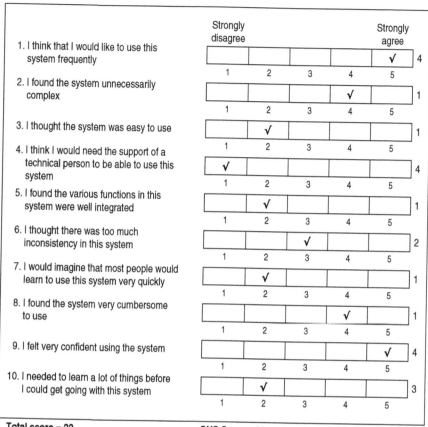

Strongly
disagree

Strongly
agree

1. I think that I would like to use this
   system frequently   √ 4
   1 2 3 4 5

2. I found the system unnecessarily
   complex   √ 1
   1 2 3 4 5

3. I thought the system was easy to use   √ 1
   1 2 3 4 5

4. I think I would need the support of a
   technical person to be able to use this
   system   √ 4
   1 2 3 4 5

5. I found the various functions in this
   system were well integrated   √ 1
   1 2 3 4 5

6. I thought there was too much
   inconsistency in this system   √ 2
   1 2 3 4 5

7. I would imagine that most people would
   learn to use this system very quickly   √ 1
   1 2 3 4 5

8. I found the system very cumbersome
   to use   √ 1
   1 2 3 4 5

9. I felt very confident using the system   √ 4
   1 2 3 4 5

10. I needed to learn a lot of things before
    I could get going with this system   √ 3
    1 2 3 4 5

Total score = 22   **SUS Score = 22 × 2.5 = 55**

© 1986 Digital Equipment Corporation

Figure 6.9 The System Usability Scale questionnaire shows a sample response and the total score.

Using the CSUQ

The CSUQ is based on a 7-point scale. Participants rate their agreement or disagreement with each statement, based on a range from strongly disagree (1) to strongly agree (7). The CSUQ is longer than the SUS but still easy to complete. Like the SUS questionnaire, the original statements use the word *system*.

Tullis and Stetson (2004) used the CSUQ in their comparative study of different questionnaires for a website study, but they changed *system* to *website* (as shown in Figure 6.10).

Overall Reaction to the Website		1	2	3	4	5	6	7		NA
1. Overall, I am satisfied with how easy it is to use this website	strongly disagree	○	○	○	○	○	○	○	strongly agree	○
2. It was simple to use this website	strongly disagree	○	○	○	○	○	○	○	strongly agree	○
3. I can effectively complete my work using this website	strongly disagree	○	○	○	○	○	○	○	strongly agree	○
4. I am able to complete my work quickly using this website	strongly disagree	○	○	○	○	○	○	○	strongly agree	○
5. I am able to efficiently complete my work using this website	strongly disagree	○	○	○	○	○	○	○	strongly agree	○
6. I feel comfortable using this website	strongly disagree	○	○	○	○	○	○	○	strongly agree	○
7. It was easy to learn to use this website	strongly disagree	○	○	○	○	○	○	○	strongly agree	○
8. I believe I became productive quickly using this website	strongly disagree	○	○	○	○	○	○	○	strongly agree	○
9. The website gives error messages that clearly tell me how to fix problems	strongly disagree	○	○	○	○	○	○	○	strongly agree	○
10. Whenever I make a mistake using the website, I recover easily and quickly	strongly disagree	○	○	○	○	○	○	○	strongly agree	○
11. The information (such as online help, on-page messages, and other documentation) provided with this website is clear	strongly disagree	○	○	○	○	○	○	○	strongly agree	○
12. It is easy to find the information I need	strongly disagree	○	○	○	○	○	○	○	strongly agree	○
13. The information provided by the website is easy to understand	strongly disagree	○	○	○	○	○	○	○	strongly agree	○
14. The information is effective in helping me complete the tasks and scenarios	strongly disagree	○	○	○	○	○	○	○	strongly agree	○
15. The organization of information on the website pages is clear	strongly disagree	○	○	○	○	○	○	○	strongly agree	○
16. The interface of this website is pleasant	strongly disagree	○	○	○	○	○	○	○	strongly agree	○
17. I like using the interface of this website	strongly disagree	○	○	○	○	○	○	○	strongly agree	○
18. This website has all the functions and capabilities I expect it to have	strongly disagree	○	○	○	○	○	○	○	strongly agree	○
19. Overall, I am satisfied with this website	strongly disagree	○	○	○	○	○	○	○	strongly agree	○

Figure 6.10 The CSUQ scale is modified for a website study.

Creating or using qualitative feedback methods

In addition to, or instead of, using a post-test questionnaire, your team can use a qualitative feedback method to end a study session. The advantage to a qualitative feedback method is that it turns over control, partially or completely, to the participant, as opposed to a questionnaire, in which you ask participants to make a forced choice in response to specific questions or statements that you give them.

The very act of framing questions or statements dictates to a large extent what participants will say (and not say). Using a qualitative feedback method, you open up the opportunity for responses that are shaped by what the participant wants to share with you. This process of giving partial or full control to the participant can provide excellent insights into the participant's experience. Two qualitative feedback methods to consider using are these:

- product reaction cards
- closing interview

Using product reaction cards

Product reaction cards were developed by Microsoft as part of a "desirability toolkit" created to understand the illusive, intangible aspect of desirability resulting from a user's experience with a product. The original toolkit had two parts: (1) a faces study, in which participants were asked to choose a photograph of a face whose expression matched their experience; and (2) a card study, in which participants were asked to choose descriptive words or phrases from a large set of product reaction cards. The cards proved so successful in the first studies in 2002 that they were adopted by other groups at Microsoft, most notably for the launch of MSN Explorer 9.

See Benedek and Miner, 2002.

See Williams, Kelly, Anderson, Zavislak, Wixon, and de los Reyes, 2004.

Figure 6.11 shows you the card set of 118 cards, with 60% of the cards being positive words and 40% being negative or neutral words. The ratio of 60% positive to 40% negative cards in the deck is based on Microsoft's analysis of the higher-than-average positive responses from participants in completing post-test questionnaires.

Chapter 7 shows you how to use the cards in a study.

The complete set of 118 product reaction cards				
Accessible	Creative	Fast	Meaningful	Slow
Advanced	Customizable	Flexible	Motivating	Sophisticated
Annoying	Cutting edge	Fragile	Not secure	Stable
Appealing	Dated	Fresh	Not valuable	Sterile
Approachable	Desirable	Friendly	Novel	Stimulating
Attractive	Difficult	Frustrating	Old	Straightforward
Boring	Disconnected	Fun	Optimistic	Stressful
Businesslike	Disruptive	Gets in the way	Ordinary	Time consuming
Busy	Distracting	Hard to use	Organized	Time saving
Calm	Dull	Helpful	Overbearing	Too technical
Clean	Easy to use	High quality	Overwhelming	Trustworthy
Clear	Effective	Impersonal	Patronizing	Unapproachable
Collaborative	Efficient	Impressive	Personal	Unattractive
Comfortable	Effortless	Incomprehensible	Poor quality	Uncontrollable
Compatible	Empowering	Inconsistent	Powerful	Unconventional
Compelling	Energetic	Ineffective	Predictable	Understandable
Complex	Engaging	Innovative	Professional	Undesirable
Comprehensive	Entertaining	Inspiring	Relevant	Unpredictable
Confident	Enthusiastic	Integrated	Reliable	Unrefined
Confusing	Essential	Intimidating	Responsive	Usable
Connected	Exceptional	Intuitive	Rigid	Useful
Consistent	Exciting	Inviting	Satisfying	Valuable
Controllable	Expected	Irrelevant	Secure	
Convenient	Familiar	Low maintenance	Simplistic	

Figure 6.11 These are the 118 words/phrases in the complete set of product reaction cards.

Chapter 9 shows you how we present the results of the product reaction cards in our reports.

In our studies, we *love* using product reaction cards because they give us an incredibly rich understanding of the user's experience. They take very little time to administer: we generally allocate about five minutes. And the most interesting discovery we've made about using the product reaction cards comes when we collate the cards from all the participants in a study and can then see how consistently participants pick either the very same card or a closely related card.

Ending with an interview

Ending a usability test with an interview provides another way for the participants to share their experience in their own words. Unlike the closed-ended questions in the interview process that was used to screen participants for the study, an open-ended interview at the end of a test session allows the participants to shed light on their experience without much more prompting than a question such as, "Tell us about your experience doing X" (a task from the scenarios).

In some cases, the interview may focus on questions from the team or observers. For instance, the moderator may ask the participant to elaborate on something the team observed so as to help the team understand the issue better. Sometimes it can be beneficial to take the participant back to a particular screen to help recall the experience. In other cases, if the product you are studying reflects a process that the user is familiar with, the moderator might ask the participant to describe it or sketch it on paper. Or if the participant currently uses a competitor's website, he or she could go to it to show the team how it compares and contrasts with the experience of working with your website.

You could start off this closing interview with a semi-structured approach using a few predetermined questions to get the interview going, but if you let it take its own direction after that, you can uncover some very useful insights. You need to keep an eye on the time, though, so that you know when the interview needs to end. For a different type of closing interview, see the next sidebar.

Retrospective recall: An in-depth review of the testing session

Retrospective recall is a specialized type of post-test interview in which you review the recorded session or parts of the session with the participant. If you decide to review the entire session with the participant, you will very likely do this instead of asking the participant to think out loud during the test.

The advantage to using this technique comes into play when you are focusing on timed tasks, in which you don't want the participant to think out loud, or when the task itself requires so much concentration that the participant would be overtaxed by being asked to talk while working.

The disadvantage—and it is a significant one—is that it takes much longer to use this technique. Not only do you have to set up the recording to review, but you may also have to stop the recording during the review so that the participant can explain what he or she was thinking and doing during the task. In planning your schedule for testing, you need to set aside double the amount of time for each testing session when you use this technique.

Testing the test

Every play needs a dress rehearsal. Without it, opening night could be full of unexpected surprises. The same is true for usability testing. With all the effort required to effectively recruit and schedule participants, it's important that the testing sessions work well for you and your team, as well as for the participants.

I recommend a two-stage process to prepare for testing:

- *Walkthrough*—a "reading" of the play to test the roles and apparatus
- *Pilot*—a true dress rehearsal with a "real" user

Conducting the walkthrough

The walkthrough provides the first chance for the team to take its places and to walk and talk through the material for the test. You get to see how everything works together, you can figure out the room setup and make any adjustments needed, and you can get familiar with the logging process. If you've set up codes for standard tasks, you can try them out and see what you want to add or change. Common codes include:

S = start task

E = end task

N = negative finding

P = positive finding

H = user consults help or calls help desk

C = catastrophe; user fails at task, gives up

S = system error, bug

M = moderator instruction or comment

Expect the walkthrough to be rough. Expect to take notes and to make changes to the test materials. Because you will need time to make these changes, you will want to schedule the walkthrough far enough in advance to do what's required afterward. Sometimes, for practical reasons, that may mean scheduling the walkthrough the day or night before testing begins, since this may be the first opportunity to get the team together or the first chance to work with the product.

Who is the participant in the walkthrough? Ideally, the participant is someone from your user pool. However, it's not necessary, and it may not be practical. Much more common is to find a "tolerant" user who will stand in for your target user. This person should be prepped to expect that the system could crash, the team may need to stop and make adjustments to the materials, or other problems may present themselves. That's why this person is called the "tolerant" user.

This person could be in the "friends and family" category. However, this person should not be a member of your team and should not be knowledgeable about your product, your goals, and so forth. Of course, the more closely this person represents the attributes of your target user, the more realistic the outcome will be.

Conducting the pilot

If you are really pushed for time, you might not do the walkthrough, but you should always do the pilot.

As the dress rehearsal, the pilot is the test of the test. It's likely to be your first experience seeing how the elements of the test work with your real user. Even if you have conducted a walkthrough, you may need to make a few more changes, now that you are testing with your real user. If you have not done a walkthrough, the changes that need to be made may be significant.

If you're doing a small study, you might have decided to recruit an extra participant for your pilot user in case you have to discard this session. However, if the changes needed after the pilot are minor, particularly if they do not affect the scenarios or post-task/post-test questionnaires, it's possible to include the findings from the pilot. I typically recruit six people for a one-day study, telling the client that if we can't use the findings from the pilot user, we will still have enough to work with from five users from a single subgroup.

If you're testing with several subgroups of the user population, you will very likely pick one of these for the pilot (unless your budget allows you to conduct a pilot for each subgroup). Your choice of which subgroup to use for the pilot depends on several factors:

- the scenarios you are most concerned about testing for timing issues or user comprehension
- the user subgroup you have easiest access to, since you will recruit an additional user from this subgroup
- the availability of a participant in the time slot
- the choice of a participant who matches some, but not all, of your screener characteristics (someone less than ideal, but close enough, so that if you have to discard these findings, there is less impact than discarding a better match to your screener)

Based on the results of the pilot, if there's time, you can conduct an analysis of the findings to help you understand the process and the types of findings you will likely see again. Even if you don't end up using these results, this practice analysis session will make the rest of the study go more smoothly.

You can also decide on any study-specific logging codes you want to add to your standard list, now that you have a better sense of what you will see in the testing to follow. You may want to start with some typical codes and then expand them. Typical findings from a study might be associated with the following codes:

N = navigation

T = terminology

MM = mental model (a match or mismatch to the user's expectation/experience)

FR = feature request; user expresses the desire for a product enhancement

Another worthwhile follow-up from the pilot, if there's time, is for the team to review the recorded session with a focus on the moderator. Because moderating is a learned skill, the team can give the moderator feedback on his or her interaction with the participant, which the moderator can use to add notes into the script.

When should you conduct the pilot? The short answer is when you're ready. Practically speaking, that may mean on the day of testing. If that's the case, you will need to schedule the pilot first, followed by a break with enough time to make the changes required to the materials before the next participant is scheduled. If you can schedule the pilot the day before testing begins, you can free up the time for the analysis after the pilot, as well as have time to make the needed changes to the test materials.

Summarizing Chapter 6

This chapter gave you the steps to take in preparing for usability testing. These include:

- Recruiting and scheduling the participants—the task that needs the longest lead time
- Assigning roles to team members during testing sessions, including:
  - developing checklists
  - creating the moderator's script
- Preparing or locating other forms you will use in testing sessions, including:
  - a video consent form for permission to record the session
  - a non-disclosure agreement for products in development
  - an observer form to standardize the note-taking process
- Creating or using available questionnaires, based on the types you want to use during testing. Choices include:
  - a pre-test questionnaire to get more information about participants before they start working with the product

- post-task questionnaires to get immediate feedback after each scenario
- a post-test questionnaire to get feedback about the whole experience; this can be in the form of:
  - quantitative feedback—closed-ended questions
  - qualitative feedback—open-ended questions
- Creating or using other qualitative feedback methods, which include:
  - Microsoft's product reaction cards
  - an end-of-session interview

With these materials prepared and ready to go, your final steps in preparation are to conduct one or both of the following tests of the test:

- A walkthrough with a "tolerant" user, not typically the actual user, to figure out how things go and what needs to be changed
- A pilot with the real user to get a final dress rehearsal, with one last chance to make changes to the materials before going on with the show

In continuing to use the Holiday Inn China website usability study as an example, this chapter ends with the moderator's script prepared for testing and examples from the pre-test and post-task questionnaires developed by the team. The full set of questionnaires for this study is included in the test plan on the book's companion website.

www.mkp.com/testingessentials

Moderator Script

Introduction

Hi, my name is Yina Li. Thank you so much for coming in today! Your participation will help our team and our sponsor learn a lot of useful feedback for improving the website you'll be working with today.

Videotaping Permission

As you know, we are going to videotape the session. The reason for recording the session is so that our sponsor's staff who are unable to join us will have a chance to look at the session and so that we can review it if we have any questions. In addition, we could potentially use some videoclips in academic and professional presentations.

Here is a permission form stating that you allow us to videotape the session. [Give the participant the permission form to review.] Are you comfortable with signing this form? [If so, ask the participant to sign it. If the participant has questions, respond to them.]

Introduction of the Evaluation Room

Before we start, I would like to give you a brief tour of this room. We have several cameras in here. [Point to the cameras.] They give the team several views of this area. Most of the time, the team will be looking at the screen you will be working on to see where you are clicking. We have a small headshot of you in the corner of the screen. We also have these two backup cameras in case we want to change the camera angle during the session. On the desk is a digital camera to record this session directly to our computer.

Here is a very sensitive microphone [point to the microphone] to pick up your voice. This is a phone [point to the telephone] that allows communication with the team during the test.

Introduction of the Team

On the other side of this room is the team observing this session. There is a one-way mirror that allows the team to see what is going on in this room. The team is made up of four Chinese students and two American students. Our advisor may also be there to help us conduct the test.

Introduction to the Test

Today, you are going to be working with the Holiday Inn China website. We'll give you some tasks to do on the site, then ask you some questions to get your feedback. You will also go to a competitor's site to do a similar task. We really appreciate your feedback about your experience, so we would like you to tell us what you are doing and why you are doing it. We understand that it may be awkward to be working on a Chinese website and having to speak in English. The reason for that is we have team members and our sponsor who cannot read or speak Chinese. They need to understand what you are doing and thinking. You may say something like "I am clicking on . . . ," "I chose this answer because . . . ," "I don't like . . . ," and "Oh, that's really cool!" If you feel that English cannot express what you are feeling, you can tell us in Chinese, but try to say it in English first. Also, we did not create this website, so you can say whatever you think without offending us.

During the session, I am just going to sit here with you, and I may ask you some questions from time to time. Before we start, do you have any questions for me or the team?

Pre-test Questionnaire

See Figure CS6.1.

To begin, I'd like you to fill out this questionnaire to help us understand your experience using other websites. While you are completing it, please tell us what you are writing down and also why you are writing these answers.

[When questionnaire is completed:] Thanks. That was really good feedback.

During Testing

We have several task scenarios for you to work through. Remember, this is not a test of you; it's a test of the website and we are very interested in all of your reactions about it. So, please remember to think out loud. After each scenario, when you tell me you are done, I will give you a brief questionnaire to complete. Then, the next scenario.

[After each scenario:] That was excellent feedback. Now, please complete these few questions and tell us what you are writing down as you fill out the questionnaire.

Post-test Questionnaire

[After the last scenario:] That was excellent feedback. Here's our post-test questionnaire. This is the last thing we will ask you to do. We would like you to do the same as you did for the questionnaire you finished during the test. Please tell us what you are writing down and why you chose the answer you did. This will help us understand your experience with this website.

See Figure CS6.2.

After Testing

That was great. We have learned so much from you.

As you know, our sponsor is offering you 2000 Priority Club points as an incentive for helping us perform the test. Are you a member of Priority Club?

- If yes, can you write down your Priority Club number/user name here? Then our sponsor will put 2000 points into your account.

- If no, would you like to register to be one? You can send your number/user name to this e-mail address: *liu@spsu.edu*. I will contact the sponsor and have the 2000 points deposited into your account.

Thank you very much for coming in today. We really learned a lot from your feedback.

Pre-test Questionnaire

Thank you for taking the time to participate in our usability test. Your participation will provide valuable feedback about your experience using a hotel's website.

Before we begin, we would like you to fill out this brief questionnaire so that we will have more information about your experience using the Internet and, more specifically, about your experience making travel arrangements.

Name (please print): _____

1. Which features impress you the most when you use a hotel's website?

   a.

   b.

   c.

2. Which features frustrate you the most when you use a hotel's website?

   a.

   b.

   c.

3. When booking a hotel room, what information is the most valuable to you

   When booking a business stay:

   When booking a vacation stay:

4. Which of the following two typical booking activities do you prefer?

   ☐ I use one or two preferred hotel websites that I'm familiar with.

   ☐ I browse different hotel websites to have as much information as possible.

Figure CS6.1 This is the pre-test questionnaire used for the website usability study.

Post-task Questionnaires

Scenario 1: Look and feel/first impressions

Please rate the following:

	Very Easy	Easy	Neither Easy nor Difficult	Somewhat Difficult	Very Difficult
Understanding the site navigation					
Understanding the site terminology (words, links)					
Understanding the first step you need to do to book a hotel room					

Scenario 2: Book a room in Beijing for 2 people

Please rate the following:

	Very Easy	Easy	Neither Easy nor Difficult	Somewhat Difficult	Very Difficult
Overall ease or difficulty of this task					
Understanding the procedures of booking a hotel room					
Understanding the search results page					

Which aspects of the site made this task easy for you?

Which aspects of the site made this task difficult for you?

Scenario 3: Cancel reservation

Please rate the following:

	Very Easy	Easy	Neither Easy nor Difficult	Somewhat Difficult	Very Difficult
This task was					

Which aspects of the site made this task easy for you?

Which aspects of the site made this task difficult for you?

Figure CS6.2 These are the post-task questionnaires used for the website usability study.

Conducting a usability test

7

Finally. After all the planning and preparation, the day has come for your usability test. If this is your first experience, you are probably nervous and excited at the same time. Even if you have been conducting testing, this may be your first time to apply the processes and procedures presented in this book. And, if you're like me, no matter how many times you have been involved in a usability test, the nervousness and excitement never go away.

Why nervous? Because you are entering unknown territory. You're testing an interface that is perhaps new to you and almost certainly new to your users. And you're using a test plan that is unique to this test.

Why excited? Because people are so amazing, and you will learn so much, including the completely unexpected, when you get to watch and work with the real users of the product.

Frankly, the thrill never goes away for me, and I'm guessing it will be the same for you.

So here we go. This chapter:

- Begins where your day begins, with setting up for testing.
- Focuses on the critical role of the moderator and the challenges the moderator faces in providing a comfortable situation for the participant before and during the test.

Usability Testing Essentials. DOI: 10.1016/B978-0-12-375092-1.00007-6

- Reviews the ways in which the moderator can administer post-test feedback mechanisms.
- Describes the ways to manage variations on the theme of testing when testing with two or more participants, two or more moderators, and in moderated remote testing.
- Presents the playbook for "customer support" when participants ask for help.
- Reviews the techniques for logging findings with software or observer forms.
- Describes the care and handling of observers and visitors and the associated logistics.
- Shows you how to conduct the test by yourself if you're working solo.

Setting up for testing

Your test day doesn't begin with the arrival of the first participant. Depending on whether you are in your own lab or a space you have reserved internally or at an external site, you need to start your day by setting up or confirming the setup for your test sessions. Using your team members' checklists, you each walk through the setup process for which you are responsible (or use a standard setup form for the lab you are using). You also want to confirm that the product is ready for the first participant. This is particularly important when you are testing a prototype or a version of the product you haven't seen before.

Chapter 6 gives you information on creating these checklists.

Sometimes setting up also means getting the room arranged to suit the study. Most studies are conducted in a typical office setup with a computer on a desk. But some products require special setup or special equipment. If you have access to your testing space ahead of time, then, of course, you will do the setup before the test day begins. But if the setup cannot be done until you get into the lab on the day of testing, you may need more than an hour to get everything ready.

In Chapter 2, I showed you a picture of our lab converted to a living room for an evaluation of the instructions for installing a digital cable box.

Meeting, greeting, briefing

Although everyone on the team has an important role to play in achieving a successful outcome from testing, the moderator has the pivotal role. That's because the moderator is the person who directly interacts with the participant. Getting this interaction right is essential to creating a positive experience for the participant and reliable results from the test. It begins from the moment the moderator meets and greets the participant and continues until the moderator concludes the session, thanks the participant, and says goodbye.

Variations on the role of the moderator in different testing situations are covered later in this chapter.

Meeting and greeting the participant

How are you going to begin the interaction with the participant? Starting off on the right foot is important.

There's a lot to do in a very short time. Not only do you want to welcome the participant and help him or her get settled in, but you also want to prepare the participant for the study, which includes reviewing the forms to sign and getting the signatures required.

In some cases, the participant has already signed these forms at check-in, so you can move through this review more quickly.

Conducting the pre-test briefing

After the usual pleasantries about the weather, traffic, or whatever you choose to chat about to get the participant comfortable and to begin your interaction, you need to brief the participant on the test setup.

Here's where the benefit of a script becomes clear. If you've done a walkthrough, you've probably made changes to your script already. If you have done a pilot, you've probably made more changes. It's OK to keep tweaking the script as you go through the day, so long as the basic information stays the same, which includes a review of

- The room arrangement, including cameras, microphones, one-way mirror, and so forth.

- The presence of observers, either in the room with you or on the other side of the one-way mirror or somewhere else. If the observers are in the room with you, you need to tell the participant what the observers will be doing.

- The think-aloud procedure, in which you describe how the participant should share his or her thinking about the experience with you.

- The study protocol, which is the process your team has devised for the test. It is typically a series of scenarios that you will give to the

There's more about how to describe the think-aloud procedure coming up later in this chapter.

participant one at a time. If you want the participant to tell you when he or she is finished, explain how that should be done, and then explain that you will give the participant a questionnaire, if you have one, or the next scenario, or whatever will happen next.

- The way in which you will interact with the participant. If you plan to leave the participant to work alone, explain why, as well as how and when you will return. If you plan to sit with the participant, explain what you will be doing, such as probing for responses to actions if the participant falls silent. Also explain what you will *not* be doing, such as answering questions about how the product works or confirming whether the participant successfully completed a task, and so forth.

- The way in which you will take notes, if you plan to take notes. If you are going to use a laptop to take notes while you sit with the participant, you need to prepare the participant for this, and you need to log consistently (and constantly) so that you are not calling attention to the fact that you are logging only certain things. And although it's very rare that a participant would ask to see what you're typing, you'd have to honor the request if it's made, so never type anything you wouldn't want participants to see.

- The important fact is that this is a test of the product, not the participant. The mantra, repeated often, is, "We are testing the product, not you." Reinforce that problems the participant may have are really helpful to the designers to understand how to improve the product. Also explain that you are equally interested in the things that work well, stressing the importance of the participant's verbal expressions of both positive and negative feelings about the experience.

- The status of the product. If you are testing a prototype and you know that the system is unstable or incomplete, you need to alert the participant. For instance, you may say that certain parts of the software are not yet built because you're working with a prototype, but you are interested in seeing where the participant wants to go, even for the parts that aren't there yet. If you're testing a product that's already in the market but is scheduled for redesign, you may want to say that. The participant needs to know his or her input will be extremely valuable in helping the designers understand what works well and what doesn't work well with the current product so that the redesigned product reflects usability improvements.

This may seem like a lot to do in a little time, but with practice you'll soon find yourself getting comfortable with all of the elements. When you do your first few usability test sessions, you'll find yourself paying a lot of attention to your script. As you gain experience throughout the day, you will want to add notes to your script to help yourself with the parts that are hardest for you to recall. Just remember: Even the most experienced moderators were new to doing usability testing at some time and had to practice, practice, practice to hone their skills.

Chauncey Wilson, a well-known usability practitioner, provides an excellent list of tips and strategies for being a good moderator in the following sidebar. Reviewing these tips before you start a study will help you focus on the essentials.

There's more about writing the moderator's script in Chapter 6.

For more on being an effective moderator, see Dumas and Loring, *Moderating Usability Tests*, 2008.

What makes a good moderator

The following tips and strategies are adapted from Chauncey Wilson:

- A successful test session starts when you meet the person and take him or her to the testing facility. A relaxed, warm (but not overly friendly) first meeting is important. The trip up in the elevator or the walk down the hall is often a place to begin establishing rapport.

- A moderator should make a list and practice neutral "prods" that can be used to elicit information, get more detail, and so on. Making a list of neutral questions or statements and practicing with them can help remove bias from the session.

- When I started lab testing, I found it very useful to videotape myself in some practice and real sessions. I discovered little tics and some poor verbal habits (*um, uh, OK*). You can also note nonverbal cues that you may be giving the participant.

- Avoid the use of loaded words such as *test* (*study* is probably fine) and *subjects* (*colleagues* or something less negative is probably better).

- I like to use the rule adopted from the American Psychological Association (APA) that a participant in a study (of any kind) should leave the situation in no worse shape than when he or she arrived and, if possible, should leave with some positive reaction to his or her participation.

- A good moderator should ensure that any observers follow a set of guidelines, such as never talking about a participant in the hallway or restrooms (this can be very embarrassing), no laughing in "soundproof" observation rooms, and so on.

- A moderator should always, always run a pilot session or two to verify that the hardware and software and tasks are appropriate. I know some people who have been in the field a long time who jump right into a study without doing a pilot, but I think that even experts need to run pilots. I also think a good moderator uses himself or herself as a pilot and goes through all the tasks, even if help is needed from a domain expert. Knowing the tasks well allows more subtle observation during the actual test.

- A good moderator is extremely careful to protect the participant's privacy. This is just as important for internal users as external users. Many companies are a bit cavalier about internal users, but an internal user who does poorly in a study might have some severe self-esteem issues.

- It is good to prepare a checklist to remind yourself of all the procedures, forms, and the like. Again, this step is useful even for experts. Something as simple as forgetting to have pens for the participants can be a bit unsettling during an actual test.

- It is useful to put together a script for a study. If you are going to read a script verbatim, tell the participant and explain that you are doing this for consistency, but also note that you will answer any procedural questions (though not product questions) at any time. Even if you don't need a detailed script (for an informal study, for example), writing one up helps make for smooth sessions.

- You might want to wear clothing that is similar to the style generally worn by your participants. If the participants are senior VPs, then a suit would be appropriate. If the participants are students, then jeans might even be appropriate.

- A good moderator knows when to end a task or when to ask the person to move on after they struggle for a long time. If a participant tries the same flawed method to complete a task six times in a row, you may not learn anything further and you may want to provide a series of "hints" to see if they will find the path to success. You may also set a time limit per task. If they don't finish a task in, say, 10 minutes, then you ask them to move on to the next one. The method for doing this has to be gentle, and you may want to have some catchphrases ready when this situation occurs (such as, "This is great. You've covered the part we needed to, so in the interests of time . . .").

Preparing the participant to think out loud

Watching what the participant does is certainly helpful. Hearing from the participant while he or she is working, and learning what pleases, frustrates, confuses, or confounds him or her is illuminating. This insight comes from the protocol called *thinking aloud*, or *think out loud*.

Some people mistakenly refer to this process as *talk out loud*, but this is not the correct term, as talking out loud is what we normally do in conversation.

Asking someone to think out loud while working is, for most, an unnatural act. So, it's necessary to stress how to do it and why the participant's thoughts are so helpful to the team. In your script, you may have written something like this:

> We want to know what you expect to happen when you make a choice and whether it meets with your expectations or not. We want to know what surprises, what delights, what confuses or even frustrates you, and why. If you find at any point that you're not sure what to do or you're trying to figure something out, tell us what you're thinking. When you share with us what you're thinking as you go along, we get a better understanding of how the process works for you. For instance, you might say, "I'm clicking on this link. . . . Oh, that's not what I expected to happen" or "Yes, it took me exactly where I wanted to go."

Several examples like this, varying the types of comments you hope the participant will share while thinking out loud, help the participant understand that you are seeking not just a description of *actions* taken but *reactions* to these actions.

Some moderators give the participant a little exercise to demonstrate thinking out loud. It could be as simple as asking the participant to load staples into a stapler and comment on the process while doing it. The demonstration shouldn't take long—usually a few minutes—and it gives you the chance to compliment the participant on his or her process of thinking out loud, or, if you want more reaction and insights, to offer suggestions for responses.

For a quick review of the research on the effect of thinking out loud on timed tasks, see the following sidebar.

Keep in mind that not everyone can handle the cognitive load of thinking out loud while they're working, so you should expect different levels of response from participants. But a gentle prompt from you, such as, "And you're looking for . . ." can help remind participants to share their thought processes if they have gone quiet. You might even tell participants at this point that if they go quiet on you, which is perfectly natural when they're concentrating, you'll ask them to share their thoughts with you.

The effect of thinking out loud on timed tasks

See Rhenius and Deffner, 1990; van den Haak, de Jong, and Schellens, 2007.

Some research suggests that thinking out loud slows down the response time for participants and therefore does not provide accurate data for timed tasks. Even in the studies for which this has been documented, the findings suggest that thinking out loud doesn't affect the *accuracy* of participants' thoughts.

See Ericsson and Simon, 1993.

See Bowers and Snyder, 1990; Olmsted-Hawala, Hawala, Murphy, and Ashenfelter, 2010; Berry and Broadbent, 1990; Wright and Converse, 1992.

As for increasing time on task, some studies show that the impact is moderate and occurs only in the early stages of familiarization with tasks. Other studies show that thinking out loud does not affect time on task or performance.

And some research indicates that the process of thinking out loud improves performance.

What does this mean for you and your testing process? If you're not sure which research to rely on for your study and time on task is a critical factor, you may not want to use the think-aloud protocol. You can compensate for this loss of feedback from your participants by using *retrospective recall*, in which you ask the participants to review the videotape after the test, or leave extra time for a semi-structured interview after the last task, working in questions you and your observers have noted while observing.

See Chapter 6 for more information on retrospective recall.

In most cases, especially when testing is for diagnostic or exploratory purposes, thinking out loud provides a rich source of information about the user's perceptions of the product's usability. And, as the most recent study by Olmsted-Hawala and colleagues indicates, the participants who were thinking out loud with active involvement by the moderator were more satisfied with the experience than when the moderator did not interact with them and they worked in silence.

For more tips and strategies for interacting with participants, see the "Methods for successful 'thinking out loud' procedures" sidebar later in this chapter.

Being an effective and unbiased moderator

To be an effective and unbiased moderator, you need to adopt the following practices:

- Monitor your body language.
- Balance your praise.
- Ask "good" questions.

Monitor your body language

It's hard to know what your body language communicates to others. But if you want to be an effective and unbiased moderator, you will need to understand what your facial expressions and body movements say and mean to the participants.

Your goal is to strike a balance between friendly and professional. Cultural, regional, and gender differences can affect what it means to be both friendly and professional, so there are no universal rules to follow. Still, you don't want to be seen as too chummy. Or too standoff-ish, for that matter. If you are the touchy-feely type (perhaps you like to hug people?), you want to resist the temptation to touch the participant, even if your motivation is encouragement. If you pat the participant on the shoulder or the hand, you could be communicating that you are in a "superior" position, which is not conducive to the partnership you want to establish with your participant.

Body language and facial expression can work for or against you. For instance, when you lean in, you indicate interest in the participant; leaning back indicates the opposite. However, changing your position, sometimes leaning in, other times leaning back, can alert the participant that you are changing your attention or interest. It's best to strike a neutral pose and maintain it.

The same goes for your facial expression. It should be neutral, if possible, or positive, no matter what the participant says or does, unless, of course, the participant says something intentionally funny. Then it's OK to laugh. Otherwise, try to avoid facial expressions that could be interpreted as responses to the actions of the participant. These include frowning, scowling, and any nonverbal expressions, such as sighing or yawning.

Watch your arms and legs as well. Crossing your arms as you talk to the participant could communicate a defensive posture, which might limit communication. Fidgeting (leg, foot, or hand) often indicates nervousness.

By studying the recorded sessions of your moderation and listening to critiques from your team members, you can become schooled in what you are communicating nonverbally so that you can focus on the things you want to change.

Balance your praise

Participants are often eager to please. They are so eager to please, in fact, that they typically complete post-task and post-test questionnaires with high marks for how "easy" it was to perform a task, even after you have seen them struggle mightily. Reeves and Nass report some fascinating findings to support this tendency to want to please in their book *The Media Equation*. As an example, they found that when study participants were asked to evaluate the performance of a computer, they were more positive when asked to respond on the computer they used as compared to using a different computer to answer the same questions. In other words, "people are polite to computers, too."

Reeves and Ness, 1996

Knowing this tendency, you can see how important it is to avoid biasing the type of response you want from the participant. That means you have to provide balanced praise, no matter what happens. Balanced praise means giving positive feedback to task failure as well as task success. If a participant knows that she failed at a task, she can be very frustrated. Your goal is to make her appreciate how helpful it was to observe this interaction. Emphasize that you learned so much from her experience. Praise her efforts.

I have seen inexperienced moderators praise only successful task completion and avoid saying anything when participants experience task failure. This unbalanced praise just reinforces participants' frustration at "failing" and can further reinforce the participants' belief that the moderator wants to hear only positive responses to the experience.

Ask "good" questions

Asking good questions means phrasing them so that they are unbiased. As with much that the moderator does, this is a learned skill. Not only do you need to learn how to ask good questions, but you also need to know how to respond to questions that the participant asks you.

For instance, the participant may ask you, "Did I do that right?" If you get this question, don't answer it. Of course, you don't want to be rude and just ignore the question, but you will learn more if you politely respond by asking a return question to get the participant to share his or her thoughts with you. For instance, in response to the participant's question, you can say, "What do you think should have happened?" or "Is that what you were expecting?" In this way, you probe for more insight rather than supplying an answer that could introduce bias into the session.

Sometimes the team will have a question or two for the participant that they want you to ask. Let's say that the team wants to know why the participant used the Back button rather than the Home button to return to the homepage on a website. You want to avoid asking a loaded question, such as "Why didn't you use the Home button?" Instead, ask, "Can you tell me how you navigated to the homepage?" Or, if you observed that the participant did not find a link to information

For more about asking good questions, see the "Methods for successful 'thinking out loud' procedures" sidebar.

required in a task (perhaps it is "below the fold" on the screen, requiring scrolling down the page), you can ask, "Where do you think you might look for a more direct route to the information you needed for this task?" Or you could ask, "Is there another way to get there?"

Good questions begin with "what" or "how" (not "why")

Good questions make the participant feel that you are interested in knowing more. They prompt the participant to share insights into the user's experience. Questions that begin with "what" and "how" tend to do this well. For instance:

- What are you trying to do now?
- What additional information would you want to see?
- How do you think you would solve this problem?

For more tips and techniques for asking good questions, see Tamler, "How (Much) to Intervene in a Usability Testing Session," 1998.

Questions that begin with "why" tend to suggest that the participant has done something wrong. They tend to put the participant on the defensive. Instead of saying, "Why did you choose that button?" rephrase the question to something less confrontational, such as "How did you decide to choose it?" Or, "Tell me your process in choosing this option . . ." and "Is that what you expected to find?"

Good questions are balanced

When asking a question that contains an adjective—such as *successful* or *difficult*—present the question using an adjective pair (*successful–unsuccessful* or *easy–difficult*), so that you avoid suggesting that you want a specific response. For instance:

- *Unbalanced example*: "So, how difficult was that for you?"
- *Balanced example*: "So, how easy or difficult was that for you?"

For more on crafting good questions, see Chapter 6.

Or avoid the use of the adjectives altogether by phrasing the question: "So, what was it like for you to do that?"

Methods for successful "thinking out loud" procedures

Adapted from Judy Ramey.[1]

In general

- When you are screening the participants for a study, notice how they respond to your questions. Decide on a strategy for engaging the participant before he or she arrives for the usability study.
- Be careful of the social dynamics you set up with the participant.
  - Don't joke, indulge in sarcasm, flirt, or betray your own nervousness.
  - Maintain a professional, neutral demeanor.
  - Keep yourself "small" in relationship to the participant. Sit slightly back from the participant, in a chair that is lower.
  - Avoid wearing heavy perfume or aftershave. The participant may have allergies to the odor or find it distracting.
  - Don't wear suggestive, revealing, or tight, uncomfortable clothes.
- Don't bias the participant.
  - Don't betray your own views or opinions of either the participant's level or skill.
  - Don't let the participant become aware of any bias you may have about the product.
- Avoid interactions with the participant that can shift the focus from the participant's domain to the designer's.
  - Don't expect the participant to tell you how to fix problems.
  - Don't expect the participant to answer other design questions.
  - Always keep the focus of attention on the participant, not yourself. Avoid "I" statements and long explanations of how the system works.

[1]From the University of Washington, with additions by Usability Analysis & Design, Xerox Corporation; available at *www.stcsig.org/usability/resources/toolkit/toolkit.html*

- ○ Stay in the relationship with the participant. Don't worry about the next question you are going to ask.

- ○ Write down design ideas so that you don't need to worry about forgetting them after the test. Just make sure you flag them in some way, so you'll know they were your ideas rather than something the participant said.

- Don't let yourself get impatient!

  - ○ When the participant seems to have a problem, the participant can often unravel it without your help.

  - ○ When you feel you should jump in, count to 10 first. The participant may need time to think.

  - ○ If you jump in too soon, you lose valuable data and the participant may become dependent on your help.

- Learn to probe in a neutral way to get information on which to base your design improvements.

Techniques that encourage thinking out loud

Here are some tried-and-true techniques you can use:

- prompting
- echoing
- "conversational disequilibrium"
- summarizing at key junctions

Prompting

- Focus on tasks, not features. Don't ask, "Do you like that dialog box?" but "Did that dialog box help you reach your goal?"

- Focus on questions, not answers.

- Explore participant thinking in a neutral way:

  - ○ Don't be too quick to assume that the participant is lost or having a problem.

○ Don't say, "What is your problem here?" but ask, "What is your goal?" or "What are you thinking you should do here?"

- Don't betray your own interests or point of view by your comments, emphasis, "waking up" and getting interested, or showing in facial expression or vocal tones that you disagree.

- Good user-focused questions:

  ○ What is your goal?

  ○ What do you want to accomplish here?

  ○ What did you expect to happen when you . . .?

  ○ How did you expect that to work?

  ○ Can you tell me what you were thinking?

  ○ What's going through your mind right now?

  ○ Can you describe the steps you are going through here?

  ○ How did you feel about that process?

Echoing

- Repeat their own word or phrase back to them as a question: "That message is confusing?" Echoing sets up a social dialogue and reinforces social conversation expectations: the participant says something, you repeat it; the participant says the next thing because that is what is expected in conversation.

- Don't put words in the participant's mouth or offer interpretations. If the participant says, "I'm not sure what to do here," don't say, "So you are confused because the menu bar is unclear?" Instead, say, "What do you see as your options?"

- If the participant says, "That didn't happen like I expected," don't ask, "So you thought that the task menu would be displayed here?" Instead, say, "What did you expect to happen?"

- Signal that you're listening ("Mmm hmm . . .").

"Conversational disequilibrium"

- Let your statements trail off and end in an upswing, as if you were asking a question. The participant will usually complete your statement.
  - "And you were expecting . . .?"
  - "And your goal is . . .?"
- Signal that you are there, you are interested, but that it is still their turn to talk ("Mmm hmm . . .").
- Speak softly. If you keep your voice at a normal or soft level, you will avoid the appearance of lecturing or speaking to an audience rather than to the participant.

Summarizing at key junctions

- When you have learned something new that is key to understanding, very briefly summarize the event and the thinking that the participant explored. Participants may offer more detail about their thought processes.
- Keep the recorder on or keep taking notes after you think that the test session is finished. Participants will often make interesting reflections about their processes during the casual remarks at the end of the session.

Know how and when to intervene

There will be times when things go wrong, and you will have to intervene. This can happen for several reasons:

- The system crashes.
- The participant struggles mightily to complete a task.
- The participant wanders off task.

Each of these situations calls for a slightly different intervention strategy.

The system crashes

If you're working with a prototype, it's highly likely that it will be "buggy," meaning that it may crash. Or other uncontrollable situations can occur, such as a loss of Internet connectivity. When these things happen, you need to intervene immediately. If you've briefed the participant on the possibility of a system crash or dead links, he or she is more likely to handle these situations without incident. You can instruct the participant to reboot, for instance, or let the participant know that he or she has just experienced a bug and that you appreciate the fact that the participant showed you it was there (again, taking the opportunity to reinforce an action with a positive response).

The participant struggles mightily

When you and your team observe that a participant is struggling with a task, your natural inclination is to rush to the rescue. Resist this temptation. Some of the best learning comes from seeing how participants handle the problem. Frequently, they solve the problem themselves, which is empowering for them and educational for you.

Of course, you don't want them to struggle for too long, with what constitutes "too long" being a judgment call. Over time, you will get better at understanding when it is time to intervene. Also, over time you will get better at handling overanxious team members who want you to rush in and save the participant at the first sign of struggle.

If you have told the participant in the pre-test briefing that you are interested in seeing how he or she solves problems, it prepares everyone—the participant and the team—to see the value in giving the participant time to work things out. However, if you've watched the first three participants fall down the same rabbit hole and the team agrees that there is a problem, you can be more proactive about helping, saying: "We've realized that this task is a problem, so I'm going to walk you through. . . ." You only want to use this approach when everyone agrees that they have seen and understood the problem, so there's no need to put participants through the struggle.

The participant wanders off task

Unlike the problem of the participant struggling to complete a task, which is educational, another problem that very likely requires intervention is when the participant wanders off task. This can happen if the participant has left the website or is hopelessly in the weeds in some part of the interface that is completely unrelated to the goals of the study.

In these cases and others like them, you won't learn what you need to know by watching the participant, and you are losing precious time. So, you will want to intervene. But you want to do it in such a way that you minimize a negative effect, which could result when the participant realizes he or she is in the wrong place. Again, being positive, while steering the participant back to the task at hand or moving on to the next task, can smooth this transition. Say something like, "Thanks so much for showing us your process because it helps us understand it. Now let's get back to the screen where you left off . . . [or] now let's move on to the next scenario."

Administer post-test feedback mechanisms

Chapter 6 describes these post-test feedback mechanisms in more detail.

When the participant finishes the last task in the last scenario, the moderator typically ends the session by administering the post-test feedback mechanisms. These could be in the form of a questionnaire, a semi-structured interview, or a qualitative feedback mechanism, such as the product reaction cards.

Using a post-test questionnaire

If you're using a questionnaire, you can ask the participant to fill it out while you watch, or you can ask the participant to share the responses orally with you so that you and the observers can hear them and the logger can take notes. If you use the oral approach, you can read the questions or you can ask the participant to read the questions.

Practical tip: If you're using an alternating positive–negative order of items like SUS, make sure you watch the participants as they complete it so you can ask them to confirm an odd-looking response.

If you're logging with Morae and using the SUS questionnaire, you can display it on the participant's computer, and then everyone can see the responses as well as listen to any comments the participant makes. What's more, Morae does the scoring, which is quite handy.

If you're using a semi-structured interview, you can take notes and record the interview, which gives you a way to review the interview later and use comments from the participant in your report.

Using the product reaction cards

As I explained in Chapter 6, in addition to getting qualitative feedback from participants' comments during the test and responses to open-ended questions, you can get a different type of qualitative feedback using Microsoft's product reaction cards.

Our methodology for using the product reaction cards is as follows:

- We place the cards at random on a table in the participant room (see Figure 7.1).

- At the end of a study (or sometimes after each scenario), we ask the participant to look over all the cards and select any—positive, negative, or any combination—that reflect his or her experience working with the product.

  We don't request a specific number, just suggest three, four, or five cards, whatever the participant is comfortable with.

- Then we ask the participant to bring the cards back to the desk and tell us what they mean as a reflection of the participant's experience with the product.

- We listen and record the participant's story of the experience.

Sometimes we switch to our document camera to record the cards that the participant picks. Other times, we simply log the card choices

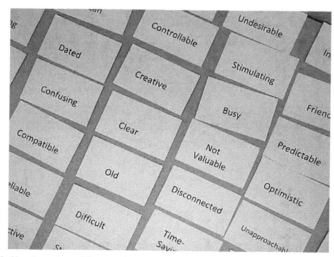

Figure 7.1 Here's a view of the product reaction cards, which the participant sees on a table at the end of a test session.

so that we have this information for our analysis. After each session, we return the cards to different places on the table so that the next participant sees them in a different arrangement.

If we are using the cards after each scenario, we replace them on the table in a different order so that the overall arrangement is always changing. If we are using them in a comparative evaluation, we may leave the cards a participant picks for Product A on the desk and then ask the participant to keep or exchange any or all of the cards when picking the cards for Product B.

Managing variations on the theme of testing

Up to now, I've assumed that your testing situation consists of one moderator, one participant, and one lab or room. But what if your situation is different from this setup? It could be different in several ways:

- testing with two or more participants
- testing with two or more moderators
- testing remotely with a moderator

Testing with two or more participants

Co-discovery

If the real-world context of use of your product involves two people working together, such as a parent and child, two friends, or two co-workers, then you will want to test under the same conditions. This testing process is called *co-discovery*. Of course, if you are using co-discovery, you have planned for this approach and recruited your participants in pairs.

In co-discovery, you're probably not going to use the think-aloud protocol because the two people will naturally talk to each other as they work together. That means the moderator will have less to do in terms of prompting for feedback and can be more focused on taking notes.

An advantage in co-discovery is that it's more comfortable for the participants. A disadvantage is that you may not see equal interaction, since one person is more likely to dominate, particularly when the two people are working together with one keyboard and one monitor (or one device).

One technique to balance the involvement of the participants is to ask them to shift keyboard (or interface) control and their seating position between scenarios. To get individual responses to questionnaires about their experience, you may want to give each one the questionnaires to complete. You may also want to use a semi-structured interview at the end of the session to get more in-depth feedback from both participants.

Multiple participants

There can also be situations in which you are testing with more than two participants at the same time. This type of testing is called *multiple-user simultaneous testing*. Your testing needs may support this approach when time is of the essence and you need to see a lot of users in a very short time.

To be able to do multiple-user simultaneous testing, you need either a big room set up with multiple stations or multiple rooms where you can schedule many users for studies at the same time. In both of these testing situations, you need multiple moderators. Or you could record these sessions without a moderator and then review all the tapes later, but that will require a huge investment in time and resources after testing ends.

Testing with two or more moderators

In addition to the multiple-user simultaneous testing situation, there are other reasons to test with two or more moderators, including:

- testing with a large number of users in back-to-back individual sessions
- testing over a long period of time
- testing in multiple locations

In testing with a large number of users in back-to-back individual sessions, you may need more than one moderator for scheduling reasons.

Remember the survey results reported in Chapter 5 on how many test sessions a moderator could handle in a day?

For instance, your testing day may go from early morning to late evening. Even if one person could be available for this entire timeframe, the schedule would be so taxing on the energy of this person that it would be more practical to share the workload with two or more moderators.

In testing over an extended period of days or weeks, even if the total number of participants is not large, you may need more than one moderator, again because of scheduling issues.

If you are testing in multiple locations and you don't have the budget to travel, you will need other moderators at these locations. Beyond considerations of budget, you may prefer to have moderators with the local language, accent, and culture at the various locations where you will be testing.

To be successful in situations where multiple moderators will be involved, you need to use one or more of the following strategies:

- *Do a walkthrough/pilot together.* This strategy works best if you are in the same location, but you can also do a walkthrough with GoToMeeting or another web conferencing tool. You can use the walkthrough to discuss various situations that might come up and how you'll handle them. This is especially important if you're collecting any kind of metrics. For purely qualitative testing, it might not matter as much.

- *Observe a couple of each other's sessions, if possible.* If testing is taking place over a period of days or weeks, you can share recorded sessions and set up a meeting to discuss the interactions. If this is not possible, schedule time to hand off to each other (if testing sequentially) or to compare notes.

- *During testing, maintain good coordination and communication among the moderators.* This coordination allows you to make adjustments, as needed, to the script and the test protocol.

Testing remotely with a moderator

Chapter 2 gives you more information on remote testing options.

Remote testing with a moderator—using a screen-sharing application such as GoToMeeting or Adobe Connect—has some of the same requirements as testing with the moderator and participant in the same place. But there are differences.

Here are some of the differences:

- the pre-test briefing
- interactions and questions during testing
- unexpected, uncontrollable events

The pre-test briefing

The pre-test briefing will dispense with the description of the room setup. In its place, you will need to cover the logistics of the remote testing process. If you have sent consent forms in advance, you need to review these to make sure the participant is comfortable with the arrangement and the use of the recording. If you haven't sent the forms in advance, you need to allow time for the participant to complete them.

If you require written consent, you need to ask the participant to mail or fax or e-mail the signed form back to you. If you don't require written consent, you can ask the participants to indicate that they agree to be recorded by responding to your question seeking permission. The recorded response becomes the archive for the video release, which eliminates the need for a signed document.

Part of the pre-test briefing requires running a test of the setup. Even if you sent out instructions on the setup requirements ahead of time, there could still be technical problems. Hopefully, any problems you uncover at this point can be fixed so that the test can go forward. It's always good to have technical support on hand at your end and, if possible, at the participant's end, to help smooth out any problems.

Interactions and questions during testing

The biggest handicap you will face as a remote moderator is that, in all likelihood, you cannot see the participant. This means you won't be able to interpret body language and facial expressions. Nor will the participant be able to do that with you. You and the participant are relying solely on voice communication. Therefore, you will need to be even more careful about what you say and how you say it.

You may also not be able to discern as easily when the participant is struggling or when the participant needs encouragement. And it may be harder to get the participant to think out loud from a distance. You'll have to decide how much prompting you want to give to encourage thinking out loud, especially when nothing seems to be happening. A good rule of thumb is to count to 10 to yourself before prompting the participant to respond.

Unexpected, uncontrollable events

Testing remotely is a learn-by-doing experience for the moderator with its own set of challenges. There's only so much you can do to manage the session. A lot is beyond your control. For instance, despite the fact that you may have confirmed that the testing conditions are working during your pre-test briefing, technical problems can still crop up, such as a loss of Internet connectivity or a situation in which the participant has to reboot the computer or re-enter the online meeting room. Be prepared for the unexpected.

Another challenge in remote testing is that the participant may need to break off for any number of reasons. These could include being called to a meeting, having to handle a job crisis, being interrupted by a phone call or a visitor, or letting other distractions intrude, such as receiving instant messages or e-mail while participating. Of course, you can request that all of these communication channels be turned off during the session, but you can't do anything about it if they are not. If the interruptions cannot be managed, it's sometimes possible to reschedule the session at a better time. Other times, you may need to break it off even when you can't reschedule the session.

Chapter 2 tells you about the advantages and disadvantages of moderated and unmoderated remote testing.

Another option is unmoderated remote testing. Because unmoderated testing does not require a moderator or observers, or any of the other strategies used in moderated testing, I don't cover it in this chapter. However, the following sidebar gives you a quick look at some research that compares the results of testing with and without a moderator.

Understanding the impact of the observer effect

Is there a difference in the results you get from conducting moderated tests versus unmoderated tests? This question comes up because the presence of a moderator introduces potential bias from "the observer effect," which is the influence of the observer on the participant.

For instance, do participants try harder when they know they are being observed? We know that participants want to please us, as we can see from the overly positive responses they give on post-task and post-test questionnaires.

Not only do we know that participants like to please us, but we also know that they view the moderator as an authority figure who is in some ways "supervising" their work. When we observe participants struggling to complete a task, we often wonder if they would spend that much time on their own or if they are trying harder because they know they are being watched. Sometimes they will tell us that if they were doing this on their own, they would have quit the task rather than struggle to get it done. Other times, they may not share this information.

A study comparing remote unmoderated testing with moderated lab testing confirmed that users being observed try harder. The participants in this study were given the same information-seeking tasks in the two testing conditions. In the moderated lab tests, the participants completed the tasks, using twice as many clicks and taking twice as much time as compared to the same tasks in the unmoderated tests. In other words, the participants in the moderated condition tried harder.

Schulte-Mecklenbeck and Huber, 2003

Keep this in mind when you are moderating usability tests, but don't let this condition prevent you from using a moderator in testing. More often than not, the moderator brings great value to the testing situation, helping the participant open up about what he or she is experiencing and providing a welcoming situation in which the participant can be made to feel comfortable.

Providing help or customer support during testing

Up to this point, I've shown you how all of the interaction between the participant and the team falls to the job of the moderator. However, certain testing situations provide the opportunity for participants

We use the help desk role routinely in our studies, regardless of whether there is technical or customer support for the product we are testing, because we find it useful to know whenever the participant feels the need to ask for help.

to ask for assistance in the form of a customer service or help desk representative. If your test plan allows for requests for help or even calls to a help desk, you should have a team member prepared to assume this role. This role is particularly appropriate when the product has customer or technical support because it matches the user's expectations for being able to get help.

If you have observers in the room with the moderator, one of these—generally a product expert—is designated to respond to a participant's request for help. If your team is in the control room, the participant can ask for help or call for help, and the designated team member can respond. An alternative technique is to set up a text chat situation with the designated team member responding to the participant's chat message.

In whatever context you offer help, when the participant asks for help, the team member acting as the customer or technical support representative has an important role to play because this interaction provides an opportunity for the team to gain insight into the problem the participant is experiencing. While some aspects of this interaction are similar to a real-world customer service call, others are different.

The first thing the designated customer service representative should do is ask the participant to describe the problem. Even though the person in this role can probably see what the participant is doing, it's useful to get the participant to explain it in his or her own words. In this way, the situation matches the real world of a customer support call or chat inquiry.

However, what happens next is not the same as would happen with a real customer service representative. That's because the goals are different for each. The real customer service representative wants to solve the user's problem as quickly as possible. The usability team's stand-in for this role wants to explore the nature of the problem for insights about the user's experience.

Taking a less direct approach to solving the user's problem, the team's customer service representative might ask the participant what he has tried or ask the participant to suggest what he might want to try next. If this approach doesn't solve the problem, the next step is to offer a helpful hint.

For instance, if the participant is on the wrong screen and can't figure this out, the designated team member might suggest going back to the homepage and trying to find the path to the information from that point. If the participant is on the correct screen, the customer service team member can tell the participant that the information he needs is on that screen and suggest that he might want to look around a bit more. If there's a tab on the navigation bar that the participant isn't noticing, the designated team member might ask whether the participant has looked along the navigation bar. Or, if the participant says that he has consulted the online help and can't find the information needed, the designated team member might ask what other words the participant could use to search the help. If that doesn't work, supplying a word or two may get the participant going again.

Still another approach is to respond to the participant's question with a question. If the participant asks, "How do I create a new form?" the designated team member might respond with, "What do you think you would want to try first to create the form?" While this approach may sound a bit circuitous, the rationale behind this strategy is to understand the problem-solving approach the participant uses. Often, with a little encouragement, the participant can solve his own problem. Knowing this point of uncertainty, though, can be very helpful to the product designers.

As these examples show, the team's designated customer support representative should provide the least amount of information needed to get the participant back on track and then encourage the participant to call again if more help is needed.

Logging observations

In a low-tech usability test, everyone may be logging observations on the observer forms created for this purpose. More typically these days, there is a designated logger using logging software. The logger has probably already established logging codes and practiced logging in the walkthrough and pilot. During testing, the logger may want to add descriptions of observations to expand the context of the codes, as well as logging comments from the participants.

In our studies, which are generally formative, we use a rich qualitative logging process within Morae, where we capture quotes from

The continuing case study at the end of this chapter shows a logged session from the Holiday Inn China website usability test.

participants, descriptions of their actions, comments from the team, nonverbal observations (sighs, leaning forward, putting head in hand, and so forth). Then we export the log into an Excel spreadsheet, where we can format it for the findings meeting and also sort on key findings.

In situations where the logger is not a subject matter expert on the product, the logger may need to designate a product expert to take good notes so that they can be added to the log to clarify any actions that the logger may not have fully understood or observed. If everyone is logging observations, one person on the team may need to collate these observations into a combined log of observations.

Handling observers and visitors

Observers are people with a direct stake in the study and are often core team members. They can be in the same room as the participant or in another room, such as the control room.

Visitors are others with an interest, either in usability testing in general or your study in particular. Visitors often observe the test from an executive viewing room.

Both observers and visitors can help bring about improvements in your product, since the more people who can see the participants working with the product, the stronger the impact will be. But they will need special handling.

Observers with you and the participant

It's somewhat of an open question, certainly debated among usability practitioners, as to whether it is an advantage or disadvantage having observers in the same room as the participant. Some usability practitioners feel strongly that observers get much more out of a session if they can attend in person and if it can be done without stressing participants. Others feel that observers are just too hard to handle.

If you can choose how and where you want the observers, you will probably make the decision on the basis of what you're more comfortable with. If you don't have options because you have only one room for the test and you want to accommodate observers, you will need to provide training for the observers in the rules of etiquette.

Here are the ground rules:

- *Arrive on time and stay the whole time.* Late arrivals will not be seated.

- *Turn off all electronic devices.* Even when a cell phone is on silent mode, if an observer pulls it out to see who's called, it can be distracting to the participant, the moderator, or both. Texting, of course, is even more distracting and may suggest to the participant or moderator that the observer is bored with the session or has other, more important things to do. So, no texting allowed.

- *No talking.* This is a tough one to police, but reinforcing the need for complete silence while the participant is working is essential for a good session. Stress how hard this may be for some, particularly if they see the participant struggle, but also stress how important it is to remain silent.

- *No adverse nonverbal communication.* That means no laughing, sighing, groaning, fidgeting, and so forth. Smiling, cheering, and encouragement of any kind are also bad. Try to stress the importance of observers looking alert and interested while not getting so engaged that they interfere with the process.

This point of etiquette needs to be sent in advance with the invitation to observe.

To enhance the observers' experience—and keep them occupied in productive ways—you can give them a job to do. If you want them to use observer forms, distribute these and show them how to use them. If you want to assign specific note-taking roles for different observers, tell each person what his or her role is. If you're going to use a laptop during the session and you won't be distracted if the observers do as well, tell them it's OK. But if you're not comfortable with observers using laptops, it's your decision to rule them off-limits.

If you distribute observer forms and you plan to collect them for review in the findings meeting, let the observers know this ahead of time. If you plan to invite the observers to participate in the findings meeting, let them know that their input is going to be important.

For further involvement by the observers, you can tell them to make a note about anything they want you to ask the participant between scenarios or after the testing session. You can give them note cards or sticky notes for this purpose. But lay the ground rules that you will decide what you can and cannot ask. Let them know that your decision will be based on the time you have and the nature of the question.

Visitors in the executive viewing room

In our usability center, we have a three-room setup that makes it easy and convenient to have core team members as observers in the control room and visitors in the executive viewing room (see Figure 7.2).

Figure 7.2 Visitors can view the session from the executive viewing room into the control room and beyond to the participant room.

If your lab setup provides for visitors in another room, this presents a great opportunity for you, and you will want to maximize its potential. If at all possible, assign a team member as the executive viewing room facilitator. This person will be on hand to do the following:

- Explain the goals of the test and the process you are using.
- If the visitors are new to usability testing, promote the value of seeing users work with the product. This is your chance to be a usability advocate.
- Answer any questions that visitors have, and monitor the conversation to "intervene" if necessary.
  - They may want to jump immediately from observation of a problem to a solution. Try to keep them in observer mode for as long as possible so that they stay open to observing and understanding users' actions and activities, rather than switching to solution mode too quickly.

○ They may experience shock and awe at what they are observing. Two reactions are likely:
  – They blame the user: "Where did you get that stupid user?"
  – They react to negative feedback: "They're calling my baby ugly!"

Stupid user syndrome

You need to be prepared for the appearance of the "stupid user" syndrome. It happens when a visitor sees a user struggling with something that seems so easy (and obvious) to the visitor. The reaction is, invariably, "Where did you get that stupid user? This person can't possibly be our real user!"

It's natural to expect a developer or product manager to want to blame the user first. It happens most often when you are testing with novice users because developers have a hard time appreciating what people *don't* know about a product they know so well. But it can also happen when advanced users are working with a new product or a new feature of a product. In both cases, it harkens back to the usability mantra: "Know thy user, for he [or she] is not thyself."

Rubinstein and Hersh, 1984

What to do when this syndrome appears? First, show the screener to the visitors, telling them how you have matched the screener to the particular user profile for this study.

We anticipate the "stupid user" syndrome and make copies of our screeners for all visitors.

In addition to sharing the screener with the visitors, encourage them to stay for the next user or, if you have already done several sessions, explain how many times you have seen a user struggle with this problem before. Ideally, if the visitors stay to see a second and perhaps even a third user struggle with the same problem, they will experience a change of attitude, in which they no longer blame the user but accept that there's a problem. Then, of course, you have to guard against their tendency to want to fix the problem in the middle of the study (unless you're using the RITE method, where fixing problems is the goal of each test.)

Ugly babies

The other common response from visitors who are developers or product managers is that they react negatively to the user's criticism because they think the user is "calling my baby ugly." And, of course, if the participant is using the think-out-loud technique, he or she may, in fact, *say* ugly things about the product.

In a website test we conducted, one of the participants got so frustrated that she blurted out, "This is the worst website I have ever seen!" That's an extreme example, but a real one, of calling the baby ugly. Again, if this happens, you will have to help your visitors get past this feeling of rejection to understand that a good usability test *should* find problems so that the baby can be treated before it leaves the "hospital."

Remote observers

There are far fewer rules for remote observers because there is far less potential for disruption and far less opportunity for control. It comes down to one rule: Put your phone on "mute."

In whatever format people are observing remotely, they cannot publicly talk during the session. You may allow them to text a team member, if this is an option during the test, and you may be able to collect their questions to ask the participant, but, as with observers on site, asking visitors' questions will be at the moderator's discretion.

Working solo

If you find yourself working alone, don't panic. You can manage the essential tasks to conduct effective testing. You just need to make some decisions about how you'll do it. Here are some options to consider when wearing several hats of moderator, logger, and facilitator:

- *Logging the findings*
  - If you are sitting with the participant, you can write the findings on your moderator script. Or you can log on your laptop.
  - If you decide that you'd like to use a template for note taking, you could create one with screen captures of the interface and make notes on these. Using a template requires up front preparation, but this effort will be rewarded in easier note taking.
  - The pace of the session might be a bit slower—as you're wearing two hats of moderator and logger. However, with practice, you can

learn to say things like, "Great, this is so helpful," while you are writing or typing; or, "Could you hold up for just a minute while I catch up."

- ○ If you are leaving the participant to work alone, you can log on a computer in the control room. But you will need to instruct the participant to wait a minute or two before getting started so that you can get to the control room without missing anything.

- *Not logging the findings*

  - ○ As you will have your hands full in the role of being an effective moderator, you may choose not to take any notes during the sessions. Some people just can't do two things at once, and that's OK.

  - ○ This option works only if you record the sessions *and* can take the time to review the tapes afterward.

- *Handling observers and visitors*

  - ○ The rules are the same for the care and handling of observers and visitors when they are in the room with you and the participant.

  - ○ When observers and visitors are in another room, you won't be able to facilitate their activities. To compensate for this, you will want to pop into their room at the end of each session to chat with them and perhaps get their observer forms, if you provided them. You can also do damage control, if needed. But you need to build in the time between sessions for this interaction.

Summarizing Chapter 7

In this chapter, I have walked you through a typical day of testing. Because the role of the moderator is crucial to the success of testing, this chapter covered the moderator's responsibilities in:

- *Meeting and greeting the participant*—planning how you will get off on the right foot.

- *Conducting the pre-test briefing*—using the script so that you say the same thing every time.

- *Reviewing the think-out-loud process*—either by explaining it or demonstrating it, or both.

- *Being a good moderator* by:
  - *Monitoring body language*—keeping a neutral posture and facial expression.
  - *Balancing praise*—complimenting the participant on successes and failures.
  - *Asking good questions*—using techniques to probe without leading the participant.
  - *Knowing when and how to intervene*—balancing the desire to rescue the participant with the desire to learn from the participant's struggles.
- *Ending the session by administering your post-test process*, which might include:
  - a post-test questionnaire
  - a semi-structured interview
  - product reaction cards or some other qualitative feedback process

You've also seen the ways to manage testing variations, including the following situations:

- testing with two or more participants
- testing with two or more moderators
- testing remotely with a moderator

Although you have planned for these situations, your role as moderator changes to suit the particular needs and constraints of each situation.

In addition to the role of the moderator, two other roles were also explored:

- *The customer support representative*—who is a product expert available to assist when the participant asks for help.
- *The logger*—who should be a fast typist to capture observations during the testing sessions, with help from a subject matter expert when needed.

Special attention was given to the potential opportunities and pitfalls when observers and visitors are present. These include:

- observers in the same room—establishing the rules for good behavior

- visitors somewhere else, with options including:
  - nearby in another room—seizing the opportunity to manage expectations and promote usability
  - remotely observing—requiring fewer constraints because of less direct involvement

For those situations when you are working solo, I presented strategies to show you how to do it all by yourself. These include:

- figuring out how to moderate and log simultaneously
- foregoing logging, with the option to review the recorded sessions later
- deciding what to do when you have visitors—using similar management strategies when observers are in the room with you but different ones when they are elsewhere

In continuing to share the ongoing activities of the team conducting the Holiday Inn China website usability study, this chapter ends with a sample log from one of the test sessions. The logger identifies the user and the scenario and enters predetermined codes for the type of log entry, along with descriptions of the action and participant comments. The software (Morae, in this case) provides the predetermined description of the code and assigns the date and timestamp.

User 2	Code		Date/Time
Scenario: Look and feel			
It is pretty good. I like to look at the promotions first.	S	Start task	3/27/2008 19:21
Color is very clean to me; it's not white, pink, and others.	Q	"Quote, User comment"	3/27/2008 19:23
The site looks very easy to navigate. You can tell what is ads, and what is other information you want.	Q	"Quote, User comment"	3/27/2008 19:26
Now I do not know what is ads on the top of the website.	Q	"Quote, User comment"	3/27/2008 19:27
The banner is kind of big.	Q	"Quote, User comment"	3/27/2008 19:27
Scenario: Book a hotel room			
I do not like the city box because there is no drop-down menu for me to choose. So I have to type the city.	Q	"Quote, User comment"	3/27/2008 19:28
She clicks more options instead of booking a hotel.	U	User action	3/27/2008 19:30
She is going the wrong way and will have to retype everything again.	U	User action	3/27/2008 19:31
She doesn't understand the choices. She wants two beds, but she chooses two rooms.	T	Terminology	3/27/2008 19:31
She looks at IATA and asks, "What is that?"	T	Terminology	3/27/2008 19:32
It [website response time] is slow.	Q	"Quote, User comment"	3/27/2008 19:33
No progress bar.	0	Team observation	3/27/2008 19:33
She does not understand the different brands of InterContinental hotels.	MM	Mental model	3/27/2008 19:33
She is focusing her attention on the information located on the left side of the website.	O	Team observation	3/27/2008 19:35
I like to see the pictures of the hotels and rooms.	Q	"Quote, User comment"	3/27/2008 19:36
She clicked the link for more pictures but a lot of information pops up.	U	User action	3/27/2008 19:37

She clicked the Crowne Plaza instead of Holiday Inn, because she says "The location is near Wangfujing" [main street in Beijing].	Q	"Quote, User comment"	3/27/2008 19:38
She wants to look at more pictures.	Q	"Quote, User comment"	3/27/2008 19:40
She says, "I guess that is the only one I can click on."	Q	"Quote, User comment"	3/27/2008 19:42
"I like to check on other hotels that are nearby."	Q	"Quote, User comment"	3/27/2008 19:44
I like to look at the features before I look at the pictures.	Q	"Quote, User comment"	3/27/2008 19:45
She does not see that she needs to input in English.	O	Team observation	3/27/2008 19:46
She types in the options box: "I like to have a city view."	Q	"Quote, User comment"	3/27/2008 19:47
She is looking for the total cost: "Where is the total?"	Q	"Quote, User comment"	3/27/2008 19:49
She inputs her English name into the name field. But she is supposed to input Chinese characters. There is no error message.	U/O	User action; team observation	3/27/2008 19:49
Response to Q: How do you choose the hotel: I like to choose the location, I like to look at the pictures, and I think the visual is very important to me.	Q	"Quote, User comment"	3/27/2008 19:50
Response to Q: What is most important in choosing hotel: I choose location because it is famous. [the street].	Q	"Quote, User comment"	3/27/2008 19:51
Response to Q: I did not know that "Enter Chinese name" means to enter Chinese characters.	Q	"Quote, User comment"	3/27/2008 19:52
Response to Q: Difficult: The total did not show up until after I had to click the link to make the reservation.	Q	"Quote, User comment"	3/27/2008 19:53
Response to Q: Navigation: It is easy but you just need to know where to click.	Q	"Quote, User comment"	3/27/2008 19:54
If I click China I like to have a drop-down menu to show the cities.	Q	"Quote, User comment"	3/27/2008 19:55
Is Beijing near an ocean? It makes me confused. [One of the options is for a room with ocean view.]	Q	"Quote, User comment"	3/27/2008 19:56

Scenario: **Cancel reservation**

She does not know how to go back to homepage.	O	Team observation	3/27/2008 19:58
She is trying to click the Priority Club to cancel a hotel.	MM	Mental model	3/27/2008 19:59
Where is the cancellation?	Q	"Quote, User comment"	3/27/2008 20:01
I do not have the confirmation number with me.	Q	"Quote, User comment"	3/27/2008 20:02

(Continued)

Session log (*Continued*)

User 2	Code		Date/Time
In the confirmation, there was no information saying the confirmation number is being sent to her e-mail account.	O	Team observation	3/27/2008 20:02
I did not write down my confirmation number so I do not think I can cancel the hotel.	Q	"Quote, User comment"	3/27/2008 20:03
She calls help desk: Qianying [team member] gives her a hint that she can go to her e-mail account to find the confirmation number.	H	Help desk	3/27/2008 20:05
I did not know because I did not write down the number.	Q	"Quote, User comment"	3/27/2008 20:06
You have to pay attention to the cancellation option under the Priority Club.	Q	"Quote, User comment"	3/27/2008 20:07
The Priority Club login and cancellation bars are in the same area and same color as hotel booking.	Q	"Quote, User comment"	3/27/2008 20:08
Scenario: **Find a Holiday Inn in Changchun**			
There is no drop-down menu so I do not know whether my spelling is correct.	Q	"Quote, User comment"	3/27/2008 20:08
She doesn't see the error message.	O	Team observation	3/27/2008 20:10
She finds the city map page.	Q	"Quote, User comment"	3/27/2008 20:10
I could not make a reservation because maybe there is no Holiday Inn in Changchun.	Q	"Quote, User comment"	3/27/2008 20:11
I still think they need a drop-down menu for cities; then I can see whether there is a hotel in the city.	Q	"Quote, User comment"	3/27/2008 20:12
Response to Q: Not satisfied at all.	Q	"Quote, User comment"	3/27/2008 20:12
Response to Q: I have to spend time to look for the hotel.	Q	"Quote, User comment"	3/27/2008 20:13
Response to Q: I did not see the error message at all.	Q	"Quote, User comment"	3/27/2008 20:13
Scenario: **Book a hotel at another website (eLong.com)**			
I like the website. It provides the airplane information.	Q	"Quote, User comment"	3/27/2008 20:14
I do not need to type.	Q	"Quote, User comment"	3/27/2008 20:19
I like this website because it provides a lot of information.	Q	"Quote, User comment"	3/27/2008 20:19
It gives me all the information I need.	Q	"Quote, User comment"	3/27/2008 20:20
I care about the rating, ranking [hotel ratings/rankings].	W	Undefined	3/27/2008 20:20
Response to Q: I like the hotel information and the prices. I do not need to look at the pictures because the rating tells me a lot about the hotel.	Q	"Quote, User comment"	3/27/2008 20:21

Response to Q: All on the same page, I do not need to click; just look at the page.	Q	"Quote, User comment"	3/27/2008 20:22
Response to Q: Very appealing.	Q	"Quote, User comment"	3/27/2008 20:22
Response to Q: (rate on scale of 1–10) 10 for eLong.	Q	"Quote, User comment"	3/27/2008 20:22
Response to Q: I do not think I will go to the Holiday Inn website, if I have this option.	Q	"Quote, User comment"	3/27/2008 20:23
Response to Q: (rate Holiday Inn on scale of 1–10) I will give a 6 to Holiday Inn.	Q	"Quote, User comment"	3/27/2008 20:24
Response to Q: Somewhat appealing [Holiday Inn].	Q	"Quote, User comment"	3/27/2008 20:28
Response to Q: In the options box, they have to pay attention. Beijing is not near any ocean.	Q	"Quote, User comment"	3/27/2008 20:28
Response to Q: Cancellation box should be bold.	Q	"Quote, User comment"	3/27/2008 20:29
Response to Q: Holiday Inn website is very basic, for basic use, it is OK.	Q	"Quote, User comment"	3/27/2008 20:29
Response to Q: Holiday Inn is a well-known hotel. They should spend more effort on revising their website.	Q	"Quote, User comment"	3/27/2008 20:30

Analyzing the findings

8

You've finished testing. That was fun, wasn't it? Exhausting, too, most likely.

Now you have logs, observer forms, participant questionnaires, session recordings, and more to somehow make sense of.

Making sense of it all can be overwhelming, but not if you have a plan. This chapter lays out a plan to help you analyze the findings quickly and make sense of the data. The process of analysis can be broken into three distinct steps, based on these questions:

1. What did we see?
2. What does it mean?
3. What should we do about it?

It's very important to take these three questions individually, and in this order. Why is this important? Because it is extremely tempting to jump from Step 1 to Step 3 without taking the time to understand what the findings mean. Once you have done the middle step—analyzing the findings—you are in a good position to decide what to do about them.

Usability Testing Essentials. DOI: 10.1016/B978-0-12-375092-1.00008-8

So, in doing Step 1—What did we see?—you will want to

- gather input from everyone, including their top positives, negatives, and surprises
- gather data more systematically, using
  - *Top-down organization*, which is a method for organizing your findings based on your predetermined markers or heuristics.
  - *Bottom-up organization*, called *affinity matching*, which is a method for organizing your findings into groups, then letting the category labels emerge from the groupings.
  - *A combination* of both organizational methods.

In doing Step 2—What does it mean?—you will want to decide

- who will do the analysis—everyone, the core team, or a designated subgroup
- how the analysis will be done—the methodology to use to find insights and problems based on
  - measuring quantitative data
  - analyzing questionnaire responses
  - interpreting qualitative data

In doing Step 3—What should we do about it?—you will want to

- establish scope and severity ratings for the findings
- recommend fixes for the problems you found

What did we see?

Everyone who observed the testing has formed opinions about what worked and what didn't. Even before you refer to the logs or observer forms from the sessions, you can probably start a list of issues off the top of your head.

Perhaps you have informally collected these findings at break points during the testing period. Or perhaps you have not done this yet. In either case, now that the last participant has finished, it's time to gather up everyone's impressions and recollections before beginning a more structured analysis.

Gather input from everyone

If you have invited observers to contribute to the analysis of the findings, you want to get their input first. There are several reasons for this:

- You want to demonstrate the value of their input by asking for it upfront.

- When input comes from others who are not part of your core team, you want to be sure to include their thoughts and observations in your analysis. This is particularly important when the input comes from managers and supervisors, whose job will be to support or implement the recommendations you will make.

- Observers often have to leave before you begin formal analysis. If you can persuade them to stay for the first part of your findings meeting, you can capture their thoughts and reactions while they are still fresh.

Collect the top findings and surprises

To gather input from everyone, ask them, one at a time, to share their

- top positive finding
- top negative finding
- top surprise, or "ah-ha" moment

By starting with the top positive findings, you stress the importance of sharing and documenting the good things in the users' experience, not just the "bad" things.

As you go through this process, you can avoid a lot of "me, too" responses for the same top finding by telling everyone that if their top positive finding is already on the list, they can acknowledge this, then offer up their next important finding. That way, the list grows as you go around the room. If you want to expand the list even further, you could repeat this process to get everyone's top five findings.

You use the same process for the top negative findings, but begin at a different place in the room so that you change the order in which people speak. It's important to stress that a negative finding is one that was observed so that the focus stays on something that happened, rather than what should be done about it.

Then, when this round is finished, you go one more round to get each person's top surprise or "ah-ha" moment. In asking each person to share his or her "ah-ha" moment, you bring to light any misperceptions people may have been harboring before testing began, as well as any surprises they experienced in seeing users work with the product.

It's quite powerful to see the top findings come to light in this informal way. There is bound to be overlap but also you're likely to get some unique findings from this process. Collating these findings on a whiteboard or laptop projected onto a screen allows you to quickly pull together a list of top positive findings, top negative findings, and top surprises, along with the unique findings.

Following this initial top-of-mind review of the findings, the core team can start the process of digging into the logs or observer forms for a more systematic approach to extracting the findings. This process ensures that the team doesn't miss anything important, and it provides additional information on the issues associated with the findings already identified in the first round.

Choose your organizational method

To organize the process of sorting the findings into categories, you choose either of these methods:

- *Top-down*—starting with categories or codes
- *Bottom-up*—starting with individual findings, clustered into groups, then labeled by category

Each method has its advantages and disadvantages. So, a combination of both methods is often what you end up using.

Top-down method—starting with categories or codes

If your team used a set of *heuristics* (usability rules or guidelines of good practice) to shape the logging process, you created codes or markers to log the findings you expected to see. Or you have set your markers based on the types of findings you got from prior studies. Organizing the findings based on these predetermined categories is called a *top-down* method.

Advantages

The main advantage of this approach to organize the findings is efficiency, which means that you save time. Because you are working with the pre-set codes for categories of findings, the team can quickly review the findings in either of the following ways:

- If you have logged the findings in a software application such as Morae, you can now export the logs into an Excel spreadsheet. If you have logged the findings directly in Excel or with word processor tables as a template, you've already got the document you need. Either way, you can sort the findings by the codes, which makes it easy to organize them for discussion.

- Or, if there isn't time to sort the findings into categories during the findings meeting, you can print out the logs for the team to review together by scanning down the printouts using the codes to identify issues for discussion.

- If you have used observer forms to code the findings, you can make copies of these and use the same process to review the findings according to the codes.

Disadvantages

The main disadvantage of this approach is that when you start with predetermined codes or markers, you might miss some findings, particularly when they don't fit into one of the categories you've established. Another disadvantage is that you could have misidentified a finding during the session, putting it into a category or code from the list before being able to analyze it.

Sometimes this misidentification happens when you aren't sure what the problem is. For instance, when you observe a user having a problem with navigation, is the problem caused by confusion over a label (terminology), the size or location of the label (design), different names or labels for the same item (consistency), or the user's lack of recognition or misunderstanding of the process (mental model)? Sometimes a finding could fit into several categories, or perhaps none.

Questions may arise as to how the logger made the decision about the nature of the finding. If observers saw the action differently and put it into a different category, some discussion of the nature of the finding will be needed.

One study showed that a detailed template for recording findings produces a better analysis for novice usability practitioners and a correspondingly better-quality report. See Howarth, Andre, and Hartson, 2007.

To minimize the impact of miscoded findings during logging, some teams use an open-topic category for any observation that's hard to categorize. This open-topic category will have to be reviewed at the end to see where to assign the findings or whether to add a category or two.

Bottom-up method—starting with individual findings

See the following sidebar for the steps in the affinity-matching process.

Your team may have decided that you wanted to stay open to whatever you observed and learned from your users, so you didn't use markers in your logs and observer forms. You now review the logs and observer forms to identify findings, then put similar findings into groupings, then assign names to the groupings. This process employs a bottom-up method called *affinity matching*.

Affinity matching tips and tricks

The information that follows is adapted from Tara Scanlon.

Steps

1. Extract the data, ideas, or information you want to analyze. Write one thought per sticky note and, if you are working from a transcript, note where in the transcript the idea came from. Or have each person on the team use his or her notes or log to do it. There could be duplicates with each person doing the analysis, but it involves the team more fully.

2. Put all of the sticky notes up on a wall or whiteboard in random order.

3. Ask participants to start organizing all the sticky notes into groups that seem to go together. Set some ground rules:

   ○ No talking. If you think a note belongs someplace else, just move it.

   ○ If a note seems to be moving back and forth, it's OK to duplicate it and put it in both places.

- Avoid predefined categories.
- If you see something that prompts a new idea or question, make a new sticky note.

4. When the grouping has finished, gather the team together to label the categories. These labels should capture the theme of the grouping.

5. Prioritize the groupings, thus creating a hierarchy. Ask everyone to vote on the top three groups they think are most important; then ask the group whether these priorities seem right. This gives you the top categories of findings.

Tips for making the affinity analysis process work smoothly

The tips outlined here can help you streamline and optimize your affinity analysis process.

- Make categories and names meaningful:
  - If you have a category that's larger than the others, you may want to subdivide this category into two or more to give each one a specific category label.
  - If you have a category called "Miscellaneous," you need to find homes for these items or start a new category.

- Facilitate the process effectively. Participants go through different stages during the affinity process. These roughly include:
  - Being overwhelmed, not sure where or how to begin.
  - Getting into the groove and doing the gross categorization.
  - Getting frustrated with the details of categorization, not sure where the process is leading.
  - Seeing the magic of data transformed into information.

Figure 8.1 shows part of an Excel spreadsheet exported from Morae and used in a findings meeting from a test of a website for students seeking information about Georgia colleges and universities. The participant in this logged session was interested in finding engineering programs, with education programs as a secondary interest.

The log describes actions and comments from the participant but does not include codes or markers. Using the log, the team quickly reads down the column containing the actions' descriptions, looking for findings and calling them out by the timestamp so that everyone can see what finding is being identified. Someone on the team writes a brief description of the finding on a sticky note and posts it to the whiteboard. This process repeats for each participant's log with new findings being added as sticky notes and posted for the sorting process, which takes place after all of the logs have been reviewed. Once everyone agrees on the groupings, names are assigned to the groups.

Figure 8.2 shows the process of a findings meeting in action. This close-up of part of the process shows findings grouped for one task in the study: Create an Account. The number on the sticky notes refers to the participant, making it easy to tie the finding back to a specific log. This example is in the middle of the process, so it doesn't show the categories of findings that emerged at the end of the process or the total number of participants experiencing each problem.

Findings Log Exported from Morae

10:19.8	Task 2: Search for college with major of interest
11:05.4	Searching for colleges and majors goes to Career Tab
12:14.4	Notices test to match interest; looks at list . . . maybe if there was high career demand link
12:53.2	Clicks on Fast Growing careers . . . not sure if this = to high demand
13:16.2	Back to career info. page . . . exploring links
13:31.8	Reading about Career Key . . . Student Career Matching Assistant . . . BEGIN
14:05.6	at logon . . . went back
14:15.8	at Matching Assistant . . . user is picking fields . . . VIEW
14:52.8	at same Career Assistant Matching
15:15.0	More engineering types seen thru scrolling and exploring
15:30.8	Scrolls and likes types of science and technology engineering. What if it was categorized? . . . now realizes in alphabetical order.
16:13.4	If a person wanted to go into Biology or Chemistry but thinks more categories of science would be important
16:37.8	Materials Engineering . . . interesting. Likes description, the experience, education and training. Abilities listing is good. Likes daily work activities.
17:54.8	On this page, likes what he sees. Really helpful if a person doesn't know what they want . . . can look at skills and description, see what you're not so good at, can either change careers or stay with this one. Scrolling . . . exploring
18:50.4	Mechanical Engineering . . . highlighting text, exploring, likes seeing abilities for Mechanical Eng. Hovers on video. Opens video.
19:44.2	Closed video
19:52.8	Error . . . end program. User closed browser by mistake.
20:09.6	User calls about technical error; instructed to close browser.
20:24.0	Control Room reinitiates browser
22:01.4	on Matching Assistant; scrolling and looking
22:26.2	Looking through Matching Assistant options . . . wonder if he can use main search . . . uses main search enters Childhood Development
23:00.0	search = no matches, tries again
23:08.8	search fails again
23:19.4	GA college tab . . . looking for engineering college, hovers over tours, back to hovering on matching assistant, hovers on Distance Search
24:03.4	distance search, enters zip . . . looks at colleges for close and far from home . . . no majors . . . says he really wants to search careers
24:42.8	Not here on GA college tab . . . decides to compare, clicks Compare View
25:00.4	Scrolling on list, likes prices, enrollment . . . likes scannable features of page. Better than CollegeBoard, which requires changing and looking, GA411 is compact and he likes the table.
26:05.6	click on UGA . . . via GA Colleges tab
26:31.4	scrolling UGA data . . . likes page information and presentation of data
27:07.2	UGA page still . . . looking . . . big paragraph of minors stops him dead for a bit . . . wants bullets instead of text or maybe columns, and easier to read. Notes teenagers don't like to read.
28:42.0	Finds Child Development . . . more reading . . . looking for Mech Eng. scrolled list . . . comments on formatting
29:54.8	Moderator interrupts
30:00.4	Moderator queries about his goal.
30:05.8	Back to Career . . . Moderator prompts to find colleges
30:29.2	looking for colleges and careers . . . List of Careers click
31:00.0	looks for Sci and Tech . . . NEXT page
31:19.2	looking for Mechanical Engineering. Next, Next, selects Mech Eng
31:36.6	Scrolls down . . . there is info here . . . I didn't scroll down far enough. Yeah, had to scroll too far . . . wanted this list up higher where he could see it earlier, maybe next to education

Figure 8.1 A log from Morae exported into an Excel spreadsheet is used to review findings.

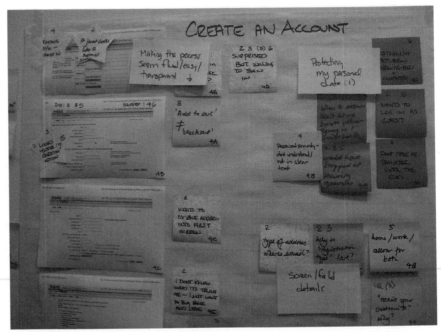

Figure 8.2 This view of affinity matching focuses on the task of creating an account.

Advantages

The main advantage of using an affinity-matching process for organizing your findings is that you stay open to whatever the process will uncover. This allows for discoveries in the findings that might otherwise be overlooked. Another advantage is that the process builds consensus about the findings and strengthens the overall team effort.

Disadvantages

The disadvantages are that the process requires a team effort, and it's generally more time consuming than a top-down approach because of the give-and-take involved in arranging and rearranging the findings into groups and then naming the categories.

To set some boundaries on the time for this process, you might want to suggest one hour for the affinity-matching process if the stickies are prepared ahead of time. Otherwise, add 30 minutes at the start for people to comb through their notes and write stickies. Then allocate another hour to discuss the top-priority categories. Anything over this timeframe is probably more time than people can sustain their interest and commitment.

Combining the methods

As you can see, choosing the method of organizing the findings depends on what you know (or anticipate finding) going into the study, how many people can be involved in the process, and, of course, how much time you have for the findings meeting. Whichever choice you make, it's often the case that you will end up using a combination of both methods:

- If you begin with a top-down approach, you will probably still need to add categories for findings that don't fit into one of the predetermined markers.
- If you begin with a bottom-up approach, you will probably also have some specific categories in mind, based on what you observed. You might even put some of these category labels on sticky notes so that you can speed up the process of grouping some of the findings.

Once you have finished the process of extracting and organizing the findings from your study, which is Step 1—What did we see?—you are ready to move to Step 2—What does it mean?—which focuses on an analysis of the findings to understand what they show you.

What does it mean?

Making sense of the findings is far easier said than done. It's not always obvious as to why something happened or what it means. This is where a team effort for the analysis is so important. Many projects require a detailed analysis and the corresponding report of this analysis. To do this analysis, you need to consider who should be involved, as well as what process you should use.

Determining who should do the analysis

If you are working as a team, the entire team should participate in the analysis of the findings. If you are working alone, you should try to elicit some help so that you can broaden the analysis of the findings beyond a single person's review. If that's not possible, then collecting the top findings from everyone who observed will give you a jump on making

The impact of a single evaluator is called the *evaluator effect*. For a discussion of this effect in usability studies, see Jacobsen, Hertzum, and John, 1998.

sense of the findings when you begin deeper analysis. If you can't get this information in person, you can ask everyone who observed, including anyone who participated remotely, to e-mail you their top-10 lists.

Why do you need more than one person for the analysis of the findings? Because studies have shown that a single evaluator will report fewer findings than the combined efforts of more evaluators. The more eyes, ears, and brains at work on a problem, the better the outcome. Not only does problem detection increase with more evaluators, but the identification of the most severe problems reaches a stronger consensus when the findings are discussed.

Collating the findings

Let's assess where you are. You've been through the logs and you've identified and organized the findings with either a top-down or bottom-up method. Now you need to collate the findings from each participant to present the results of your study. If your findings are in spreadsheets or word processor tables for the individual sessions, you can merge these easily and quickly. You can then sort the findings by using a keyword, which will identify the participants who experienced each problem. And don't forget the importance of collating the positive findings. Once the findings are collated, it's a simple matter to count up the number of participants experiencing each type of finding.

For instance, if you determined that terminology was a category, you could sort for terminology to locate all the terminology findings for all the participants. Collating this category of finding, you see that five of six participants experienced confusion over terminology. Then you can give examples of the words that caused confusion, and you can further dissect the finding by indicating how many participants had a problem with each word that caused confusion. Or, if you used affinity matching and listed the participant number on the stickies for each person experiencing a problem (as shown earlier in Figure 8.2), you can add them up easily at the end of this activity.

An implicit point about counting and presenting the findings is that the tasks need to be the same for all participants using the same product. In cases where the product changed (such as revisions made between participants or after the first day), the tasks changed because of product revisions, or you had optional tasks that some but not all participants did, you need to account for these variables in your analysis. For instance:

- When do you count data from a pilot participant? *Answer:* If the pilot participant is reasonably representative of the target audience and you didn't change the task afterward.

- What if you cover a task in only four of six tests? *Answer:* Make sure you report the "four" part, and mention why the task was dropped (usually because it was either too easy or too time consuming, or maybe because you deliberately planned more tasks than you expected everyone to complete).

- What if fixes are made mid-test? *Answer:* Report the findings as, "On the first day, two of the four participants experienced … but then change *X* was made, and the remaining two participants had no difficulty." Granted, in formal (summative) usability testing you wouldn't do this, but in an increasingly agile world, our methods are being pushed to adapt.

Remember, too, that you need to decide what to do about *outlier* data, a problem experienced by only one person.

> There's more about how to analyze outlier data coming up in this chapter.

Presenting quantitative data

If your study focused on obtaining metrics to match business goals, you will want to present quantitative data. However, the proper way to present the data you collected can be problematic, particularly if you do not have grounding in statistics. It's easy to mislead with statistics, as is well documented in a classic book by Darrell Huff called *How to Lie with Statistics*. Although it's not likely you will deliberately misrepresent the findings in the ways Huff points out, you might inadvertently misrepresent the findings by citing statistics when you don't have statistical validity.

> Huff, 1954

In this part of the chapter, I give you some simple guidelines on how to present common metrics and how to avoid misrepresenting them. If you don't have a background in statistics, you will want to read more in the books that are devoted to this subject. And you will want to get help from a team member or someone you can recruit from outside your team to make sure your data are accurately and appropriately presented.

> A great resource for user experience practitioners is Tullis and Albert, *Measuring the User Experience: Collecting, Analyzing, and Presenting Usability Metrics*, 2008.

Quantitative data are findings that can be *measured in numbers*. Because the data can be counted, quantitative data can be *validated* from the findings.

In your planning meeting, you very likely determined that you would measure certain actions and activities, such as the following:

- time on task
- success/completion rates
- errors (and recovery)
- failure (could not complete task or abandoned task before completion)
- assists (calls for help or use of help within the system)
- search (how often, what terms were used, and whether results were effective)
- optimal or preferred path (if there is more than one way to complete a task, which one was chosen the most often)
- other (for those conditions you might not think of until you see them in action)

Counting and collating this information provides the measurement of success or failure for each of these actions and activities. Once these findings are counted, the question then becomes one of how best to represent them. The correct representation depends on the numbers you counted. In large studies, you can present these findings as percentages; in small studies you should not.

Working with statistics

Many usability studies are *formative*, conducted during product development to diagnose and fix problems. Other studies are *summative*, conducted at or near the end of product development to obtain metrics to confirm achievement of the goals for the product. Whether the study is formative or summative, size matters when it comes to presenting findings as statistics.

However, the exact minimum number is not universally agreed upon. It can range from fewer than 20 to 50 or more participants, with even larger numbers typically associated with strict experimental methods.

Although the number is not set in stone, what is clear is that larger numbers increase the *confidence interval*, which is the measure of the accuracy of your claim that your percentages represent findings that are likely to be duplicated in another study and, with really large studies, in the general population.

Moderated studies that are designed to produce statistics often fall within the 12-to-20-participant range. These studies are likely to use *descriptive statistics*, which reflect the results from the sample used for the study. In contrast, bigger studies provide the numbers for *inferential statistics*, since these allow you to make statements that can be inferred for the population at large. These large studies are generally automated (unmoderated), and the results are generated by the automated tools associated with the study.

Presenting data as mean, median, or mode

In presenting descriptive statistics, you have a handy assistant in the form of the analysis toolpak in an Excel spreadsheet. A typical example of a descriptive statistic is time on task. Not only can you present the actual time on task for each participant, but you can also set up an Excel spreadsheet to calculate various measures of *central tendency*, which reflect the middle of the distribution.

The most common methods are to calculate the *mean*, the *median*, or the *mode*. To consider these options and choose the best one, you need to know what each represents:

- *The mean*—is the most often used of the three representations because it is the *average* for all the data points.

- *The median*—is best to use when the range is widely distributed, with a big difference between the highest and lowest point on the range. It shows the *midpoint* in the distribution. This is the point at which half of the data are above this point and half are below this point.

- *The mode*—is the most commonly recurring value. It shows the data point that *occurred most often*. It's not as typically used in usability analysis as the other two methods, but there could be reasons to choose it. For instance, you would use the mode if you want to show that most people completed the task in four minutes rather than reporting the average time to complete the task across all users.

Jeff Sauro, a usability and human factors engineer, has produced a handy confidence interval calculator, which you can access at *www.measuringusability.com/time_intervals.htm*

More about how to use the toolpak for these calculations can be found in Tullis and Albert, 2008.

Whichever method you use, you will find that it is helpful to use the same method in iterative studies so that you can establish benchmark metrics and track improvements in the results as the product continues in development and testing. In addition, you can use these metrics to compare one product against another or one design against another in a competitive analysis. If you're testing with more than one type of user, you can use these metrics to compare one user group against another—for example, performance by novices as compared to performance by experts.

Using quantitative data in small studies

For more on the pitfalls of misrepresenting data in study reports, see Gray and Salzman's classic article, "Damaged Merchandise? A Review of Experiments that Compare Usability Evaluation Methods," 1998.

When your study is small, you want to consider very carefully whether to use metrics, since they could misrepresent the findings. For instance, small variations in time on task within a small group of users could make it problematic to report average time on task, particularly when one of the participants was a "wildcard" on time, either using much less time or much more time. Eliminating this one data point may leave you with too few data points to present results in any meaningful statistical way. In these cases, it's best to use a table of the actual time on task for each participant.

Dealing with outliers

In small studies, every person counts. An outlier is a single instance of a finding, something you have observed in one user only. What should you do about an outlier?

The tendency may be to throw it out of consideration because you observed it in only one person (the wildcard effect). However, in small studies, a single person could point up a significant finding. Some say, although it's risky to even mention this as a data point, that if you are testing with five users and one person's experience is an outlier, that finding could represent 20% of your users. But don't report this single finding as a percentage, since it is too small a data point to be meaningful. What the 20% (one in five) value suggests is that every outlier should be reviewed and discussed because a problem for one user could represent one that will be experienced by others.

In taking a closer look at each outlier—which may mean reviewing the recordings—you should go back to the three-step process of analysis: What did we see? What does it mean? What should we do about it?

To determine whether to report an outlier or ignore it, you need to consider these points in your analysis:

- Is the participant truly representative of a target user? Sometimes outliers are the result of a recruiting mismatch when it turns out that the participant is not in the target user group. Maybe the person lacks the required domain knowledge or the motivation to use the product or the service. In the case of a mismatch for any reason, the findings from this session may need to be tossed out.

- Would others have the same problem? You see a problem but need to understand whether it is representative so that you can determine whether you need to address it. Let's say a participant is texting on a mobile phone and can't hit the right keys because she has long fingernails. No one else had this problem in your study, but would others have this problem? Very likely. So, it should be included in the analysis.

- If you're not sure about the finding, does it require further study? In some cases, you can't quite understand why the participant had the problem or whether others would have the problem. You don't want to just set it aside, though. So you might decide you need to note the problem and see whether it happens in the next iteration of testing.

Of course, a single problem is still "good enough" to indicate an issue that needs to be discussed and addressed, particularly in small studies. If it can be fixed easily, why not go ahead and fix it?

Presenting findings in numbers versus percentages

In small studies, it's customary to count occurrences. You did this as part of your analysis, adding up the number of participants experiencing a particular problem. Now you want to pick the right way to represent these findings.

Numbers work best. You will report that, for example, four out of six participants could not complete the task, rather than representing the number as a percentage, such as 67% of the participants could not complete the task. In reporting numbers rather than percentages, you avoid suggesting a validity that is not borne out by the small number of participants in your study. You also want to be careful to avoid generalizing to the whole user population, which is especially important to guard against when you are using small numbers of participants from one subgroup of your user population.

Keep in mind, though, that findings can be *significant* without being *statistically significant*. Also keep in mind that not all findings are self-evident. They need to be analyzed, in many cases, to be understood. A typical example is how to count success or failure for a task. If you haven't already decided this before testing, you will need to discuss it during your findings meeting. Among the many variations in determining success or failure are considerations of

- successful completion of the task within the predicted timeframe
- successful completion of the task beyond the predicted timeframe
- successful completion of the task with assistance
- failure to complete the task—recognized by user
- failure to complete the task—not recognized by user (user thinks the task was done correctly)
- other—for those conditions you might not think of until you see them in action

Analyzing questionnaires

In addition to analyzing the findings from the logs, you also want to analyze the participants' responses from the post-task and post-test questionnaires. Participants' responses on these self-reporting questionnaires can be of two types:

- *Quantitative responses*—responses to questions or statements using a rating scale, in which the participants select the rating from a range of options.
- *Qualitative responses*—comments, opinions, and perceptions expressed in response to open-ended questions.

Quantitative responses on questionnaires

Self-reported ratings by participants can be readily counted and collated, so these are typically reported as quantitative data. If the study is large enough, you can represent these ratings in percentages using the mean, median, or mode. In small, formative studies, you will want to present the findings as numbers, such as five out of six participants reported that they were satisfied with the product's performance (based on their choice of a 4 or 5 on a 5-point Likert scale).

However, you need to consider the biases prevalent in self-reported questionnaire responses. You probably observed during testing that the participants didn't want to be seen as unpleasant, so they didn't want to complain about their experience, especially in front of other people or in the recording. In addition to this tendency to want to be pleasant, other traits in people that can, and do, affect the way in which they complete questionnaires include these:

- People tend to avoid the extremes on a scale. This is called the *error of central tendency*. So, if they are rating their satisfaction on a 5-point scale, they're likely to avoid either extreme, picking a rating close to the middle or above it but not too often at the top or bottom of the range.
- People tend to rate responses consistently. So, if they chose a 4 out of 5 for the first couple of responses, they are likely to stay close to that response throughout.

Timing of the questionnaire, it turns out, may also affect the result. One study reported that it does.

Participants were asked to rate task ease and enjoyment in three conditions:

1. During a task, in which they were asked to respond to two questions.
2. Again, after task completion, in which they were asked to respond to the same two questions.
3. And for another group, in which they were asked to respond to the two questions only after task completion.

Here's what the study found:

- Participants responded with higher ratings after task completion than they did during the task.
- Participants who were asked to respond only after task completion responded with *significantly* higher ratings than the other group.

For more on the nature of people to want to please, see Chapter 7.

Some questionnaires, including SUS, alternate the statements between a positive statement and a negative statement in hopes of getting the respondent to think about each statement and the appropriate response. For more on SUS, see Chapter 6.

See Teague, De Jesus, and Nunes-Ueno, 2001.

Given this potential for ratings that might not accurately reflect users' experience, you will likely want to weigh these findings as one piece of the whole puzzle of user experience.

The best way to analyze the results from questionnaires is to notice when a participant marks one or two responses very differently from the rest: There's very likely a reason behind this different rating that you'll want to explore. If you didn't follow up with the participant during testing, you can still study the log or the recording to see whether you can understand the reason for a particular rating.

Qualitative responses on questionnaires

Many questionnaires include open-ended questions soliciting qualitative responses. These are responses expressed in the participants' own words. Analyzing these responses can give you additional information and insights into your users' experience, which you can use in two ways:

- You can go through the responses to find representative comments—positive and negative—to reflect the range of comments.
- If you think others will want to review the questionnaire responses, you can plan to include them in an appendix in the report, file them in the participant folders, or scan them for electronic distribution.

Using qualitative feedback from the think-aloud process

A rich source of qualitative feedback, and one that can often be more reliable and revealing than responses from open-ended questions on questionnaires, comes from the comments participants make while they are thinking out loud.

Chapter 9 is all about the ways to report your findings.

These comments from users while they are engaged with the product can shed light on the nature of the problems they experienced, as well as what pleased them. Quoting users' comments to support your findings makes for a better understanding of the users' experience. These user quotes make for powerful statements in your report of the study findings.

Depending on the type of study you are conducting and how the results will be used, you may want to collate the participants' comments. You can do this in one of the following ways:

- If you typed users' comments into your log, you can export them into a spreadsheet, then sort the comments by keywords or by issues. If you created your log files in a spreadsheet or word processing document, you can sort within this document.

- If you used observer forms or some other format that doesn't allow for quick sorting, you can organize the notes about user comments into positive and negative groupings.

Collating responses from the product reaction cards

If you have used the product reaction cards for qualitative feedback, you can now collate the choices participants made to show:

See Chapters 6 and 7 for more on using the cards.

- how many positive words were selected
- how many negative words were selected
- how many of the same words were selected
- how many similar words were selected
- how many unique words were selected

As is the case with participants' responses to questionnaires, their selection of cards is a subjective process that can be quantified by grouping the findings and counting the results. These findings can be added to the findings from the other feedback mechanisms.

What should we do about it?

You've come this far by answering the first two questions: What did we see? What does it mean?

Now you're at the point in your analysis where you need to make sense of what you saw and heard, which answers the question: What should we do about it?

This third and final step in your analysis brings together all of your data sources, ranking them in some systematic way, and putting them into recommendations.

Triangulating the data from findings

Triangulation is a research technique, used often in qualitative studies, to demonstrate the dependability of the findings by examining the data from multiple perspectives. Triangulation is the process of comparing separate sources of findings to look for consistencies or discrepancies (see Figure 8.3).

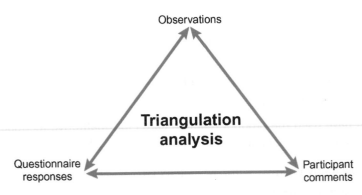

Figure 8.3 Triangulation brings together different data sources to enrich the analysis of findings.

In analyzing your study findings, you might employ triangulation by comparing your qualitative and quantitative data. Here's an example of how it works. Let's say you set a metric for completion of a particular task at under five minutes. You would like to use this metric as a baseline in future studies once you confirm that it is valid. To do that, you look at the time-on-task results to see whether all participants completed it in five minutes or less. Then you look at the logs for each participant to see how they went about doing the task, what they said while they were doing the task, any questions or uncertainty they may have expressed, whether they successfully completed the task, and how they responded to a post-task questionnaire to rate their satisfaction with the process.

You find that most participants took closer to 10 minutes to complete the task, but it was partly because they were learning useful things along the way. They commented positively about the task as they were doing it, although you observed that they did not take the most direct navigational route to task completion. In their post-task questionnaires, they rated time on task as satisfactory. What are you going to make of these findings?

When data from different sources support a finding, it helps the team assess the strength of the finding. When data seem to conflict, you need to examine the data for insights. In the case of the time-on-task example, the metric could have been wrong. Other data supports the positive experience users had, taking twice the time projected to complete the task but being satisfied with the outcome.

In addition to triangulating the data sources from your study, you can triangulate across other sources of data collection, such as server log data, call center data, and so forth.

In iterative studies, you can triangulate the data across the usability studies, looking for evidence of improvement (or not). If you use the same questionnaires in these studies, it makes it easy to compare and contrast results.

Characterizing findings by scope and severity

You've analyzed the findings, counted the number of times each finding was experienced by participants, categorized them by type, and compared or contrasted them with other data sources. You now need to categorize them by scope and impact. That means

- determining whether a finding is *global* or *local*
- determining the *severity* of the finding

Determining global and local findings

One way to sort findings is to organize them into broad (global) findings affecting product design and narrow (local) findings affecting a particular screen or page. This first cut at organizing the findings will help you see the scope of the findings, making it easier to attach severity ratings to them.

Joe Dumas and Ginny Redish introduced these ways of categorizing findings in *A Practical Guide to Usability Testing*, 1999.

Global findings

The beauty of small studies is that they can give you big results. Even though your participants may be engaged in tasks in only one part of the product, the problems they experience are often indicative of problems of design or implementation that occur throughout the product. A finding that reflects an issue of this scope is called a *global finding*. A finding uncovered in one place may point to the need to fix it not only where you saw it but also throughout the product. Thus, a global finding is usually a significant finding.

What are typical global findings? A short list of typical global findings often includes:

- *Information architecture/navigation*—participants can't find what they're looking for because things aren't clearly seen or they are in the wrong place.

- *Consistency*—items are called one thing in one place but something else in another place (terminology); or a person working to complete a form cannot tab through the form consistently or from one form to the next; or page design is different on different pages, causing users to be unsure about where they are or where to find certain objects.

- *Feedback*—participants complain about not knowing what to do or not understanding what happens when they perform an action; or the system doesn't tell them they have successfully completed a transaction or that it is processing a transaction (no progress bar); or they don't have embedded assistance to tell them how to enter information in a field.

These are not, by any means, all the types or examples of global findings you will uncover. But they suggest the ways in which global findings are important outcomes of usability studies.

As you can see, global findings are often related to the top-down or bottom-up categories resulting from your analysis. You may know the type of global finding you will get—terminology issues, for example—but you probably won't be able to anticipate all of the examples. Your collated findings, organized under the category of terminology, give you the examples.

Local findings

A *local finding* is one that occurs in only one place—that is, on a single screen or page of a website, in a particular step in instructions, or in a particular feature of a product. Local findings—a typo or a missing entry box on a form—are generally easy to fix (at least easier than most global findings). Many local findings have little or no impact on the user's experience, but some can have serious consequences, such as not being able to complete a form because a box is missing.

Because local findings are isolated issues, developers will very likely want to fix them right away, frequently before the analysis is complete. And that's OK as long as everyone recognizes the problem for what it is. However, some local findings can turn out to be global, indicating a problem of design or implementation that needs to be addressed throughout the product. Looking at the types of local problems you have found and seeing whether they represent global patterns is an important part of the analysis phase. No doubt you will end up with a list of local and global problems, with various effects on the user's experience. For that reason, you want to establish severity ratings for your findings.

Establishing severity ratings

Characterizing the significance of each type of finding and each group of findings is the last part of your analysis. In this part, you prioritize the findings by the severity of their impact on the user's experience.

Severity rating scales vary, but they all have an extreme condition on each end of the scale with varying degrees of effect on user experience in between. The type of rating scale to use might have been determined in the planning meeting. If not, your team needs to decide how to rank the findings by severity so that the priorities for fixing them can be established.

The discussion surrounding the assignment of severity ratings to the findings is strengthened when it is a team effort, since consensus is needed on how to determine what a rating means. For instance, you can rate findings by:

- *Frequency of occurrence*—measured by how often you saw it or how often it is likely to occur.

- *Impact of the problem on user experience*—measured in terms of success or failure, as well as ease or difficulty of the process for users; ability to recover from error; and so forth.

- *Persistence of the problem*—measured by observing whether users who experience a problem can learn to avoid or overcome the problem going forward.

A simple 3-point severity rating scale might look like this:

1. *Catastrophe*—user cannot complete task; or user can complete the process but expresses extreme irritation at the process; or user needs assistance (business goal is to make the process independent of user assistance).

2. *Serious problem*—user is frustrated but gets through it; suggests that others may be less inclined to put up with the inconvenience or that frustration level will be high.

3. *Cosmetic problem*—user may hesitate or pick the wrong option, but user corrects it without incident; or user expresses minor irritation or annoyance, but it doesn't affect ability to complete tasks.

A more finely tuned rating scale might have four rating categories, like this:

1. catastrophe
2. major problem
3. minor problem
4. cosmetic problem

A very basic rating scale uses the following categories:

- high
- medium
- low

Of course, you also want a category for positive findings, since you don't want to ignore these. And, depending on the type of study you are doing, you might want to add other categories, such as "bug" and "comment" (for feature requests, patterns in behavior, or other interesting things users say). You could get even finer in your scale, adding more categories, but you need to consider the likelihood that each new category will increase the discussion of how to rate a finding.

Making recommendations

Now that you have completed your analysis of the issues and set priorities for fixing them, you have one task remaining: making recommendations on how—and when—to fix the problems you have identified.

There are a lot of issues to consider here:

- Do you have the developers in this meeting who can provide specific recommendations?
- If you do not, are you expected to make more general recommendations based on your understanding of issues that users faced and problems that need to be addressed?
- In either case, how should the recommendations be prioritized? You could set priorities on the basis of
  - easy to fix first
  - showstoppers first, regardless of complexity
  - some combination of these
- Are there time constraints that affect the types of recommendations that you make?

These issues need to be addressed, based on your team's expertise, since they affect the types of recommendations you will make.

Some recommendations are easy to make

Some recommendations are so obvious and intuitive that everyone easily agrees on them at the findings meeting. For example:

- *Enable Back on browser*—Users wanted to use Back to return to a previous screen.
- *Expand Advanced Search field*—Screen real estate is sufficient to display the information in Advanced Search.

Other recommendations may be specific or general

If your team includes the developers who will make the changes, you can be very specific in your recommendations and actions. In fact, you may not need to document them beyond providing a list with priorities, since everyone knows what needs to be done as a result of their participation in the findings meeting.

If, however, you are making recommendations *to* the developers, your recommendations will likely be couched more generally, since you might not be able to tell them *how* to solve the problem, only that the problem has to be addressed.

Figure 8.4 shows an example of a recommendations list that comes *from* the usability experts *to* the course developers. It doesn't tell the developers how to make the changes, but it does identify the types of changes that the team recommends. The study focused on the user experience for a new course template for a large organization.

All recommendations should be actionable

No matter what your relationship is to the product, your recommendations need to be specific and actionable. If you do not have developers participating in the analysis of the findings, this requirement for actionable recommendations can be the most challenging part of the process.

Time is a factor in determining the type of recommendations you can make. If you have little time—or maybe no time—after you complete the study, your recommendations have to be somewhat high-level, turning the implementation over to the developers to fix the problem. If you have more time between the study and the due date for the report and if your team has product knowledge, you can design solutions for the findings. These can be presented as prototypes or wireframes to suggest the direction of the recommended changes.

Time is also a factor in what gets done, and when. You may have established your severity scale on the basis of what can be changed now. This happens frequently when the product is tested late in development. If testing takes place early, you can make recommendations for now and others for later in development. If testing takes place at the end of the development process, the recommendations may be stored away for the

---

Usability Team Recommendations for Course Developers

Based on the findings from this usability study, we recommend the following actions:

- Condense content on screens, using a minimalist approach, as favored by participants.
- Conduct a final edit for spelling, punctuation, etc., to maintain a high level of professional presentation in the course.
- Reduce the amount of information on screens; isolate to specific features or functions only.
- Provide information on what happens if NO is selected for any option; provide information on user's ability to leave and return at any time.
- Determine learning goals for content so that they are fully supported in the module. For example, if the goal is to teach users how to enter data, design "Let Me Try" to work without prompts, so users can learn on their own versus following prompts.
- Reduce the number of visual icons to keep the essential ones and avoid confusion over those that are similar but not intuitive.
- Consider visual strategies to provide more separation between the system and the content module when content involves training on using a software system.
- Consider screen design for:
  - Location of information on the left side of the screen divided by the vertical rule (users didn't see it).
  - Breadcrumbs—users didn't see them.
- Clearly delineate between chapter reviews and the final test; consider including assessments at the ends of chapters, as users expressed a preference for this strategy.
- Determine the role and relationship of instructions within each module so that they support learning for a single course, as well as learning the course/template design:
  - Consider embedded assistance, rather than providing the overt instruction for each module and each lesson.
  - Consider a training module for new users of the learning program.

Figure 8.4 These recommendations are based on analysis by the usability team for the course developers to implement.

next product release or for the next new product. Don't miss the chance to document the findings and recommendations you believe should be made, even if you know they can't all be addressed in the near term.

Prioritizing the recommendations is also important. You might, for example, decide to fix a lot of small things now that are technically simple, leaving some of the bigger, more complex problems for later or for the next release. In some cases, a serious problem could be fixed quickly but not ideally now. Then, with more time, the problem could be addressed more systematically. Or you might decide that the problems are so systemic that there is no point in fixing any of them now, since the recommendation (supported by everyone) is that the product (or a feature within the product) needs to be scrapped and rethought.

This kind of recommendation—to rethink the product rather than try to fix systemic problems—is best made when you are looking at a product at an early stage in development, but there could be reasons to recommend this action for products about to be released or already released to users.

Summarizing Chapter 8

This chapter gave you a strategy to make sense of the findings from a usability study. With so much data to work with and so little time—everyone always wants the results "yesterday"—you need a method to work quickly and effectively through the mounds of data. You now have that method, which follows this process:

- You begin by collecting quick highlights and takeaways from everyone who observed testing.
- You then settle down with the team to conduct a detailed analysis. If you have been doing testing on your own, you should make every effort to get someone else to work with you on this critical analysis phase because two (or more heads) are definitely better than one.
- You choose your data-sorting methodology between:
  - top-down, from predetermined categories
  - bottom-up, letting the categories emerge from affinity matching
  - or a combination of the two methods
- You collate these data to see how many participants had similar experiences.
- You take a close look at outliers—those findings from a single person.
- Depending on the number of participants in your study, you either:
  - Present the findings in number counts when your study is small.
  - Present the findings as descriptive or inferential statistics when your study is large enough for each type of data analysis.
- You then review the post-task and post-test questionnaires to analyze:
  - *Quantitative feedback*, in response to Likert-scale or other fixed-scale questions or statements.

- ○ *Qualitative feedback*, in response to open-ended questions or semi-structured interviews or other methods, such as the product reaction cards.
- You triangulate the findings to strengthen the outcomes from the review.
- You categorize the findings by scope (global or local) and severity rating.
- You organize the findings into recommendations, for now and for later.

The usability testing team for this study did its first analysis of the findings following testing with three of the six participants. They used a top-down approach, which matched codes for anticipated problems, such as layout, navigation, and translation. When they didn't have a category for a finding, they called it "other," to be analyzed later.

The findings in the table that follows are excerpts from the team's meeting notes for the first two scenarios. Qualitative feedback from the three participants was also collated, using comments and responses to open-ended questions. The team organized these into positive (likes) and negative (dislikes) comments. At this point in their analysis, they did not include global and local designations or severity ratings, since these came at the end of the testing period in a more extensive findings meeting. The full findings report is on this book's companion website.

Scenario 1: Look and Feel

Participant 1

Category	Findings	Comment
Layout	Log in for Priority Club on the left confused the participant. For a moment, she thought she would not be able to book a hotel unless she joined Priority Club.	
	Disliked advertisements.	"So many advertisements!"
Translation issue	Translated directly from the English-language site, the wording for king-sized bed on the Chinese website makes no sense.	
	"TRUST" symbol was not recognized. She does not feel safe to give her credit card number. However, she said that having safety guarantee is very important.	
Aesthetics	Does not like colors on the site.	"Colors do not match."
Brand identity	Confused when she saw the log in/name and password boxes for Priority Club.	"I assume that I would not be eligible for any discounts because I am not a member of Priority Club."
Navigation	Business Conference button confuses her. She thinks she can only book if she's coming for a conference.	

Participant 2

Category	Findings	Comment
Brand identity	Confused by the different hotel logos/graphics at the bottom of the page.	"Are they sister hotels?"
	Initially only interested in using the site because of the Holiday Inn name/reputation.	
Aesthetics	Liked the color scheme.	
Layout	Thought that only the search box in the center of the page was related to the hotel site.	
Navigation	Thinks the design is intuitive.	

Participant 3

Category	Findings	Comment
Aesthetics	Liked the color scheme.	
	Did not know what the advertisement was for; thought banner was excessively large.	
Navigation	Navigation is clear.	

Scenario 2: Book a Hotel Room

Participant 1

Category	Findings	Comment
Aesthetics	The listing for the same hotel should not have two background colors—white and gray—which makes this hotel look like two separate ones.	
Layout	She thought she was at a different page than Holiday Inn when booking her hotel because there was a Priority Club banner at the top now. Did not notice that some of the booking options in the results page are not Holiday Inn.	"The results page should have some way to categorize the results."
	Could not find the Submit button.	

Scenario 2: *Continued*

Navigation	Confused the "Start Over" and "Finish Booking" buttons. She accidentally clicked on "Start Over."	
	When she went back, she was actually in the Priority Club, but she did not notice.	
	Some hotels that are not Holiday Inn appear in the search results page.	
Translation issues	The word used on Submit button does not translate well.	
	"CNY"s [currency] confused her. This term has no meaning.	
User options	On the reservation page, there is a check box on the left to let people select personalized choices, which she tries three times with different options. The website still could not find any matched rooms for her. She was very frustrated.	
	Wants a drop-down for cities where Holiday Inns are located.	"Typing wastes my time."
	Wants a drop-down for calendar/dates.	
	Wonders why she must put in an English name.	"Why is an English name needed?"

Participant 2

Category	Findings	Comments
User options	Hopes to see the hotel ranking from users.	
	Wants to know price range (drop-down).	
	Wants a city-search option.	
	Wants more detailed info on what hotel offers.	
	Prefers that a credit card verification # is requested.	
Layout	Missed the required agreement checkboxes when trying to book the hotel. He caught the error with the error message.	
Other	Slow response	"Website speed is toooooo slow."

Participant 3

Category	Findings	Comment
Layout	Did not like that there was no drop-down menu for city selection.	
	Wanted to see a progress bar.	
	She wanted to see real pictures of the hotel locations she was reading about, including interior pictures. (Many shared the same generic exterior image photo.)	
	Displayed room choices that she was not interested in. She chose rooms with two beds but was shown more choices than that.	
	Had difficulty finding price total.	

The following are some qualitative findings from comments and open-ended questionnaire responses comparing Holiday Inn and competitor (eLong) websites.

Participant 1

Likes

Liked the pop-up for city names that have hotels because she did not have to type in a city name and try finding where hotels might be located.

Thought eLong was much clearer for information input.

Liked the one-column style.

Liked the color and look of the site better than Holiday Inn China.

Thought the select bar on the homepage was very convenient so that she did not need to input anything.

Liked the table layout for the results page when searching for a hotel. ("Easier to view the information.")

Dislikes

Did not like the moving advertisement. (Advertisement that moved on the page as she was scrolling up and down.)

Participant 2

Likes

Upon first impression, already prefers e-Long's search box.

Liked that it auto-translated English name to Chinese characters.

Liked that there was a price-range filter; however, he would prefer to enter in his price-range manually rather than being limited to certain price ranges.

Liked that city selections were provided.

Liked seeing hotel ratings and user ratings. (Would have preferred an explanation of rating system, i.e., what criteria are met to warrant the ratings.)

Dislikes

None.

Participant 3

Likes

Liked the look better.

Liked that airfare prices were shown. (Not sure this is relevant for the Holiday Inn website since it is not intended to be a full-fledged travel site.)

Liked that she didn't have to type in a city name. (Because a selection box was present.)

Liked the information presented to her on results page.

Liked seeing hotel ratings.

Dislikes

Did not like eLong's advertisements. (Scrolling ad)

Prefers eLong to Holiday Inn site by far.

Combined Negative Findings

- All three participants disliked that there was no drop-down selection or pop-up box for the city selection.
- P1 and P3 did not notice the error message when trying to find a hotel in Changchun.
- P2 and P3 initially liked the color scheme; however, after seeing eLong and the English-language Holiday Inn site, they liked those better than the Chinese version.

- Website performance was extremely slow. (Multiple reasons for why this could be possible. Not at fault but could be worth investigating.)
- Priority Club information confused all three participants throughout the whole process.
- P2 did not like that there was not a credit card verification number check during payment process.
- "Days staying" selection next to calendar option confused all three participants.

Preliminary Recommendations

- The site would look more professional/credible if it followed a similar design to the English-language Holiday Inn site. (Much cleaner look than the current Chinese site.)
- Remove "days staying" selection from hotel search page. Calendar feature is sufficient.
- Generate an error message box telling users what they did wrong or create a more visible error message for when users fail to provide all required information for search fields.
- Create a city selection drop-down menu or pop-up box for where hotel locations are available.
- Consider resizing advertisements or locations of advertisements. Currently they are overwhelming or confusing to users.
- Create an "in-between" (progress) loading page to show users that the site is processing search results. The blank page confuses users and leaves them wondering if the site "died" on them during the search process.
- Create a section to enter a credit card verification number during checkout process.

Reporting the findings

The medium is the message.

—Marshall McLuhan

Understanding Media: The Extensions of Man, 1964

There are so many media to choose from to communicate your findings from a study. You may have a hard time choosing which one is best. Yet each one, as Marshall McLuhan reminds us, makes a unique impact on the message.

For many, testing is the fun part. The reporting part is hard, not terribly exciting (to most), but essential for communicating what you learned, what the findings mean, and what should be done about them. If you choose the right medium and craft the message well, your chances of seeing the recommendations put into action increase dramatically.

This chapter looks at how to get started by following Aristotle's ancient but relevant advice to know:

- *Your audience*—the people who are likely to receive your report
- *Purpose*—both yours in preparing and delivering it, and theirs in receiving it

Usability Testing Essentials. DOI: 10.1016/B978-0-12-375092-1.00009-X

277

- *Context in which they will receive it*—the medium for the message:
  - a written report, informal or formal
  - an oral report with presentation software and video clips

Once these issues are resolved, you need to decide how to organize your findings for the type of report you'll be preparing:

- writing an informal memo report
- writing a formal report
  - preparing the parts for a formal report
  - writing the executive summary
  - organizing the rest of the report to match your audience needs
- presenting the study findings—positive and negative—using strategies for:
  - summarizing the findings in tables
  - illustrating the findings with screen shots, figures, participant quotes, or video clips
  - ordering the findings by severity, category, or some other ordering scheme
- presenting post-task and post-test feedback results, including:
  - survey responses from your own or a standard questionnaire such as SUS
  - qualitative responses from product reaction cards or some other feedback method
- recommending solutions or actions
- presenting an oral report, which entails:
  - planning
  - preparing video clips
  - practicing
  - delivering
  - handling questions
- advocating for more testing and other UCD methods to confirm the improvements in user experience

I'll start with Aristotle, and you'll soon see why.

Following Aristotle's advice

Aristotle's *Rhetoric* is as relevant today as when he first presented it to his students. An effective communicator (he would have said "orator") is someone who considers the three essential elements of the rhetorical situation:

- *Audience*—Who are you delivering the message to? Are you directing your message to the manager who allocates resources, the developer who makes the changes, the stakeholder who has oversight of the process? If there are multiple members of your audience, how are they alike, and how are they different? How much do they already know about usability in general and what you did in this particular study?

- *Purpose*—What is *your* purpose in presenting this information, and what is *their* purpose in reading/listening to/viewing it? Do they already believe that changes are needed, or must you persuade them? Are you documenting known findings that everyone understands because of their involvement in the study, or are you presenting findings and recommendations to an audience who will be learning about them for the first time? Will the key stakeholders be prepared to act?

- *Context of use*—How will the information be received, and how will it be used? Will everyone be gathered in the same space in a meeting? Or will they get the report in some distribution medium? Do they have time to review the report when it arrives? Will the delivery of your report kick off a discussion of possible solutions? Or will your audience be taking the recommendations and putting them into immediate action?

Preparing the message for the medium

Although you have many media to choose from to present your study results, most study results are written up in some sort of report. The context of use can vary considerably. Some reports are delivered on paper and in person. Others are delivered as a PDF document sent as an e-mail attachment. Still others are uploaded to a shared project workspace. The report recipients might print out the report or read it online. If they're reading your report online, they might be seeing it on a computer or mobile device.

You can also report the results in person. This can be in the context of a meeting called for this purpose or as part of another meeting. You might be delivering the report in the same room with the meeting attendees or using meeting software to connect to others in different locations. The meeting could be archived and shared with others in various ways, such as via a podcast.

Keeping Aristotle in mind, you need to sort out the issues of audience, purpose and contexts of use. You should start by thinking about the audience for your report(s) and what you want to accomplish. Then, if you're writing a report, you need to decide how to structure it and what level of formality or informality to use to present the findings and recommendations. Then you need to think about the life of the report (including recorded oral reports and video highlights) and whether it will go beyond the time of delivery.

Writing an informal memo report

If the context is informal, the report might be a memo like the one shown in Figure 9.1, which documents what you did and what you learned. A memo report can generally be written up quickly and distributed widely as an e-mail attachment. This format and approach are often used in rapid development projects, since the actions need to be taken as soon as possible after testing ends.

You will notice that the report begins with a summary, which is a very important part because it sets the context for the report, explains what was done, and provides a brief description of the types of findings. A good practice to keep in mind when writing this important part of the report is to apply the journalistic 5 Ws and an H: *Who, What, When, Where, Why,* and *How.* The answers to these prompts give you the structure for an effective summary. In the summary, I show you how each of these prompts is addressed.

You will also notice that the report documents the positive findings first—always a good organizational strategy—followed by the issues users experienced, the number of participants experiencing each issue, the recommendation, the department responsible for the action, and a deadline for completing the action. These assignments were made in the findings meeting, so the memo merely documents them.

Destination Teaching/Teacher Career Center Usability Study Report

Summary

A usability study of the Destination Teaching website [what] was conducted on June 24, 20xx [when] by a team of Usability Center and client members [who] at the Usability Center at Southern Polytechnic [where]. The purpose of the study was to determine whether users can easily find information about becoming a teacher and to learn how well the site supports their need for specific information to help them in their goal [why]. Six participants were prescreened to match the study screener criteria:

- The user has a college degree in an area other than education.
- The user is interested in becoming a teacher.
- The user is not familiar with university system institutions or the Colleges of Education.
- The user has not visited the website being tested.
- The user is proficient in using a computer and is familiar with searching for information on the web.

Each participant was given four scenarios to complete. All were asked to "think out loud" so that their words and actions could be recorded and reviewed. At the end of each session, the participant was asked to pick four or five words (from the product reaction card deck) that best described his or her feelings about using the site [how]. In both their comments and card choices, users reacted positively to the potential for the site as a resource for prospective teachers; however, certain aspects of the site impeded their ability to succeed at the tasks. These included confusing terminology, unclear navigation, misconceptions about the site's purpose and use ("mental model"), and level of content (too much or too little information) [quick overview of findings, positive and negative].

An overview of the results from the study follows, with recommended changes for areas where the users found difficulties.

Findings and Recommendations

Favorable Findings

- Users liked the fact that when they selected a university's website it opened in a new window so that the user did not have to leave the Destination Teaching site when researching schools.
- All found the site attractive, two citing the "pleasing colors."
- Users commented that the homepage fit on the screen with no need to scroll.
- All users indicated that the financial information was easy to find and "very informative."
- After quickly reviewing the homepage, users could easily explain the purpose of the site.

Problems and Recommendations

The following is a list of the top problems users experienced and a correlating recommendation (unranked), along with assignment of responsibilities and targeted completion dates.

	Study findings	Recommendations	Responsible	Completion date
1.	Three of six users had difficulty finding the subheadings on the left navigation bar.	Redesign the left navigation bar to better highlight the subheadings for easier navigation.	System office	July 21
2.	Three of six users noted that the site uses lots of text. One user thought the font was too small.	Edit site content to streamline content and increase usability and readability.	DT staff	August 12

Figure 9.1 A memo report of a usability study of a website for prospective teachers documents the essential information for the team. (*Continued*)

	Study findings	Recommendations	Responsible	Completion date
3.	Three of six users said they know about financial aid in general but are unfamiliar with the state scholarship (HOPE) information on financing.	Move HOPE scholarship information to the top of the page.	System office	July 21
4.	Three of six users had difficulty finding the degree information on the university's pages.	Change default page to "degrees" and leave tab for general information.	System office	July 21
5.	Five of six users found the Statistics and Reports page confusing and said it does not offer expected information.	Remove this link from the site.	System office	July 21
6.	Four of six users do not understand the significance of the colored boxes in the grid on the Routes/Programs page.	Redesign the grid or consider removing the grid and creating a glossary of terms page.	DT staff	August 12
7.	Three of six users found Search feature very difficult to use. The degree option throws them off correct use of Search.	Remove degree option from Search feature. Add reset button.	System office	July 21
8.	Three of six users were confused by top University System of GA (USG) navigation bar and search engine.	Leave USG link at the bottom of the page and remove top USG navigation bar.	System office	July 21
9.	Five of six users did not understand the differences between the MAT and M.Ed. degrees.	Clarify definitions and post throughout the applicable pages on site.	DT staff	August 12
10.	Three of six users wanted more information on subjects to teach and suggested that there should be a list.	Beef up content on Subject page to include list of subjects to teach, or at least general areas.	DT staff	No date assigned (need content developer)
11.	Two of six users found the homepage right navigation links confusing because of terminology. One user did not notice the links.	To be determined.	DT staff	No date assigned

Post-test Product Reaction Cards Results

The following words were selected by participants to describe their reaction to the website, with almost all being positive.

Positive:
- useful (chosen by all six participants)
- organized (chosen by three participants)
- usable
- comprehensive
- accessible
- relevant
- connected
- simplistic (user elaborates by using the words "simple to use")
- easy to use
  - time saving
  - fast

Negative:
- overwhelming

Figure 9.1 A memo report of a usability study of a website for prospective teachers documents the essential information for the team. (*Continued*)

Writing a formal report

The main difference between writing an informal report and writing a formal report is in scope. Formal reports are typically much longer than informal reports, and they have prescribed parts and a formal structure.

For samples of complete reports, visit the book's companion website at *www.mkp.com/ testingessentials*

Preparing the parts of a formal report

Formal reports will likely contain the following parts, listed where they are usually placed in relation to the other parts of the report:

- *Cover or title page*—usually includes the identification of the study, the date of submission of the report, the group/author of the report (and study), the person or group to whom the report is directed, and, sometimes, a screen capture of the product that was tested.

- *Cover memo* (from the author of an internal report) *or letter* (from the external project consultant)—optional, and often not used these days when the report is sent as an e-mail attachment.

- *Executive summary*—provides a snapshot of the purpose of the study and includes the top findings and action items.

- *Table of contents*—starts with everything in the report that *follows* the table of contents and usually indicates first- and second-level headings and corresponding page numbers in the report. Also includes a list of appendices.

- *List of illustrations and/or tables*—groups and lists figures and tables (if both are included) with a number and a caption for each and the corresponding page number. If only figures or only tables are included, this section can be called "Tables" or "Figures." Screen shots could be included in the list of figures if they are identified as figures. However, if they are embedded within the report and are not formally labeled as figures, they would not be included in this list.

- *Body parts*—provide the meat of the report (no pun intended); they are identified by section headings. Common section headings include:

  - *Introduction/Background*—the information needed to fully inform those who may not know why the study was done, how it fits into the development cycle, whether prior studies have been done, which version of the product is being tested, and so forth.

- ○ *Methodology*—the testing methodology used, including:
  - – type of test—formative or summative, formal or informal
  - – testing conditions—in a lab or elsewhere, including specifics about the participant's computer and monitor (size and screen resolution), software, operating system, or browser, and so forth.
  - – characteristics of users (user profiles/personas), number of participants, and recruitment method (internal or external)
  - – length and format of sessions
- ○ *Test goals and objectives*, linked to the product's business goals
- ○ *Metrics* used to evaluate user experience, such as time on task, task success or failure, and so forth
- ○ *Participants*—screener data, typically compiled in a table
- ○ *Tasks/Scenarios*—a description of the tasks or the actual scenarios used. If actual scenarios are not included here, they can be included in an appendix or, if they are included in your test plan, this document can be referenced.
- ○ *Findings/Test results*—positive and negative (combination of text, visuals/screen captures, and tables)
  - – For each finding:
    - a. number of participants
    - b. example of finding, participant quote/video clip, screen capture to illustrate the finding
  - – For each result:
    - a. severity rating (for negative findings)
    - b. impact (global or local)
- ○ *Post-task, post-test results*:
  - – summarized/collated post-task and post-test questionnaire results
  - – frequently shown in tables and figures
- ○ *Recommendations*—can be combined with findings or addressed separately; each recommendation is:
  - – described and, where appropriate, illustrated
  - – prioritized, based on severity rating as well as feasibility of fixing the problem now or later
- ○ *Next steps*:
  - – assign actions to individuals or groups
  - – advocate for more usability testing and other UCD practices

- *Appendices*—also called "back matter"—provide optional supporting materials:
  - labeled A, B, C, with the appropriate heading for each to reflect the contents
  - typically contain completed screeners, post-task and post-test questionnaires, logs, study protocol, moderator script, and so forth. Can also include full-page screen shots for reference.

Although all of these report parts have their uses, some are more important than others. Perhaps the most important part is the executive summary, which, despite its name, is generally read by everyone. Other report parts are read selectively by those with a need and an interest.

Writing the executive summary

The executive summary got its name because it is targeted at executives and managers who often just want to read the key issues in a report, as long as they are put into a context that tells them what they need to know. Like the informal summary shown earlier in Figure 9.1, the executive summary needs to cover the journalistic prompts of the 5 Ws and an H.

It turns out that executives aren't the only ones who like executive summaries. Everyone does. That's because everyone benefits from having the big picture of the report, even those who go on and read other sections or the whole report.

Figure 9.2 shows an executive summary for a formal report. I've indicated where the journalistic prompts are covered, as well as the place where recommendations are included.

Organizing the rest of the report to match your audience needs

After the executive summary, the report should give readers the information they want and need in the order in which they expect to read it. If the next thing your readers want to read is the section on results and recommendations, put this information next. If, however, they want to be filled in on the background, give them this information

Executive Summary

A usability testing team with members from Southern Polytechnic's Usability Center and Acme Software Company's development group [who] planned and conducted a usability test of the FTP software product [what] at the Usability Center [where]. This was the third usability evaluation of this product, with this evaluation's focus on the version (v. 7) currently under development. The screener previously developed for the advanced user was used. The objective of the test was to understand the advanced user's experience resulting from a significant redesign of the interface [why].

On March 16 [when], a walkthrough with a recruited user was conducted in the morning, and the pilot test was conducted in the afternoon. Numerous changes were made to the scenarios between the walkthrough and pilot; fewer changes were made following the pilot [how].

Testing with four more participants took place on March 16 and 17, with the findings meeting held directly after the last test [how]. A spreadsheet of the findings was distributed to the team after the meeting.

The top findings are grouped into the following categories [summary of top findings]:

Positives	Users commented positively about the colors being fresh and making the product feel "current"; they liked the new design with the tab interface and Windows skin; they also liked the new e-mail notification concept and the presence of context-sensitive help.
Aesthetics	Users commented that the interface seemed busy and overly complex.
Workspace manager	Users did not understand the concept of a workspace manager. It did not match their mental model for a specific task or activity; even when they understood the concept, users could not "add new" workspace successfully.
E-mail notification	Users had trouble with the dialogue box, the meaning of "location," and the configuration for testing e-mail (including how they wanted to receive confirmation/feedback); they also had problems with the e-mail option under "General" in "Program" options.
Right-click options	Users wanted right-click functionality to match their Microsoft mental model (e.g., for "compression" and "transfer" of files).
Learnability	Users complained about the startup wizard but all used it successfully; many users went to help; most wanted to search for terms with the index, which had not yet been developed.
Feedback	Users did not understand "mode" feedback.

This report describes the goals of the test, the characteristics of the user population identified for this test, the scenarios, and the findings. [This is called a *forecasting statement*, as it provides a brief description of the order of the parts of the report.]

Figure 9.2 The executive summary provides the key findings for the report of a File Transfer Protocol (FTP) software usability study.

next, so that they are prepared to understand the results and the recommendations. But don't blithely assume that everyone wants or needs the background before they can understand the results.

As Aristotle reminds us, these decisions are all about audience.

A report organized for readers who are primarily interested in the results and recommendations, but who need some context first, can be organized this way:

1. Executive summary
2. Results/recommendations
3. Discussion/findings
4. Methodology used in this study
5. Participant demographics/characteristics
6. Background/problem/study goals

When the report is for a fully informed audience, you can use another journalistic technique, called the *inverted pyramid.* It begins with the *lead*, which for journalists is the top news of the day, working backward to the starting point of the story (for those coming into the story who aren't up on the prior news). A usability report organized for a well-informed audience of readers would look like Figure 9.3. You notice that it doesn't have the executive summary, because everyone is up to speed. But it should still begin with a clear statement of purpose—just a sentence or two—so that readers can say to themselves: "Oh, this is the report of the findings from the usability study of Product X."

Another option for organizing this report for well-informed readers, especially if they were all in the findings meeting, is to reverse the first two main headings to present the report parts as shown in Figure 9.4.

If, however, your readers need some background and context to understand what you did and why, you can organize your report as shown in Figure 9.5. This arrangement works well for mixed audiences—a combination of readers, some who know a lot and others who know a little or nothing about your study—because all readers can get the high-level overview of findings in the executive summary and then read the report straight through, if they need to, or skip around to the parts that interest them.

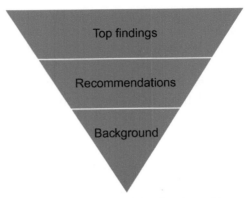

Figure 9.3 An inverted pyramid organizational structure is used in a report for informed readers.

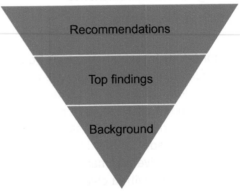

Figure 9.4 A report for very well-informed readers can begin with the recommendations.

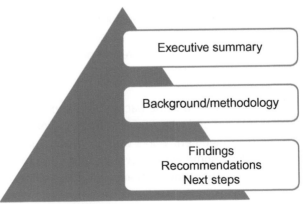

Figure 9.5 The organizational structure of a report for a mixed audience begins with an executive summary.

To learn about a standardized format created specifically for summative evaluations of software, see the following sidebar. You'll also learn about the work being done to create guidelines for formative evaluations.

Development of the common industry format

Development of a standardized formal report format, called the Common Industry Format (CIF), was initiated in 1997 by the National Institute of Standards and Technology (NIST). The CIF became an ISO standard in 2005.

Its purpose is to establish a report format structure that gives decision makers, typically purchasing agents at large companies and government agencies, the same type of information to evaluate software solutions from different vendors. The report structure includes the requirement to document usability methods and metrics, which places usability front and center as part of decision making. With use of the CIF, internal human factors and usability reviewers can evaluate the usability aspects of the vendor's proposed solutions.

The primary use of the CIF is for summative evaluations of software solutions. Because most usability testing done during development is formative, some of the CIF's sections don't apply to formative tests. To create a corresponding format for formative evaluations, a committee was formed to identify common (and best) practices for communicating information in less formal formative evaluations. In 2004, I participated in the first of several workshops, which was held in Boston, to shape these guidelines. For an excellent summary of the workshop findings, see the Theophanos and Quesenbery 2005 report, "Toward the Design of Effective Formative Reports."

For information about the CIF, see *http://zing.ncsl.nist.gov/iusr/*

For a template of report elements, see *http://zing.ncsl.nist.gov/iusr/formative/*

Presenting the findings

Once you have decided on the type of report you want to write—formal or informal—and the audience that will be receiving it, you need to plan how you will present the findings—the major part of your report.

As you know from your meeting that discussed findings, there are often many, many findings from a study. Choosing what to report is an important decision, but you should be guided by the fact that you want the report to result in actions for product improvement. If you present *everything* you saw, you can overwhelm your readers. Instead, you want to focus readers' attention on the key findings and their impact on product usability.

There are so many ways to present the findings that there isn't sufficient room to give examples for all of them. But a number of elements from studies tend to be commonly used. Among these are

- observations
- metrics
- severity ratings
- questionnaire responses
- qualitative feedback
- recommendations

You will want to illustrate the findings with

- screen shots
- figures
- participant quotes
- video clips

To show you some ways to present your findings and make your recommendations, I've collected the examples that follow. The point of these examples is not to set them in stone but to give you some ideas to devise your own best way to present the findings and link them to actions and recommendations. Because your goal is to improve the usability of the product you tested, you want your report to support action and improvements in user experience. You are in the best position to determine how to craft a report that will do just that.

The examples are presented in the following groups:

- *Summarizing findings*—presenting the top-level findings visually in tables

- *Illustrating findings*—using screen shots, figures, quotes, and video clips
- *Ordering findings*—ranking them by priority or grouping them by categories
- *Making recommendations*—determining how and at what level of detail

Using tables to summarize the findings

Although you provided a high-level summary of the findings in the executive summary, you now need to present more detailed information about your top findings.

Why do this twice in a formal report? For readers who will go beyond the executive summary, they are looking for more information about the top findings so as to get a fuller understanding of the issues. Tables that show task success/failure, summaries of behaviors, sample strategies used by participants for accomplishing the tasks, usage of particular features, and so forth can present the study findings quickly and efficiently, but also more fully than in the executive summary.

Figure 9.6 shows the findings grouped by category with the number of users affected. The study was for a new application for hotel call center operators.

Figure 9.7 summarizes the findings for task success and failure. The section presenting these findings in the report begins with an explanation of the findings shown in the table. This is a good way to present tables because the explanation helps users understand what they're seeing in the table.

In the next example shown in Figure 9.8, results for a category of finding are presented in a table showing the number of users experiencing the problem and the specific instances of the problem within the category. The study was for a university library's website for distance learning students. As you saw in Figure 9.7, the explanation of the table precedes the table.

Category	Users affected
Confirmation of data entry	6 of 11 participants wanted to see a confirmation statement following an action.
Help assists	A total of 31 requests for help were made: • 7 to confirm tab was correct for the task • 5 to query search functionality of system • 4 for prompt on how to complete task • 3 to confirm correct entry format for data (dates, numbers) • 2 to query about grayed-out Force Register
Autofills (zip code)	4 of 11 participants indicated they would like autofills based on zip code entry.
Overwrites	10 of 11 participants overwrote contact information [wrong path] because they didn't see how to add an e-mail and an address and didn't know they had overwritten rather than added information.
Advanced search	7 of 11 participants didn't see advanced search (or didn't select it, if they did see it).
Confirmation number	5 of 11 participants could not find where to enter the guest's confirmation number.
Mouseovers and clicks	11 of 11 participants moused over fields and clicked, at some point in the test, to see whether the field was editable or whether more information was presented via a popup.
Back button	2 of 11 participants wanted to use the back button (possibly indicating lack of confidence in correct path to exit screen).

Figure 9.6 The key findings for a call center usability study are grouped into categories with the number of users experiencing each problem.

Route Task Results

Three out of six users found the route map feature without prompting; two failed to find it after prompting, and one failed but did not ask for assistance (see Table 1). Failure was counted as not finding the route map without prompting.

Those who did not find the map without prompting, or failed to find it at all, thought that this feature would not be available and that they would have to use outside sources, such as Google Maps, to determine the route and the place to find a hotel along the way.

Table 1. Route Task—Success and Failure

	Success	Fail	Saw additional search options	Without prompting	After prompting
User 1	x		x	x	
User 2		x	x	x	
User 3	x		x	x	
User 4		x	x		x
User 5	x		x	x	
User 6		x			x

Figure 9.7 A description and a table present a summary of findings for a task on finding a route map for a hotel website usability study.

Findings for Mental Model Issues

The user's mental model refers to the difference between actual site structure, content, and functionality and what the participants expected or assumed. The users needed to match their experiences of getting information on the library's website with the navigation and terminology used on the site. Issues arose when users' mental models were not matched with the site's structure and labeling so that users were uncertain about which path they should take to reach their goal. To perform the tasks in this study, users wanted to know:

- Where do I start?
- How do I do this?
- What is this?

The table shows the problems users experienced.

Mental Model Issues for Users	P	1	2	3	4	5	6	7	Total
Where do I search for a book?	x	x		x	x	x			5
Where is Course Reserves?	x	x		x	x	x		x	6
Where do I search for articles?	x	x				x	x	x	5
Where do I go if I'm doing research on a topic (need books and articles)?	x	x	x	x					4
What's the difference between GIL and GALILEO?		x		x	x	x			4
What would be in "Resources" and what would be in "Services"?	x	x			x			x	4
How do I find out what my password is?	x				x	x	x		4

Figure 9.8 Each of the issues within a category—in this case, mental model—shows the number of users who experienced the problem.

Illustrating the findings

Illustrating the findings allows you to show as well as tell your readers what the issues are. You can illustrate the findings using screen shots and callouts that explain specific problems, using figures such as charts and graphs, using participant quotes, and embedding video clips.

Using screen shots

Using screen shots really helps readers who are not familiar with the product. Screen shots are also useful if the product is changing, so that you can document the issue in the version you tested.

Figure 9.9 shows screen shots with callouts to illustrate terminology problems experienced by users in the library website study.

Do terms used match what the user thinks/wants? Usability issues in the terminology category include unexpected or missing keywords, vague or ambiguous language, or unnecessary jargon.

GIL versus GALILEO: Participants were not confident they knew what these terms meant.

"Database"—this term has two meanings: computer database or reference database?

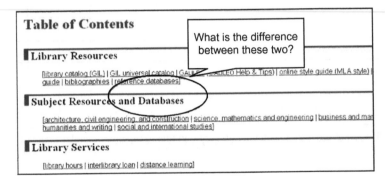

"Request"—this term has a two meanings: request book or request password?

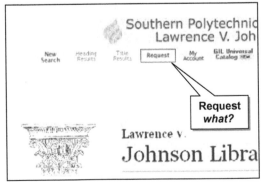

Figure 9.9 Terminology issues are presented using screen shots from the library website study for distance learning students.

Using figures

You can also illustrate findings using figures, which include charts and graphs of various types. Figure 9.10 shows a graph that compares user preferences when working with one of three versions (A, B, C) of a health-related prototype website.

A final question at the end of the tasks was: How does this website compare with other health information websites you have used? The scale was −3 to +3. The figure is introduced with an explanation of what is presented in it, which helps readers interpret the findings.

What you can see in the graph is that professionals overall liked the site they were testing better than another site they had used (though none of them thought it was outstandingly better). But the real findings illustrated here are:

- The B version compared very poorly—much worse than the other two—for consumers.

- The C version was not the best rated by professionals but was the highest rated by consumers (patients, friends, family members).

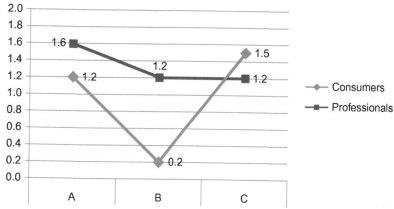

How does this website compare with other health information websites you have used? (range −3 to +3)

Figure 9.10 A graph shows user preferences for a health information website, with responses from two user groups.

The next example (Figure 9.11) shows the percentage of successes across all tasks for the same health information website usability study. As you can see, it is possible to present a lot of information in this way.

Percentage of successes across all tasks with a 95% confidence interval

	Consumers (N = 36)				Professionals (N = 36)			
	A	**B**	**C**	**All**	**A**	**B**	**C**	**All**
Average success rate	55.2%	63.5%	71.9%	**63.5%**	77.0%	70.0%	76.0%	**75.0%**
Upper limit	64.8%	72.5%	79.9%	**68.9%**	68.8%	61.0%	67.7%	**70.0%**
Lower limit	45.2%	53.6%	62.1%	**57.8%**	85.3%	79.0%	84.4%	**80.0%**

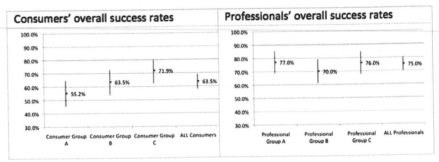

Figure 9.11 A lot of information from a big usability study is presented clearly and concisely here.

The next example (Figure 9.12) presents the results of a comparative evaluation of two versions of an election ballot, in which half the participants received the A version first and half received the B version first. The study was a formal, summative usability test comparing the language of instructions on ballots.

See Redish, Chisnell, Laskowski, and Lowry, 2010.

The bar graph shows that test participants (voters) were more accurate on Ballot B (the plain-language version) than on Ballot A (the version with traditional ballot language). It also shows the effect of which

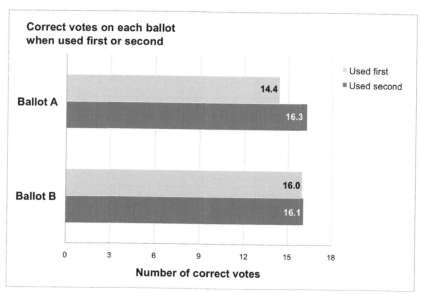

Figure 9.12 This bar graph shows the impact of accuracy on voting based on the order of ballots used.

ballot participants worked on first. With the plain-language ballot (B), order of use mattered very little. With the traditional-language ballot (A), however, order of use mattered a lot. Participants who had already voted the plain-language ballot were significantly more accurate on the traditional-language ballot than participants who voted the traditional-language ballot first.

Using participant quotes

Another way to illustrate the findings is by providing participant quotes. Participant quotes can persuade readers of the severity of a problem, reveal the users' thought processes, or simply make the findings more vivid and interesting to read. Figure 9.13 shows participant quotes associated with a category of findings.

Participant quotes can also be used to show positive findings and suggestions for new features or different ways of using the product, as the quotes in Figure 9.14 illustrate.

Report of Labeling Issues

Users expressed concern about the lack of labeling on cables and equipment. Comments from users who had trouble with labeling are shown in the following table.

User No.	Comment
U1	"These labels [on the cable box] don't match [the labels in the instructions]."
U3	"The cable box is not labeled."
U4	"These cables aren't labeled, so how do I know which is audio?"
U8	"The back of the DVR does not say 'cable in' as in the manual. The box says RF IN, but I guess this is where it goes."
U10	"It doesn't say 'OUT' [user is looking at back of cable box]."
U17	"It says RF IN here [on DVR box]. In the instruction book it says 'CABLE.'"
U19	"It's a little confusing because it says RF IN."

Figure 9.13 Findings with regard to labeling issues are presented with representative participant quotes from a study of the instructions for the self-installation of a digital cable TV box.

Positive Comments and Suggestions

Positive impressions

- "I love this page because I know exactly what I'm looking for."—User P (pilot), searching for a book on the GALILEO search tab
- ". . . and that's it! That's really cool!"—User 2, locating a book with GALILEO
- "Once I got to a search box, I knew what to do."—User 5
- "This task was the easiest of all so far . . . I wouldn't have started here without [the tutorial]."—User 6, finding a book in GALILEO after viewing the tutorial

Suggestions

- "Why can't I have a search button?"—User P, looking for links to research a topic
- "A universal catalog should do a universal search on all resources."—User 3
- "If it said 'Reserves' on the resources page, that would make it easier for me."—User 5
- "They should have a standard 'Forget your password?' option if you don't know it."—User 5
- "The interface needs some rearranging . . . I'd like some bifurcation of the links, side-by-side title and explanation."—User 6
- "There should be some kind of help for the password . . . I'd like to know in advance that I'll need a password."—User 6
- "Better subcategories would help."—User 8, on navigating the site links

---

Figure 9.14 Positive comments and suggestions are presented from the library website study for distance learning students.

Embedding video clips

Nothing beats the experience of seeing users, up close and personal, struggling with your product. But the next best thing, for those who could not be present during testing, is embedding video clips in the report. If the format of your report and the medium of delivery support it, this can be an effective way to illustrate the findings.

System software that ships with Windows PCs and Macs makes this fairly easy to do, particularly for those who know their way around the tool. Or, if you recorded the sessions in Morae and used markers to identify the findings, you can search on the markers to find the clips you want to include.

Ordering the findings

In addition to illustrating findings, you also need to establish a hierarchy for ordering them. As you know, you want to begin with the positive findings, but after that you need to present the findings in a ranked or prioritized list.

If you assigned severity ratings in your findings meeting, you want to order the findings on the basis of severity, beginning with the highest level of severity. Figure 9.15 shows severity ratings and the number of people experiencing the problem for the library website study.

Of course, there are other ways to order findings. If the tasks covered several different parts of the product, it often feels natural to organize the findings into those categories, especially if the responsibility for making changes also falls along those lines. Or if there's a predictable sequence to the screens, then you've got a chronological order to follow.

These methods are by no means all that can be used to present the findings from a study. Every situation—audience, purpose, and context of use—is potentially different, so you will want to consider the approach that works best in each, including creating your own approach for reporting the results of your study.

Collated Findings, Ranked by Severity

The following four levels of severity we used to rate the findings:

- Level 1—Prevented completion of a task
- Level 2—Frustrated participant and caused significant delay on a task
- Level 3—Had a minor effect on usability
- Level 4—Caused no significant impact on performance, but participant indicated a preference or a suggestion for future changes

Usability problem	Number affected	Severity
Confusion over how to find Course Reserves	7	1
Confusion over where to go to search for books	6	1
Confusion over where to go to search for articles	6	1
Password: Failed to retrieve password	4	1
User Support: Wanted explicit on-screen descriptions	7	2
Tutorial: Went too fast; couldn't stop it or change the pace	6	2
Misunderstood function/connection of GIL and GALILEO	5	2
Wanted password warning/help	5	2
Terminology: Resources page confusing	3	2
User Support: Title and TOC pages confusing	3	2
User Support: How do you reserve a book in another library? (interlibrary loan)	3	2
Tutorial: Was not helpful	5	3
Layout: Poor layout—cramped, hard to read	4	3
Tutorial: Animation distracting	4	3
Tutorial: User control (start/stop) not explicit	4	3
Terminology: Confused by meaning of "universal"	3	3
Tutorial: Couldn't see everything	3	3
User Support: GALILEO: Is this article really the full text?	3	3
User Support: SPSU book search gave incorrect match (graduate student task)	3	3
User Support: Wanted help: site map, search, etc.	5	4
Tutorial: Wanted volume control	3	4

Figure 9.15 The findings are ranked by severity, with the number of users affected.

Presenting post-task and post-test results

In addition to presenting the findings from your observations, you will want to present your collated post-task and post-test questionnaire data. You will also want to collate the responses you got from qualitative feedback methods, such as the product reaction cards.

Presenting survey responses

Some survey responses produce quantitative data. If you asked for satisfaction ratings, for example, you can present the mean, median, or mode for these across all users. Or, if you are working with a small response sample, you can present the results as numbers of responses, saying that four out of six users rated the task a 4 or 5 (on a 5-point scale), indicating a high level of satisfaction with the task.

Other responses, such as those from open-ended questions, produce qualitative data. Figure 9.16 shows participants' responses to a post-task

There's more about when to use numbers and when to use statistics in presenting these findings, as well as an explanation of the mean, median, and mode, in Chapter 8.

Post-task Questionnaire Responses

Scenario 4: Post-task Questions with Responses

1. How easy or difficult was it to separate the FTP servers into a new group?
   - ○ **1—very easy**   **P 1 2 3 4**
   - ○ 2   5
   - ○ 3
   - ○ 4
   - ○ 5—very difficult

2. How easy or difficult was it to turn off the monitoring on everything?
   - ○ 1—very easy   P
   - ○ 2   5
   - ○ 3   1 3
   - ○ 4   2
   - ○ 5—very difficult 4

3. What's your opinion about the time it took to complete the tasks in this scenario?
   - ○ 1—took less time than I thought it would
   - ○ **2—took about what I expected P 1 3 5**
   - ○ 3—took too much time   2 4

Comments on any answer(s) above:

P: Once I found it, it was easy—re #1 rating above.

2: I would like the interface to allow me to disable notifications instead of polling.

3: Re Q2—It would have been easy to turn off monitoring for everything if the first option was available.

4: Some things seem to be more difficult than need be. All in all, things are clear though.

5: When both FTP servers were selected, I right-clicked and chose a new group. I expected the new group to control the selected FTP servers, but it did not. I could not find a way to put multiple machines into maintenance mode.

Figure 9.16 Individual post-task questionnaire responses are shown with the most frequent response indicated in bold. (P = pilot participant)

questionnaire, with the most frequently chosen response indicated in bold. It also shows the comments provided by participants, which represent qualitative responses. The study was for an FTP software product.

Presenting SUS results

If you used the popular SUS survey, you should present the average score for all participants, since this score can then be used as a baseline for comparison with other studies. You can also present individual responses to give readers a closer look at the results.

There's more about the SUS and other standard post-test questionnaires in Chapter 6.

Figure 9.17 shows the individual scores and the score chosen most often for each statement as well as the average score. Minor changes have been made to the standard SUS statements to suit the study.

	Strongly DISAGREE				Strongly AGREE
	1	2	3	4	5
1. I think that I would like to use this software frequently.			2 4 5	w	1 3
2. I found the software unnecessarily complex.	2 3 5	1	w 4		
3. I thought the software was easy to use.			4	1 2	w 3 5
4. I think that I would need to consult technical support to be able to use this software effectively.	w 3	1 2 4 5			
5. I found the various functions in this software were well integrated.			w 4	1 2 3	5
6. I thought there was too much inconsistency in this software.	2 3 5	w 1	4		
7. I would imagine that most people with a need to monitor network devices would learn to use this software very quickly.			4	2	w 1 3 5
8. I found the software very cumbersome to use.	w 2 3 5	1	4		
9. I felt very confident using the software.			w 5	2 1 4	3
10. I would need to learn a lot of things before I could get going with this software.	w 2	1	4	5	3

Figure 9.17 The results from the SUS are presented with a description of the scoring methodology. (W = walkthrough/ pilot user.) Yellow cells indicate the point on the rating scale that was picked the most for the corresponding statement. Light blue cells indicate the items on which the six evaluators overall produced a favorable rating—all of the items except the last one. The positive/negative split on that item was 3-2, barely positive. The average SUS score obtained from the six participants was 77.5 on a 100-point scale.

Presenting qualitative responses

In addition to the qualitative responses you may have used as quotes in your report, you can also collate and visually display the results of qualitative responses you get from other methods, such as the product reaction cards that were used.

Chapters 6 and 7 tell you about the product reaction cards and how to use them.

Figures 9.18, 9.19, and 9.20 show several examples of different ways in which to present the results graphically from use of the product reaction cards.

Straight-
forward
Efficient
Accessible
Useful
Usable
Time saving
Valuable
Inviting

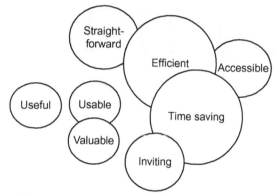

Figure 9.18 A word cloud presents the product reaction cards that the participants selected, with the size of the cloud reflecting the number of times a specific word was chosen.

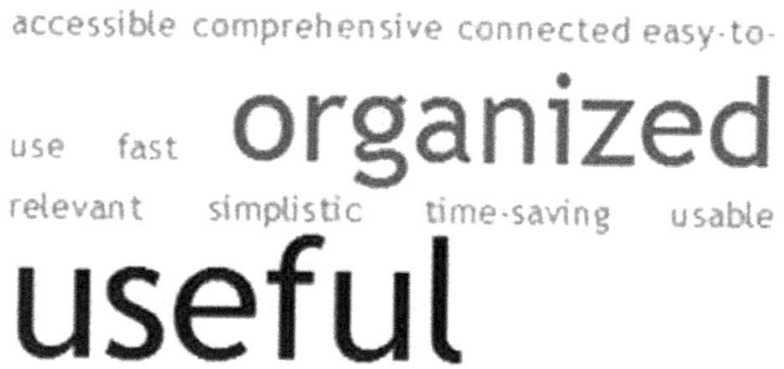

accessible comprehensive connected easy-to-
use fast organized
relevant simplistic time-saving usable
useful

Figure 9.19 The two most often chosen words are the largest, and all the others—chosen only once—are the same size.

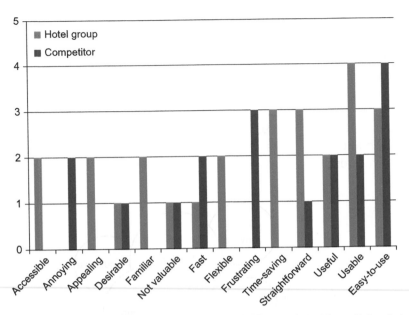

Figure 9.20 A bar graph presents a comparison of the words selected by participants in a website study of a major hotel group and a competitor hotel group.

Making recommendations

The recommendations section of your report is arguably the most important section, perhaps only bested by the executive summary, which also contains the top recommendations, but in brief.

After all is said and done, if the report doesn't motivate action—or more to the point, specific actions—to address the issues uncovered in the usability test, it will fall short of the goal to improve the product. However, as I covered in Chapter 8, the level of detail provided in each recommendation is dependent on the experience of the person or team writing the recommendations. If you know what the action should be, state it. If you do not know specifically—because you are not an interaction or graphic designer, for instance—then you will make more general recommendations for action, pointing out the need for change based on the study findings.

The approaches to take in presenting recommendations are almost as varied as the ways to present the findings. A few examples will show you some options.

In Figure 9.21 the recommendations are combined with a list of the findings labeled "areas of concern." The study focused on the activities associated with artists creating a personal web space on a website for an artists' organization. This approach works well when you can connect a specific recommendation to a particular problem.

When you can illustrate the proposed solutions, you make the recommendations crystal clear. Figure 9.22 shows a problem called out—links should focus on what users want to do—and the proposed solution, which uses mouseovers to provide a tooltip to explain confusing terminology. The study is of a library website for distance learning students.

Findings and Recommendations

Area of Concern	Recommended Fix
Excessive scrolling • Too much text on the screen • Horizontal line breaks at the bottom of the screen (under some screen resolutions)	• Move instructions to a pop-up window accessed via a link • Use Next and Back buttons between each field instead of requiring scrolling to the field • Eliminate all scrolling throughout the tool
Inadequate error handling • Messages do not display near actual error • Messages don't clearly identify the error • Inconsistent format of messages (some in windows, some in red text)	• Highlight actual errors on screen • Move error message next to error
Confusing/Inflexible form behaviors • Errors on forms clear all fields, not just the field in error	• Highlight form input error without clearing all fields

Figure 9.21 Findings and recommendations are grouped by type of issue.

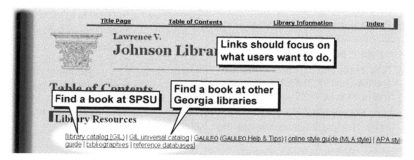

Figure 9.22 The problem with terminology is illustrated with a callout, and a proposed solution is illustrated with tooltips.

The example in Figure 9.23 shows a report format that presents the scenario, the number of participants having a positive experience or a problem, some sample participant quotes, a screen capture in one

Scenario 2.

You are a research administrator working for a researcher who would like to apply for funding from NIAID for a tuberculosis vaccine project. You are looking for information on how to apply for funding and what kind of funding is available.

Findings	Recommendations, comments
Going to Research Funding All participants selected Research Funding as the main topic for this scenario. Research Funding ▶ Initiatives ▶ Grants ▶ Contracts ▶ Small Business Awards ▶ more on Research Funding	Keep Research Funding as one of the major labels on the home page.

Selecting from the Research Funding list
 	
☐ Only half of the participants thought they knew what "Initiatives" meant.
 	
☐ Of the 5 researchers:
  – 2 chose Initiatives
  – 1 other chose it because he did not know what it meant
  – 2 ignored that option
	Consider using another term, not Initiatives, as the first and most general link about Research Funding.

Finding what they were looking for Both the public participants and the research participants were topic-oriented. They wanted to find information about tuberculosis vaccine. No public participant found it. Only 2 research participants found it and they had to do a lot of exploring and hunting before they did. Even the researchers complained: ☐ P7: "I'm lost. I just want to get the information and to get there quickly." ☐ P9: "Do I have to slog through…?" ☐ P10: "I want it to be quick. I just want to pull up my topic."	Create a searchable database that encompasses all funding opportunities. Allow users to search just within funding opportunities by topic as well as by type of funding. (Although, as P12 pointed out, there may be more general opportunities that would work for a researcher that do not include that researcher's key words. As P12 said, researchers would need to look for both "the forest and the trees.")

Figure 9.23 A sample from a report by Ginny Redish, a well-known usability consultant, shows a combination of text, graphics, participant quotes, and other elements.

Findings	Recommendations, comments
Understanding different funding mechanisms	Rename <u>Initiatives</u> to something like <u>Funding Opportunities.</u>
Even researchers are not always clear about the different funding mechanisms:	Offer a page that gives quick and easy explanations of the differences between grants, contracts, and other funding mechanisms with links to look at each one.
☐ P8: "As investigators, we're supposed to know, but it's a haze."	Cross-link from all types of funding opportunities to the others.
5 of the 7 public participants and 4 of the 5 research participants first chose <u>Grants.</u>	
A few eventually got to one of the other pages, such as Special Announcements that recommends checking many different types of opportunities. However, neither the Grants page nor the RFP page links to these.	

Figure 9.23 (*Continued*)

example, and generalized recommendations to either keep or change an aspect of the website based on the findings.

Presenting an oral report

It is widely reported that the fear of public speaking is greater than the fear of death. While this may or may not be true, it is true that many people dread speaking publicly, even more so when it must be done professionally. That's why Toastmasters International is such a popular organization.

See *www.toastmasters.org*

Whether you are someone who fears public or professional speaking or someone who relishes the opportunity to present your work, you will often find yourself asked—or perhaps volunteering—to deliver an oral report of your usability study. In some cases, the oral report may be the only deliverable.

In other cases, the oral report may be delivered at the same time as a written report of the study's results. In either of these situations, the following are the key components of an oral presentation of the results of your study:

- visual support, typically using PowerPoint slides
- a handout of the slides to be distributed before or after the talk or saved as a PDF file to distribute electronically after the presentation or on request
- video clips showing examples of the key findings
- and, of course, *you*

You may be presenting your study results at an on-site meeting, but it is increasingly common to present the findings using a web-based meeting application such as WebEx or GoToMeeting, especially when your audience is at different locations.

Some of the people hearing your presentation may not have much background information about your study, so in these situations you will need to set the context for the study. Including this background information, when needed, will not be a problem for those who are already aware of the study, since it gives everyone the same starting point for receiving the information you will present. To get you ready for this presentation, I will give you some suggestions for

- planning your presentation
- preparing video clips
- organizing your presentation
- delivering your presentation
- handling questions

Two popular books are *Confessions of a Public Speaker* by Berkun, 2009, and *Presentation Zen* by Reynolds, 2008.

Of course, the information I share with you is just the tip of the iceberg in terms of what you need to know to be an effective presenter. But there are some excellent books to help you learn more.

Plan your presentation

It's essential to plan your presentation. You don't want to look like you don't know what you're doing in the presentation, because this could adversely affect your credibility regarding the usability study. So don't skimp on the time needed to plan, organize, and, most of all, practice your presentation before you deliver it.

Prepare video clips

Earlier in the chapter, I mentioned that you can illustrate your findings in a written report with embedded video clips if the medium and delivery support doing this. I suspect that most reports are delivered as PDF documents attached to e-mail, which limits the use of embedded clips.

However, when it comes to preparing an oral presentation, video clips are typically built into it in one of two ways:

- embedded in PowerPoint slides
- presented as a stand-alone DVD or CD of the highlights with audio and/or text commentary

An example of a stand-alone video highlights presentation for the Holiday Inn China website study can be found on the book's companion website at www.mkp. com/testingessentials

Even with today's tools to make this preparation easier than it once was, it still takes time, so you need to plan for this as part of your planning for the oral presentation.

Whatever you choose to show from the recorded sessions, you are shaping your audience's experience. There is no way to completely avoid bias in selecting some findings and not others and in deciding how you present them, so you will want to consider which is best for your situation. Should you:

- Show one clip from each user to present the complete participant pool?
- Show multiple clips of users experiencing the same problem to demonstrate the extent of the problem?
- Show fewer but longer clips to fully contextualize the problem?

There's not a right or wrong answer. As with so many things associated with usability, "It depends." If you want to present a sample from each user to represent all participants, you would go with the first choice. If you want to demonstrate an issue shared by several users, then shorter, back-to-back clips drive the point home. If you want to present the complete picture of a problem, you would show full, unedited clips.

And don't overlook the importance of showing positive findings. It's best to begin with these, in fact, because it puts the audience at ease. They won't feel attacked or defensive if they see that you plan to balance your presentation by showing the positive as well as the negative findings.

If your audience is receptive to seeing video highlights and you choose your approach well, you have the opportunity to let your users speak for themselves, which can be highly motivating.

Practice, practice, practice

Just like an actor preparing for a play, you must practice your part to ensure that you have a successful show. And if your presentation is a team effort, you must practice with your team members as well as with your slides and any other media you will use, such as your video clips or stand-alone video.

If technology is involved, especially if you are using conferencing software, you will want to have at least one practice run with the technology. It is best if you can get someone at a remote location to tune in for a test drive of the audio, desktop sharing, connection quality, and whatever else you need to check. Then, before the meeting starts, you will want to check your systems again so that you can address any newfound technical issues. Whether you are presenting in person or remotely, you want to avoid the embarrassing and stressful situation of holding up the start of your presentation because of technical issues.

Whatever the time expectations are for your presentation, make it your very first priority to honor this expectation. If your presentation is scheduled for 30 minutes, use your practice sessions to make sure you can deliver it in under 30 minutes. If the question-and-answer period is included in this 30 minutes, cut your presentation by 10 minutes to allow time for questions.

Why is timing so important? For every minute over the audience's expectation for when you should conclude your presentation, you lose "points" in your performance. A presentation that runs too long may be completely counterproductive to your efforts to be effective and persuasive. In some meeting situations, where meeting rooms are at a premium and have to be reserved in advance, you might not get to finish if you run beyond the allotted time.

Deliver your presentation

You've probably heard the old adage:

- Tell them what you are going to tell them.
- Tell them.
- Tell them what you told them.

It's still good advice for an effective organizational strategy.

Delivering your presentation means establishing a beginning, middle, and end. The beginning sets the context, answering the audience's questions of "Why am I here?" and "What will I hear?" Providing this information prepares your audience to know what to expect.

In the main part of your presentation, you summarize your findings. You may be able to use the same organizational approach as in your written report, or you may need to change up the organization for the context of the meeting situation and the audience. Whatever you do, don't make the mistake of thinking you have to tell *everything* you learned in the study. You won't have time. So, pick the best parts to summarize.

In general, the audience will want to know the same things they want from the written report but in less detail:

- key findings, positive and negative
- severity of negative findings
- solutions/recommendations
- next steps (this is the advocacy part)

Know how and when to ask for questions

Unless your situation dictates otherwise, you should expect and plan for questions. That means you will have to set aside time for questions within the time allocated to you to present your report.

As part of your introduction, tell your audience how you want to handle questions. If you don't mind being interrupted as you go along, let the audience know that they can ask questions at any time. With this format you need to decide how much time you can allow for questions and still get finished on time. You will then need to manage the questions as they come along.

Or, if you want to take all questions, you may have to let the audience know that you will have to cut some parts of the presentation short to allow for all the questions. In some cases, you can ask the audience if they would like to run longer (10 minutes, perhaps?) to allow for all the questions. In other cases, you may have to delay answering some questions until after the meeting so that you can finish your presentation on time.

Some presenters prefer that the audience hold questions until the end. Perhaps the format of the presentation shapes this expectation. It certainly makes it easier to manage the time you have, although it puts the burden on the audience to remember the questions they want to ask during the presentation but wait until the end to ask them.

If your expectation is that the audience should hold questions until the end, tell them this upfront, suggesting that they jot down questions as they are listening. Or, if you are presenting in a web conferencing format, they can text their questions to you during the presentation, and you can answer them at the end, as time permits.

Advocating for more UCD

In any situation where you are reporting the results of testing and your audience includes people beyond your core team of committed UCD practitioners, you should seize the opportunity to "sell" usability. That means becoming an advocate for more user-centered design practices.

Here's where we return to Aristotle and the premise behind his rhetorical principles: *persuasion*. Aristotle knew it was vital for his students to learn how to be persuasive in their oral arguments. His *Rhetoric* is all about how to do that.

Chapter 3 offers up some cost-justification strategies for usability advocacy.

Before concluding your report—in whatever context you deliver it—don't miss the opportunity to take Aristotle's advice and use it to advocate for more usability practices. Your written or oral report should be convincing on its own merits about the value of usability testing. But don't assume that this is enough to persuade management to do it again, do it earlier, do it more often, and use other tools in the UCD toolkit. You have to tell them what the next steps should be and why it is in their best interests to do more.

This advocacy can be handled in a separate section at the end of your report called "next steps" or at the end of your oral report. Or it can be slipped into the recommendations part of your report.

Here are some ways to implement the advocacy strategy:

- If you recommend design changes, stress the importance of testing the effectiveness of the changes with another small study. Emphasize the cost savings in using the same scenarios, screeners, and other parts of the test to do another study.

- If you demonstrated that much of what you learned is valuable but cannot be used in this product release because of the late placement of the usability test in the development timeline, stress the product improvements and savings that can derive from testing earlier.

- If you found things that would be best confirmed by contextual inquiry (site visits) or a card sort or another tool in your UCD toolkit, emphasize the benefits of adding more tools to the user experience feedback loop.

- If your study established a baseline of metrics, stress the importance of measuring improvements against these metrics in future studies.

- If you debriefed the process with the team and have decided to make some changes to your process next time, explain what these changes will be to demonstrate continuous improvement.

You get the picture. Push, quietly or forcefully, as the situation requires, for more UCD practices. This is your chance to advance the cause of user-centered product design.

Summarizing Chapter 9

This chapter presented options for reporting your findings in various media. The most common method to report study findings remains the written report, which can be informal or formal, as the situation requires.

It all comes down to your audience (your readers), your purpose, and the context in which they will receive and use the information from your study. We have Aristotle to thank for these guidelines, and they are as valid today as when he advocated them.

No matter who your audience is or how formal or informal the reporting context is, it's very important to begin your report with a summary so that everyone knows the goals of the study, the top findings, and the top actions/recommendations. Busy readers may drop out at this point, if that's all they want. But that's OK because you have served their needs and respected their time.

Once you've provided an introductory or executive summary, you have to get down to the nitty-gritty of reporting the findings in detail. Although there are many ways to present your findings, I suggested some options:

- using tables to summarize the findings
- illustrating findings with screen shots, figures, participant quotes, and video clips
- ordering findings by severity, category, or some other way
- presenting questionnaire results
- using visual displays of qualitative information, such as the product reaction cards
- making recommendations at whatever level of detail is appropriate and expected

Next, I presented the challenges (and opportunities) in preparing and presenting an oral report, dividing the process into three steps:

1. Preparing the presentation, including the content that will likely be molded into PowerPoint slides and supported with video clips or a stand-alone video.
2. Practicing the presentation with the slides and other elements and in the context in which you will be making the presentation.
3. Delivering the presentation, including managing the time expectations and the way in which you will ask for questions.

I ended this chapter by stressing the importance of advocating for more usability testing and other tools in the UCD toolkit. Once you have done this, you are done! For this project, anyway. But if you have been successful and persuasive in reporting your results, you will be doing more usability work soon.

The complete report for this case study is on the book's companion website. A sneak peek is provided in the executive summary shown here.

www.mkp.com/testingessentials

Executive Summary

Test Objective

Karen Bennett, Manager of User Experience at IHG, presented her concerns for the usability study of the Holiday Inn China website as follows:

- Do users connect better with the Holiday Inn or a competitor site such as *www.elong.com*?

- Which features do the users connect with and like (IHG vs. competitors)?

- Does the booking process work for the Chinese user; if not, why?

- Does a competitor's site have a better booking process; if so, why?

Our study focused on gathering qualitative and quantitative data to address IHG's concerns about the site's usability.

Based on IHG's concerns and the heuristic evaluation we conducted, we assessed the ease and difficulty of the following hotel booking tasks on *www.HolidayInn.com.cn*:

- The general feeling/layout of the site:
  - Is it easy to find the information users want to know the first time they visit?

- The procedure of booking a hotel online:
  - Basic searching: Is it easy to use?
  - Entering personal information: Does the website require reasonable and suitable information for Chinese users?
  - Do users understand all of the information requirements?

- Language: Can users understand the language on the Holiday Inn China website? Are there any translation mistakes?

- Satisfaction with the site: Which aspects of booking a room do users like and which aspects do they dislike?

- Perceived reliability of the site:
  - Do users trust the website?
  - Do they readily provide the personal information requested?
- Navigation: Can users find clear and efficient navigation when booking a hotel room or browsing the website?
- Compare Holiday Inn China website to competitor site: How do users feel about the *elong.com* website in comparison to the Holiday Inn site?
- Compare Holiday Inn China website to the Holiday Inn U.S. website: How do users feel about the U.S. version of the same site?

Note: Since we concluded our usability testing on the Holiday Inn China website, the following changes have been made to the website:

- There is now a map feature available when search results are displayed.
- The input fields have been changed from the upper right corner to the center of the page.

Our Process

The purpose of the Chinese *www.HolidayInn.com.cn* usability test was to collect feedback about how users use the website, what problems they encounter using it, what improvements they would like to have made, and what additional information they need. Following industry-standard methods of usability testing, our team undertook an evaluation of the site, developed user profiles, and developed a six-scenario test plan to conduct testing with six users.

Our Results

The team found many consistent issues among users that were areas of concern. Our findings have been divided into the following seven categories:

1. *Aesthetics:* The look and feel of the website, and whether it is seen as trustworthy.
2. *Navigation:* How well users can find their way around the website.
3. *Feedback:* Information that tells users where they are or what is happening.
4. *Layout:* The arrangement of page elements and their effectiveness at guiding the user.

5. *Feature requests:* Options that users want and expect but do not find.

6. *Brand identity:* How well users recognize Holiday Inn and other IHG hotels as a brand.

7. *Mental model:* The process flow and design users expect to find and how well the website matches their expectation.

Based on the qualitative feedback we received from participants, as well as our analysis of the quantitative data from testing, we identified 13 usability issues with the Holiday Inn China website. The following table lists these issues from high severity to low severity and indicates the number of participants who experienced each problem.

Usability problem	Number affected	Severity
Feedback: Loading screen has no progress bar. This confuses users as to whether their information is being processed.	6/6	high
Mental model: Users are confused as to whether they are required to input a full Chinese name, or just family name.	5/6	high
Layout: Error messages were not seen by the user or they were misinterpreted.	5/6	high
Layout: Users found the Priority Club Login options confusing.	4/6	high
Feature request: Users want more information on hotel amenities.	4/6	high
Feature request: Users want to see a drop-down list of cities instead of having to type city names.	3/6	high
Layout: Users want the total price for their stay to be listed, instead of a per-night rate only.	3/6	high
Layout: Users have trouble finding the cancellation link to cancel their reservation.	3/6	high
Feature request: Users want to see hotel rankings by different categories (customer experience and price).	4/6	medium
Layout: Users think advertisements are overwhelming.	3/6	medium
Aesthetics: Search results of hotels are displayed in a two-color format, confusing users' perception of how many results are being displayed.	2/6	low
Feature request: Users complain about not seeing promotional rate information.	2/6	low
Navigation: The "start over" and "finish booking" options on the "confirm booking" page confused one user.	1/6	low

International usability testing

10

Know thy user, for he is not thyself.

—Rubinstein and Hersh

*The Human Factor:
Designing Computer
Systems for People,* 1984

Although this statement is written in language that reflects its time—the book in which it appears was published in 1984—the principle remains valid today; even more so when you are testing products for international users. In the chapters leading up to this one, I have presented the essentials for usability testing. This chapter narrows the focus to the specific challenges in testing for and with international users. These include:

- Learning about your international users and creating personas to represent them
- Understanding cultural differences and adapting to them
- Planning the test, including such issues as:
  - where you should be—here or there
  - how you should organize the planning—on your own or with help from local vendors
  - how you should localize the test protocol
  - how you should select the moderator to suit the context of testing
  - how you should prepare for other aspects of international testing

Usability Testing Essentials. DOI: 10.1016/B978-0-12-375092-1.00010-6

Learning about your international users

It's always an important first task in planning for testing to learn as much as you can about your users and to then use this knowledge to plan a test that involves them in real tasks that match their goals. This requirement is the same in international testing, but the added challenge is that it may be more difficult to learn about these users, unless they are readily available to you. Some are, because there are international and intercultural users in your own country. Others, of course, are in their countries, not yours. Getting to know them, wherever they are, and creating personas to give them a shape and personality will help you plan a study that matches their goals for your product.

Some international users are here

"Here" is wherever you are.

For starters, you don't need to think of another country to consider your international users. They might be right here at home. In an increasingly multicultural world, we often need to consider our "non-native" users from the perspective of their cultural and language backgrounds. In the United States, this might mean testing with first- or second-generation Hispanic or Asian immigrants. (Both of these groups, of course, represent many countries and cultures, so it's easy to overgeneralize.) They may be bilingual in English and their first language, but they may be more comfortable working in their first language and dominant culture.

You may also need to consider English first-language speakers who represent specific cultures, such as African Americans or Native Americans. In your planning meeting, you probably discussed the level of diversity appropriate to your product and your study. If ethnic diversity is a goal in recruiting, your screening criteria included the characteristics of this diversity.

Chapter 5 has more about planning for ethnic diversity in your study.

Other international users are "there"

"There" is where your users are.

You may have users that are both "here" and "there." In the case study of the Holiday Inn China website, the primary users are in China. The secondary users are Chinese-speaking U.S. residents. The team developed personas for each user and tested with the ones who are in the United States. Although they could not test with the ones who are "there," they recommended that testing be done in China in the next study.

To understand the in-country, in-context experience of your international users in other countries, you have to test where they are. If you know who these users are—as, for instance, the persona of "Tony" Chen reflects—you can begin planning for a test. If you do not know who these users are, you will want to find out what you can from the research that's available to you. This will likely be your starting point in planning an international study.

Chapter 4 shows the Chinese persona of Tai "Tony" Chen as well as the U.S persona of Min He.

Create personas for your international users

Personas should be based on research, and international personas are no exception. But doing this research may not be as easy as it is for your domestic users, particularly when your international users are in many countries around the world.

A full-scale, multicountry study of your international users can be cost prohibitive for all but the most well-financed products, so you are much more likely to narrow your scope to perhaps a single country or a group of countries with a shared language or culture, such as Latin American, Spanish-speaking countries or Chinese-speaking countries or cultures.

Even when you are focusing on only one language, there could be many subgroups who speak that language, as well as many variations of the language in both spoken and written forms. Take Chinese as an example. If you decide to test your product with Chinese users, you need to consider which language you will use. If you settle on Mandarin, which is the official language of mainland China and Taiwan as well as one of the official languages of Singapore and parts of Malaysia, you then need to decide which version of the written language you will use. In Hong Kong, the official language changed from Cantonese to Mandarin with the handover to China in 1997, but the older population still speaks Cantonese. And in mainland China, a considerable part of the rural population does not speak or read Mandarin, using its indigenous language instead.

You also need to choose the character set. In mainland China, the choice would be simplified characters (introduced in 1955), but in Hong Kong and Taiwan, it would probably be traditional characters.

Next you have to consider the reading capabilities and preferences of your users. Taiwan and Hong Kong users primarily read characters displayed in right-to-left orientation, but in mainland China, they read characters displayed from left to right. The layout of the rows is another distinction: In mainland China, they read in the Western style of horizontal rows from left-to-right; however, in Taiwan, they might read from the top of the page to the bottom and from right to left because Taiwan only recently (2004) mandated the left-to-right horizontal reading orientation. And it's not unusual to find a crazy-quilt combination in the streets. Figure 10.1 shows an example from the streets of Hong Kong. The top line displays the characters from left to right, the middle line displays them from right to left, and the bottom line displays them from left to right.

Depending on your product's intended audience, you may need several personas for a single language group. As you know from developing domestic personas, you must also consider differences in age, economic level, education, product familiarity (or lack of it), shopping habits, and other factors. These differences can be particularly important in international testing, when economic level, age, and gender can have a huge impact on product awareness and adoption.

Figure 10.1 This photograph of a Hong Kong street sign displays the text running in two directions; it is from *http://en.wikipedia.org/wiki/Written_Chinese*

But don't let this vast unknown overwhelm you. Just as there are huge potential differences among users in your country, which require you to narrow your focus to one or more subgroups, you have to decide who your targeted users are for a particular international study, then create personas for those users.

Focus on specific cultural characteristics

Aside from the need to consider the usual characteristics that form the basis of a persona, you need to consider culturally based characteristics that might have an impact on your international personas. The following topics will help you focus your research and data gathering on learning the ways in which culturally based differences within international user groups need to be reflected in the personas you create:

- *Learning styles*—Is there a cultural preference for the way in which information is presented in the context of learning, for receiving information from an authority figure, for working with peers to learn something new, for working alone to figure things out, for using or avoiding help or instructions when learning a new system?

- *Reading patterns*—Is there a cultural expectation for the amount of information provided, for the type of visual support (if any), for the use of icons, or for a reading orientation from left to right, right to left, or top to bottom?

- *Trust*—What constitutes a trusting situation, and how can this situation be engendered? Are the users a risk-averse or a risk-taking culture? Are they open to new experiences or more comfortable with the familiar and known experience?

- *Relationship*—Is the need for relationship-building stronger than the need for efficiency in task completion? If establishing a relationship is an important precursor to speaking candidly with others, how is a relationship fostered with others? With the company? With the product?

- *"Face"*—When users make a mistake, who do they blame—themselves or the product? Will they expect the product to support them in a face-saving interaction? How will they express their feelings about the product to friends, family, co-workers, their employer? Do they risk shame or "losing face" if they are disappointed by the product? Can they express their frustration or disappointment candidly without a loss of "face" to themselves or to you?

Understanding cultural differences

You could spend a lifetime learning about other cultures—even one other culture—and it's a wonderful undertaking. But when time is of the essence and you want to jump in and learn what you can to prepare for international usability testing, help is available in the form of books and articles that address international and cultural dimensions of people and how they use products.

I've organized some excellent resources to give you the background information to begin your persona creation and to start planning for testing. The book's companion website has a list of resources on international usability testing for a wide variety of products. By far, the largest number of these is about the cultural influences on website design, since websites are the most obvious focus for design adaptation and international usability testing.

Books to learn more

A growing number of books are available that focus on international design and user research, including:

- *Handbook of Global User Research,* a collection of chapters written by and for user experience professionals, with chapters covering testing in 20 countries, edited by Robert M. Schumacher, 2010.

- *Usability and Internationalization of Information Technology,* a collection of chapters edited by Nuray Aykin, 2005.

- *The Culturally Customized Web Site: Customizing Web Sites for the Global Marketplace,* in which the authors, Mitish Singh and Arun Pereira, go well beyond the surface issues of localization to present true customization strategies for different cultures, 2005.

- *Beyond Borders: Web Globalization Strategies,* by John Yunker, which presents an overview of the issues with spotlights in every chapter on specific company strategies and solutions to going global, 2003.

Articles to learn more

www.mkp.com/testingessentials

This book's companion website also includes references and links to articles on specific issues relating to cultural differences in international users. To give you a sense of the topics and coverage in the articles,

some intriguing highlights are previewed starting on page 326. You
will notice that a disproportionately large number of the studies involve
Chinese users. You might wonder why that is. The sidebar that follows
should give you a sense of the answer.

If the world were a village of 100 people . . .

There would be

- 61 Asians (20 would be Chinese, 17 would be Indian)
- 14 Africans
- 11 Europeans
- 9 Latin Americans and South Americans
- 5 North Americans

Of these 100,

- 18 would not be able to read or write
- 33 would have cell phones
- 16 would be on the Internet
- 27 would be under 15 years old
- 7 would be over 64 years old
- there would be an equal number of males and females
- there would be 18 cars in the village
- by the end of the year, 1 villager would die and 2 children would
  be born, making the population climb to 101

The numbers keep changing, but they suggest where the focus of
international user research is, or should be, these days. Just follow
the numbers to Asia.

These numbers are from *www.
About.com*, August 5, 2007

Asia is of interest to Westerners in particular not just because the
world's population growth is there, with China and India now the
two most populous countries in the world, but also because, for

Westerners, Asians are the most "different" from us and therefore the most challenging to try to understand.

And Asia is a booming place for usability and user research. The Chinese have been hosting User Friendly, an annual conference on usability, since 2004, and their lineup of international speakers is testament to their desire to connect what they do to what is happening elsewhere in the world. China and India have well-established HCI communities that work to grow the profession and that conduct usability studies that expand the global reach of usability testing to include in-country experts.

For a wonderful insight into the Asian mind, I highly recommend Nisbett, The Geography of Thought: How Asians and Westerners Think Differently . . . and Why, 2003.

Internet shopping characteristics

See Mahmood, Bagchi, and Ford, 2004.

Cultural differences affect attitudes toward risk, which range from cultures that are risk averse to those with little concern for risk. One study compared several Western cultures for differences in attitudes toward risk in Internet shopping. This study looked at the impact of a culture's feeling of trust toward others as a basis for understanding the culture's willingness to trust a website. The researchers reported that country-specific levels of trust of others differ widely. The data are pretty fascinating:

- 5% of Peruvians trust each other
- 36% of people in the United States trust each other
- 44% of people from the United Kingdom trust each other
- 65% of Norwegians trust each other

See Barnes, Bauer, Neumann, and Huber, 2007.

Another study reported the results of a survey to determine attitudes toward risk for Internet shoppers from three countries: Germany, France, and the United States. The researchers organized the responses into three clusters:

- *Risk-averse doubters*—are critical of online shopping. This cluster, the smallest, is dominated by the French respondents (66.3%).

- *Open-minded online shoppers*—have the lowest perceived risk in shopping on the Internet. This cluster, the middle group, is dominated by U.S. respondents (44.5%).

- *Reserved information seekers*—are open to purchasing on the Internet, but they like to use the Internet first for information and comparison shopping. This cluster was the largest group and was dominated by German respondents (37.9%).

Knowing the potential impact of culture on trust can help designers address the needs of cultures in product development. A goal of international usability testing can be to determine whether the product, particularly when the product is a website, is seen as trustworthy by the users.

Information architecture

Cultural differences affect users' expectations for information architecture on websites. One study compared Chinese websites and American websites and found that the most striking difference was in the large number of content links on a Chinese portal page compared to a U.S. portal page. Figure 10.2 shows the Chinese portal page for a popular website, *www.sina.com.cn*.

See Rogers, 2008.

The study reported that most Chinese websites use a portal design like Yahoo! or MSN portals, regardless of whether the site is a portal or not. However, the design of the Chinese portal is more often 10 times longer than the comparable U.S. portal page design.

Another difference in the two designs is that the American portal will very likely be organized by categories with unique pages for each category, whereas the Chinese portal will put all of the information on a single page and in what appears to Americans as "a bewildering hodgepodge of categorized hyperlinks, with ad banners, large menus, and ad links interspersed with links to content."

Part of the reason for this design approach is that it addresses slow dial-up connections, still common among Chinese users. Once the page loads—which can take a minute or more—all links open in a new window and therefore open quickly. This design works for the Chinese user, who is accustomed to seeing a large amount of information on a

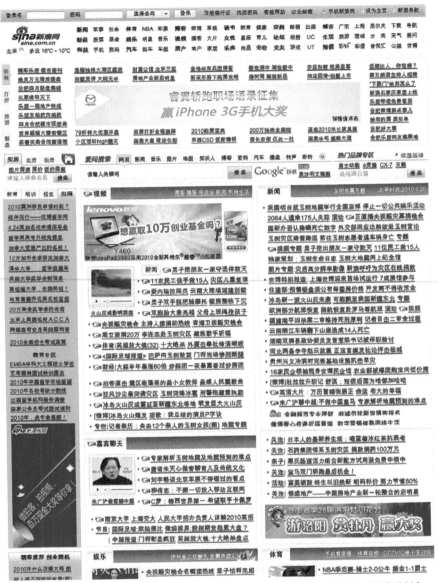

Figure 10.2 Part of the homepage for *www.sina.com.cn*, captured on April 27, 2010, shows a huge number of links.

page without having to use the search feature. And Chinese users are accustomed to browsing with multiple windows open simultaneously. According to Rogers, Chinese users prefer this arrangement and are not frustrated by this way of presenting information because they like having all of the information available to them at once. Chinese web designers cater to these preferences.

Another study looked at the impact of user experience based on the culture of the web designer. The study compared websites designed by Chinese and American designers with Chinese and American users. The results showed that users performed information-seeking tasks faster when the web content was created by designers from their own country. The authors conclude that the designers' cultural backgrounds influence their cognitive style in presenting the information on the website.

See Faiola and Matei, 2005.

Search patterns

Cultural differences in gaze patterns, as well as the amount of time spent on a search results page, are noted in eye-tracking studies of Chinese and Western users.

A study of Baidu (a popular Chinese search engine) versus Google showed that gaze patterns are markedly different for Chinese users of Baidu versus Chinese users of Google and even more different when compared with North American users' eye-tracking patterns with Google.

The study found that Chinese users of Baidu search the whole page down to the bottom, look at more results, modify their search queries more often, and spend much more total time on the Baidu results page than on the Google results page. (See Figure 10.3.)

The full report, by Tobin, Hotchkiss, and Lee, 2008, is available at www.enquiro.com/ whitepapers/pdf/chinese-search-engine-engagement.pdf

However, when Chinese users are on the Google site, they tend to conform to the "triangle" gaze pattern at the top left of the page, which shows the first several results in much the same pattern as North American users of Google. (See Figure 10.4.)

Technology adoption

Culturally based usage patterns affect new technology adoption. Studies examining technology adoption issues include:

- *German versus Indian users of washing machines,* emphasizing contextual/environmental differences, labeling/terminology issues, mental model differences, and differences in clothing.
- *The introduction of ATM machines in China* and Chinese attitudes and concerns affecting usage and adoption.

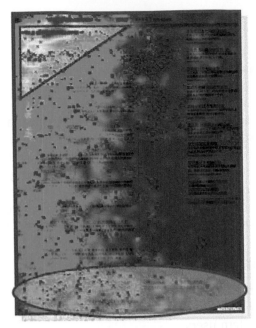

Aggregate Baidu
(showing clicks)

Figure 10.3 The heat map and mouse clicks shown here are from the Baidu search results page.

Aggregate Google
(showing clicks)

Figure 10.4 The heat map and mouse clicks shown here are from the Google search results page.

- *The introduction of a voice/video kiosk for Chinese migrant workers* with low literacy and low technology skills.

- *The design of advanced driver assistance software systems,* focusing on differences between Swedish and Chinese drivers.

- *Mobile interaction design* for low-literacy cultures in Africa.

- *Texting practices* and the cultural influences affecting how (and why) people use mobile messaging technology, including gender identity differences in use and preference.

- *Performance perceptions of MP3 players* influenced by cultural expectations of effectiveness and efficiency in design, comparing the perceptions of Taiwanese and North American users.

- *The design of e-learning courses* and the impact of culturally based expectations for teacher- or student-centered learning, collaborative or individual learning, cooperative or competitive learning environments, and other factors.

Applying the work of Hall and Hofstede to understand international users

You can't read much about international or intercultural usability without coming across references to either Hall or Hofstede. Edward T. Hall is best known for his introduction of the concept of high context and low context to describe differences among cultures. Geert Hofstede is best known for his analysis of cultural differences based on five cultural dimensions.

See *Beyond Culture,* Second Edition, 1989.

See *Cultures and Organizations:* Software of the Mind, Third Edition, 2010.

Hall's concept of high-context and low-context cultures

Hall's categorization of cultures places them on a continuum from high context to low context. In a nutshell, *high-context cultures* seek meaning from the unspoken signs and signals in the communication context. In contrast, *low-context cultures* seek meaning in the explicit words themselves. Although Hall doesn't provide a breakdown of countries to show where each sits on the continuum, he provides examples of countries, as shown in Figure 10.5.

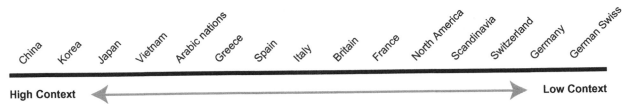

Figure 10.5 Hall provides some examples of countries from high context to low context.

As you can see, the high-context cultures cluster around Asian countries, and the low-context cultures cluster around North American and Northern European countries.

Hofstede's concept of five cultural dimensions

Hofstede studied national cultures within organizations using survey responses from IBM employees worldwide. This study resulted in his definition of the first four dimensions of culture. He later contracted research in Asia to add the fifth dimension for Asian countries. Here's a quick review of the five dimensions:

- *Power distance*—the extent to which the less powerful members of institutions and groups expect and accept that power is distributed unequally.

- *Individualism vs. collectivism*—the extent to which a culture values individual emphasis (achievement focus) versus collective/group welfare (affiliation focus).

- *Uncertainty avoidance*—the extent to which the culture's members feel threatened by uncertain, unknown situations or embrace these situations.

- *Masculinity vs. femininity*—the extent to which cultures value assertive (masculine) behavior versus modest (feminine) behavior.

- *Long-term vs. short-term orientation*—the extent to which cultures are influenced by Confucian philosophy. This dimension was added when Hofstede realized that the first four dimensions were European-centric. The Confucian philosophy defines the relation of individuals within the hierarchy of a family and social organizations and places a high value on hard work and education, and the need for patience and perseverance in waiting for rewards.

Hofstede positions the countries and regions of the world on a scale that roughly ranges from 0 to 100. The usefulness of the scale is not so much in the specific place of a country on the scale but in comparing the dimensions of a country or culture in relation to others.

For example, if we use Hofstede's scale (based on the numbers in the 2010 edition) to compare the dimensions of the United States and China, we see the following differences:

Cultural dimension*	United States	China
Power distance (104)	40	80
Individualism vs. collectivism (91)	91	20
Uncertainty avoidance (112)	46	30
Masculinity vs. femininity (110)	62	66
Long-term orientation (118)	29	118
*The number in parentheses after each dimension shows the highest possible value for that dimension.		

China scores high on power distance and extremely high on long-term orientation, relatively low on uncertainty avoidance, and extremely low on individualism. The U.S. scores place that country generally on the opposite end of the scale from China (with the exception of similar scores on masculinity). The most extreme differences are reflected in individualism—the United States has the highest score—and long-term orientation—China has the highest score.

So, how does this information help you understand the two cultures? Although any distinctions you can draw from the differences in these dimensions must be tested with real users, you can use this information as a benchmark to learn how your users respond on the basis of cultural distinctions such as these. You could test your current product to learn what the cultural issues are. Or you could redesign your product to address the potential cultural differences, then test to see whether your design matches users' expectations.

Not everyone is a fan of Hofstede's work or its application to interaction design. For insights into the issues some have expressed, see McSweeney, 2002, and Light, 2009.

For an analysis of websites applying Hofstede's cultural dimensions, see Aaron Marcus and Associates' report, "Cultural Dimensions and Global Web Design: What? So What? Now What?" 2001.

For instance, if you are designing or modifying a website for Chinese users, you might want to study the user's experience reflected in the following dimensions:

- *High power distance*—Is this dimension addressed through a focus on authority figures, certifications, expertise?
- *High collectivism/low individualism*—Is this dimension addressed through an emphasis on loyalty to customers and easy access to people who can answer questions and be available to help? Does the site properly focus on the greater good of society rather than the gains of the individual?
- *High uncertainty avoidance*—Is this dimension addressed through a clearly stated and easily located return policy and warranty information? Are users' needs met by the inclusion of customer reviews? Can users navigate the site with confidence because of links and labels that are clear and obvious? Can they avoid making mistakes? If they make a mistake, can they easily and obviously recover?
- *High long-term orientation*—Is this dimension addressed through a prominent display of information about the company's longevity and its success in building strong relationships with partners or customers?

For an example of how to apply Hofstede's cultural dimensions in designing or redesigning a website, see the case study analysis of the UPS website for Costa Rica at the end of this chapter.

Planning for international testing

Planning for international testing has many of the same requirements as planning for domestic testing. However, a number of important requirements are unique to international testing. These include:

Chapter 5 is all about the essentials of planning.

- where to test:
  - "there"—in the country where your users are
  - "here"—from your country, but connected to your users remotely
- how to organize the test planning:
  - on your own
  - with help from local resources
  - with local resources testing for you

- how to structure the test protocol:
  - localizing the scenarios
  - localizing the questionnaires
  - scheduling single-participant sessions or co-discovery sessions
  - choosing the think-aloud or retrospective recall method
- how to select the right person as moderator
- how to anticipate other aspects:
  - preparing for the prospect of participants arriving with others
  - needing more time for greeting and establishing rapport
  - needing more time between sessions
  - interpreting nonverbal communication cues

Some of these decisions may be made for you before you start planning an international usability study. Others may be dictated by budget or time considerations. Still others need to be anticipated so that surprises are minimized. For each decision, whether made for you or by you, it's important to consider the impact on the outcome.

Where to test

If you have a choice about where to conduct the testing, you will want to weigh the advantages and disadvantages of testing in the country where your users are or from your home base with a remote connection to the participants. Another possibility is that you don't conduct the testing but instead hire a local organization to do the testing for you. More is coming up about that later in this chapter. For the moment, let's set aside the option that you won't be doing the testing and focus on your options for testing with your users in their country or remotely from yours.

Testing "there," where your users are

Advantages of testing in the country where your users are include:

- If you speak the language of your participants, you can engage in dialogue with them before, during, and after testing. If you do not speak their language, this advantage disappears.
- If you're testing in a lab or a room reserved for testing, you can see a lot of people in a day in back-to-back testing sessions. Even

with cancellations, it is possible that backups can be scheduled quickly, since they can be recruited from a local pool of qualified participants who may be willing to be called on short notice.

- If you're testing in people's homes or offices, you get to learn about their environment.

  Figure 10.6 shows a Chinese man using a computer in his home. In the picture you can see that the desk is crowded with various objects—numerous eyeglasses, a watch, a card file stuffed with perhaps cards and correspondence, a mobile phone, a modem, speakers, and several other devices—and a laptop connected to a large monitor and a keyboard. Directly behind the man is an open lateral file drawer. He's not wearing glasses and he's not using the external keyboard, so perhaps he shares this computer and desk with someone else. Because a typical Chinese home is small and space is at a premium, this contextual insight can help shape the requirements for your product as well as your understanding of the effects of the environment on the usability of your product.

- You can increase your understanding of the culture by using your free time to explore the streets and parks, video arcades, and Internet cafés. This can be particularly important if you want to understand the context of use for your product "in the wild."

Figure 10.6 This photograph of a Chinese man using his computer at home tells us a lot about his environment.

Figure 10.7 shows young people playing video games in Shanghai, which can be critically important to understand if you are testing a video game.

Figure 10.7 This photograph of a computer center in Shanghai, China, shows a public arcade where people play video games.

Disadvantages of in-country testing include:

- The cost of travel and accommodations for one or more people.
- The jet-lag issues associated with crossing time zones. An extra day, at the very least, is needed to adjust to the time difference.
- The language barrier, if you do not speak the participants' language.
- The cultural barrier, if you are not able to acclimate to the culture in the short time in which you will be there.
- The logistics of the testing setup, which you may have to handle from afar. These could include locating and renting the space, securing the computers, and arranging for Internet connections, DVDs, and so forth. Again, if you are handling these arrangements yourself, you will probably need to arrive at least a day before testing begins to get everything ready.
- The testing arrangement itself, which may require that a team of foreigners sit in the room with the participant, making the situation potentially unnerving for the participant.

Testing from "here" to reach your users remotely

For more on remote testing, see Chapter 2.

Testing remotely, with you "here" and your participants "there," gives you the ability to learn about your users' experience from a diverse pool of users in a relatively short time. There are many decisions to make about how to set up and conduct international usability testing remotely. And, as with most things, there are advantages and disadvantages to testing from afar.

Advantages of testing remotely include:

- You can test people from many different countries so that a single study can get a wide diversity of participant responses.
- You can schedule testing at different times to accommodate participants' availability and time zone differences. With this flexibility, and if your schedule permits, you could conduct fewer tests per day, testing over a period of days while making changes to the product as you continue to test remotely.
- If your participants are testing in their home or office environment and you are using conferencing software, you can see what programs are installed on the participant's computer. If the participant has a webcam, you can begin the session by seeing both the participant and his or her workspace.
- You can connect a number of observers to the test session from one location or many locations. There is little or no cost associated with having a lot of observers, and the result is that more people get to see the session and learn from the users, with the added advantage of not disturbing or distracting a user by their presence.

Disadvantages of testing remotely include:

- You may have to test at very odd hours, including the middle of the night, to be able to accommodate time-zone issues and the availability of your participants.
- You generally cannot record the participant's body language, just his or her voice and interactions with the interface. So you miss the nonverbal communication cues and the quick adjustments that can be made when you see a user struggle or become frustrated.
- You may experience firewall issues, Internet connection issues, and other technical problems that prevent the session from being held.

You will have much more difficulty controlling these in advance, no matter how well you plan.

- If the participant is speaking by phone, he or she may not have a speakerphone and will therefore be trying to speak to you and think out loud while holding the phone receiver and working with the product, which may be awkward or impossible.

- It's harder to "train" participants on thinking out loud when you're not there to help.

- If your participants do not speak English, you will have to work with an interpreter, which makes the business of listening to the interpreter, in addition to observing the participant, doubly challenging.

For more about working with an interpreter, see the following sidebar.

Working with an interpreter

There are many reasons to need and want to work with an interpreter. First off, you need to consider the *preferred* language of your participants. Even if they can speak your language, there can be considerable advantages in having them work in their dominant language:

- They are generally more comfortable in their dominant language.
- Their ability to concentrate on the tasks they will be doing with your product will be enhanced when they can speak in their dominant language.

When working with an interpreter, you need to work out the logistics of how the translation will be done. Some options to consider are these:

- Where will the interpreter be in relation to the participant—in the same room or somewhere else?
- Will the interpreter be doing a simultaneous translation or will the translation come later in a transcript or audio voiceover on the recordings of the sessions?
- If the moderator has dual-language capabilities, will that person also be the interpreter? If so, how often will the moderator stop and explain what the participant is doing, and what effect will

this have on the session in terms of continuity within scenarios and the session length?

- If you are the moderator, how will the process work to allow for the interpreter to translate your statements for the participant? And how will the interpreter translate comments from the participant?

- If the logistics of stopping frequently during the session to allow for translation are too difficult to manage, you might decide that the interpreter will take notes and review them with you after the sessions. Or you can review the recordings with the interpreter after the sessions.

How to test

Are you going to do the testing yourself? If so, will you be testing in your language or in another language? Are you going to subcontract with a local vendor to assist you in testing? Or are you going to contract with a local vendor to do all the activities associated with in-country testing? As with the decisions you made about where to test, each of these options presents advantages and disadvantages.

Conducting testing yourself

If you speak the language of the country where you will be testing, you may be able to conduct the testing yourself. This approach works best when you have contacts in the country who can handle some of the logistics, such as recruiting participants, renting space, and buying the needed supplies. If your company has offices in different countries, this simplifies matters because you can very likely use your own company's space and support to set up and conduct the testing. If you don't have a company location or in-country contacts helping you get ready, you will be at a disadvantage and it will make the planning and arrangements more time consuming.

If you're recruiting the participants yourself, you will need to confirm their participation and do the follow-up work to get them to the testing facility, and you will need to purchase the appropriate gift or provide the appropriate honorarium. This topic, on its own, is fraught with potential pitfalls, since gifts and rewards are highly culturally specific. You will need to do your homework to be sure you are providing the appropriate compensation for participation.

Testing with help from local resources

Without company connections to help you plan and conduct a usability study, you will very likely want to get help from local resources. There are a lot of reasons to work with a local vendor, not the least of which is the vendor's knowledge of the country, the culture, and the conditions under which you will be testing. Local resources can be hired for parts of test preparation, such as participant recruiting, or they can partner with you on planning and conducting the testing, such as providing a moderator and helping you create a script that is culturally appropriate.

When you subcontract with a local vendor, you will need to communicate effectively about what you want. If the vendor is recruiting the participants, you will want to review the recruiting script. If the vendor is providing the moderator's script, you will want to review it. If you're providing the moderator's script, you will want the vendor to review it to be sure it is culturally appropriate. And if you don't speak the language, all the documents will need to be translated.

Hiring a local vendor for the testing

If the logistical challenges of testing on your own in another country or subcontracting with a local vendor for part of the testing prove too daunting, you should consider the option of hiring a local vendor for everything. If the vendor is large enough to provide resources for all the countries in which you will be testing, you could simplify the process by hiring one vendor. If this isn't feasible, you could hire a local vendor for each country in which you will be testing.

Finding a local vendor for in-country testing may require a longer lead time than you would normally need for testing yourself, particularly if you have to locate different vendors in different countries. The trade-off for this additional lead time is that you get a "turnkey" operation, where the local vendor does the participant recruiting, the testing, and the translation of results. In choosing a vendor for everything, it's important to select one that has both translation and usability testing experience. This dual experience will make your communication back and forth much more effective, allowing you to focus on your specific goals for the study.

Structuring the test protocol

It's often the case in testing internationally that you want to compare the experience of international users with domestic users. This type of comparative evaluation typically invokes reuse of a test protocol created for domestic usability testing. Comparative evaluation is certainly valuable, but to do it well, you need to localize the test protocol to make sure that the elements of the test are presented in appropriate ways to match cultural expectations.

Localizing the scenarios

Although it is common practice to use scenarios in testing, you may need to modify the approach to suit the cultural context of your users. If you're testing in a task-driven culture that is comfortable performing tasks and is goal-driven to do so, the types of scenarios you create for domestic testing will likely work as well in your international context. However, the details that make the scenario come alive will very likely need to be changed to fit into the context of the participants' experience. If you're testing in an affiliation culture, where the task goals need to be stated in terms of what will benefit others or provide support for community-focused goals, the scenarios may need more drastic revision.

Localizing to match usage patterns

See Liu, Coventry, Johnson, Zhang, and Chen, 2007.

If the tasks will be done in a culturally specific context, you will need to customize your scenarios to fit local usage patterns. One research study shows how far you might need to go. In testing the introduction of automated teller machines (ATMs) in China, the usability testing team found that Chinese users do not withdraw cash in the same way that Westerners typically do. Whereas Western users might stop by an ATM frequently to withdraw enough money for a day or a weekend or an event, Chinese users prefer to take out all of their salary for a month. ATMs that restrict the amount that can be withdrawn are not effectively designed for these users. Scenarios in which participants are asked to withdraw a small amount of money might not feel realistic to Chinese participants.

Localizing for a different frame of reference

In some cultures, localizing the scenarios may require that you contextualize them in a completely different frame of reference.

In testing conducted in India, Human Factors International (HFI), an international usability consulting company with an office in Mumbai, uncovered the fact that the typical scenario technique did not result in the desired outcome. Participants seemed undermotivated and unresponsive to the tasks they were given. So, the test team devised a strategy called the *Bollywood method* (Bollywood is India's Hollywood), which put the tasks into the context of a complicated movie plot with dire consequences if the information was not provided in time to rescue the person in distress. With this approach to presenting the problem, the participants became much more engaged in pursuit of the solution and grew much more verbal about the problems they encountered in trying to reach their goal.

See *www.humanfactors.com/ services/crossculturaldesign.asp*

Localizing the questionnaires

In addition to shaping scenarios to suit the cultural context, you will also want to review the types of questions you ask and be attuned to the way in which culture influences responses. Face-saving cultures may be acculturated to avoid giving negative feedback because this avoidance saves face for both the participant and the moderator. As a result, post-task questionnaire responses may be even more positive than responses you get from participants in your domestic studies.

Several studies involving testing with international or non-native English speakers shed light on the challenges of localizing questionnaires.

Vocabulary concerns

One study looks at non-native English speakers in the United States and the difficulty they have with one statement from the System Usability Scale (SUS) questionnaire. The difficult word is *cumbersome,* which

See Finstad, 2006.

I have found that the word *cumbersome* also causes problems for lower-literacy native English speakers, so I am always prepared to explain that it means *awkward*.

appears in Statement 8: "I found the system very cumbersome to use." If a more commonly understood word, such as *awkward*, is substituted, the statement is more easily understood.

Since this single word in a widely used questionnaire causes problems for non-native English speakers, it points up the necessity and the challenge of creating localized questions for international testing.

Preferences for questions about others

See Anderson, 2008.

In a usability study of Latino users of the Spanish version of a bank's website, Cliff Anderson, a well-known usability practitioner, reported that Latino users were uncomfortable answering questions about their own experiences but were quite comfortable speaking for others. Localizing questions to reflect this cultural preference, he found that if he asked whether others in the community would be likely to use the product, the responses were more revealing.

Preferences for response-scale displays

See Chavan, 2007.

Another discovery HFI made when testing with Indian users is that they did not understand the semantic differential scale, which shows a range of possible responses to a question or statement. In typical use of this scale, the options are presented along a horizontal line, as shown in Figure 10.8.

HFI found that Indian participants—particularly those with low-level socioeconomic status—tended to pick one end or the other of the scale and nothing in between. The test team felt that the choice the participant made did not correspond to the user's experience. They

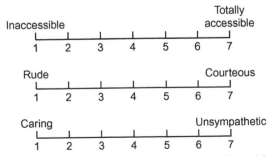

Figure 10.8 A semantic differential scale like this one is typically used for questionnaire responses.

concluded that it was the presentation of the scale as a horizontal line that caused problems for the participants, because they could not pick from a scale that presented everything on the same plane. So the team redesigned the representation of the scale to make it a radio volume control knob with the numbers representing low to high volume on the knob, as shown in Figure 10.9. This representation allowed the participants to choose low to high responses to post-test questionnaires, which resulted in scores that were more reflective of their experience.

Figure 10.9 A visual representation of the response ratings scale as a radio volume control knob produced better results in an Indian usability study.

Preferences for what makes something usable

Another cultural consideration is being able to understand what's important to users when it comes to their assessment of usability. One study showed that culture affects the weight of factors determining usability. In this study, Chinese and Danish participants responded to the same post-test questionnaires, but they valued usability factors differently. The Chinese respondents found "satisfaction" far more important in its impact on usability than the Danish respondents. "Fun" was also considered more important for the Chinese than the Danish respondents.

See Frandsen-Thorlacius, Hornbaek, Hertzum, and Clemmensen, 2009.

In contrast, "nonfrustration" and "effectiveness" were significantly more important to Danish respondents than to Chinese respondents. The takeaway from this finding is that you cannot assume that all cultures value the same aspects of usability equally.

In doing post-test questionnaires, you will need to analyze responses within the cultural context of the participants, then compare them between cultures for insights.

Scheduling single sessions or co-discovery sessions

For more about co-discovery, see Chapter 7.

While it is generally the norm in U.S./Western testing to invite one participant at a time to evaluate a product and provide feedback, there are situations in which co-discovery—testing with two people—is the preferred method. In certain international contexts, this method might be much more common, particularly in a collectivist culture, as is the case with most Asian cultures. For example, if it would make participants more comfortable while using a product to talk to a friend rather than to a moderator, the co-discovery approach will likely yield better insights. However, if it would be inappropriate for an employee to work with a supervisor during a study, you will want to match participants in co-discovery in such a way as to avoid issues of status differences.

Choosing think-aloud or retrospective recall

If the participant is a non-native English speaker, it might be a burden to ask him or her to think out loud as he or she is working with the product. Or it may make the participant too self-conscious to think out loud while working, particularly in a collectivist culture where speaking one's independent thoughts may not be encouraged in a setting outside the home. Even in co-discovery, the participants may be much more inclined to speak to each other about what they are doing, not about what they are reacting to or responding to, positively or negatively. In these situations, retrospective recall, in which the participant or participants review the recording of the session and share their reactions, would be more likely to produce better insights.

For more about this finding, see Hall, de Jong, and Steehouder, 2004, and Shi and Clemmensen, 2008.

Selecting the moderator

Chapter 7 tells you all about being an effective moderator.

Putting all other considerations aside, the most important factor in conducting an effective usability study is the role of the moderator. Aside from the usual guidelines about how to be an effective moderator, in international testing you have the additional fundamental question about whether you should be the moderator or turn that job over to a native.

In any testing situation, the hardest challenge for the moderator is to keep a neutral stance and avoid biasing the participant in any way. In an international study, this challenge is increased by considerations that are beyond the moderator's control. They can come down to considerations of

- ethnicity
- age
- gender
- status

It's very likely that your ethnicity will be different from that of the country/culture where you are conducting usability testing. This fact may make your participants uncomfortable or perhaps uncommunicative for reasons beyond your control.

The same is true for your age, your gender, and your status as an outside expert. If you are obviously either older or younger than the participants, this can cause problems for them in the testing environment. Older moderators may be seen as too dignified to hear of problems expressed by the participant; younger moderators may be seen as too inexperienced to receive such information.

Gender has its own set of complications. If you are male and the participant is female, or the opposite, this difference can cause problems. On the one hand, female participants may not feel comfortable speaking candidly to male moderators. On the other hand, male participants may not trust the authority of female moderators. If the culture in which you are testing does not make such exchanges common among strangers, you inadvertantly will affect the outcome of the test by nothing more than your gender.

Likewise, if you are viewed as an outside expert or authority (a position of high status), participants in cultures that accept unequal status differences (Hofstede's cultural dimension of power distance) may not feel comfortable being critical of the product. One study of the cultural impact of the moderator on the results showed that when Indian participants had Indian moderators, they found more usability problems and made more suggestions for improvements than those in the control group with an Anglo-American moderator.

See Vatrapu and Pérez-Quiñones, 2006.

This finding is more likely to occur in collectivist cultures where a bond of shared culture fosters greater comfort and ease than would perhaps be the case in Western, individualistic cultures where the individual's pursuit of the goal is less likely to be influenced by the characteristics of the moderator.

Weighing all of these factors, you will want to consider whether you can accomplish your goals in testing if you assume the moderator duties. In situations where you may adversely affect the outcome—for no other reason than that of being "different"—you will most likely want to hire a local moderator and then work with that person to communicate your goals.

Anticipating other aspects of international testing

There is always a lot to consider in setting up any usability study. But when you're testing in an international context, there's even more to consider. Among the aspects requiring special consideration are these:

- What if the participant arrives with someone else?
- Does the time for preliminary greetings need to be extended?
- Do the breaks between sessions need to be longer to allow for cultural variability in participants' adherence to time commitments?
- Do you know how to interpret nonverbal communication cues?

What if the participant arrives with someone else?

Aside from deciding on the condition of testing with one at a time or two at a time, you will also need to decide how you will handle situations in which the participant arrives with someone else. Perhaps the other person is a child or a spouse, parent, friend, co-worker, or supervisor.

You may think your response should be to bar anyone else from the testing session, but the cultural context may require that you rethink this view. If the person is required to have a "chaperone," as might be the case with a female who must have a friend, her husband, or supervisor present, you will need to accommodate this situation, even if it means that the other person introduces potential bias into the situation.

If the participant has a child in tow, it may be expected that you will accommodate the needs of the child. So, you will need to prepare for this accommodation or allow the participant to have the child present during the test.

You may want to set up a waiting room for the friend, family member, or supervisor to use while you are testing. In this case, you need to think about refreshments, magazines, or other forms of entertainment that would be appropriate for the person who is asked to wait. If your testing facility does not provide space for a waiting room, then you will have to have a Plan B, in which you provide a way to accommodate the presence of another person during testing.

Another possible consideration for accommodating someone else is in the context of double-booking participants to ensure that you have at least one person for each testing session. This requirement to double-book may be most appropriate if you are testing in a high power-distance culture such as India. In such a culture, potential participants may agree to participate in deference to the direct request from a high-status person, but then fail to appear. According to one study conducted in India, this tendency results in Indian participation rates as low as 0%. So, continuous and multiple participant booking may be necessary. In the case where more than one participant shows up, you need to decide how to handle the situation.

See Beaton and Kumar, 2010.

Should more time be set aside for meeting and greeting?

If you're accustomed to a few minutes of chit-chat as you are greeting the participant and then immediately getting down to business, you may need to extend the time and effort for meeting and greeting your participants to allow for the cultural expectations of socializing before business gets underway. Cliff Anderson reports on learning this about U.S. Latino users in a usability study of a bank's Spanish-language subsite of its website. Not only did the test protocol need to allow more time for social pleasantries, but Cliff wondered whether this need to establish rapport would make remote testing inappropriate.

Should breaks be longer between sessions?

Some cultures view schedules as strict commitments. Others place a higher priority on the relationships and interactions taking place at the

See *Beyond Culture,* 1989.

moment. Edward Hall studied these culture-based relationships to time, dividing cultures into two groups according to their orientation to time:

- *Monochronic (M-time) cultures*—emphasize schedules, segmentation of a day into discrete blocks of time, and promptness.
- *Polychronic (P-time) cultures*—emphasize the involvement of people and completion of transactions rather than strict adherence to a set schedule.

As an example, North American cultures tend to be M-time cultures; Latin American cultures tend to be P-time cultures. If you are testing in a P-time culture, you should be prepared for possible delays because someone got held up in another activity. Within reason, you can accommodate these delays if you plan extra time between sessions.

Can you interpret nonverbal communication cues?

Whenever you are observing a test and reporting on the results, you want to consider the potential cultural differences in interpreting nonverbal communication cues. Gestures, head nodding, eye contact, and other aspects of body language all signal responses that can be readily misunderstood if you don't know how to read the signs.

See Yammiyavar, Clemmensen, and Kumar, 2008.

One study compared nonverbal communication differences in usability testing between Indian, Chinese, and Danish participants and found that hand and head gestures differed among the cultural groups. Although the frequency of gestures did not vary among the three cultures, the type of gesture was different, particularly when it preceded a usability problem. Thus, being attuned to these gestures can help you understand the presence of usability problems experienced by the participants. It may not be possible for you to decode these nonverbal communication cues entirely on your own. This is another reason to get assistance from a local person, either as an observer or an interpreter for your studies.

In situations where you cannot understand the language of the study and you do not have simultaneous translation, you can focus entirely on the nonverbal communication cues from the participant and between the participant and the moderator. Think of it like turning off the sound on the television and just focusing on what you observe. This level of concentration can be extremely interesting, particularly if you take notes and use these notes to ask questions when you get the translation or the report of the study.

Summarizing Chapter 10

This chapter exposed you to the special considerations associated with international usability testing. Although the basics of testing are generally the same no matter where testing takes place, testing with international users requires that you make adjustments to suit the norms and expectations of the culture. These include:

- Creating personas that reflect the users from the country and culture in which you will be testing.

- Adjusting your lens of understanding to account for cultural differences, which you can do by:

  - Consulting the growing body of research that focuses on international usability testing. The book's companion website has a list of resources and references to help you get up to speed.

  - Reading up on the work of Edward Hall and Geert Hofstede, the two most widely cited resources on cultural influences affecting human behavior.

- Planning the test for the international context and users, including making decisions about:

  - where you should be—in country or remote

  - how you should organize the testing—assessing your capability to do the testing on your own, or with help from a local vendor, or farmed out entirely to a local vendor

- Structuring the test protocol, considering the need to:

  - localize the scenarios

  - localize the questionnaires

  - conduct single sessions or co-discovery

  - use think-aloud or retrospective recall

- Choosing the right moderator.

- Anticipating other factors, such as:

  - preparing for the arrival of friends, family, or a supervisor with the participant

www.mkp.com/testingessentials

○ setting aside appropriate time for welcome

○ allowing for extra time between sessions

○ understanding how to interpret nonverbal communication cues

That's a lot to consider. But this chapter has given you the basics to plan, prepare, and conduct an international test. And I have provided you with resources to show you what others are doing and learning about international usability testing.

When you are presented with the chance to conduct testing to understand international users and their experience with your product, embrace it. One of the unending joys of usability testing is that it always provides you with the opportunity to learn *from* your users while you are learning *about* your users. That's what keeps usability testing so exciting!

This case study is an analysis of the Costa Rican website for UPS, based on the application of Hofstede's cultural dimensions and a comparison of the UPS site with other shipping websites. This study includes an analysis of the target user from a cultural perspective and presents designs for several pages to show how the cultural dimensions discussed in the report could be applied to a redesigned website that would be more suitable for the Costa Rican user. The executive summary is here. The full report is on this book's companion website at *www.mkp.com/ testingessentials*

One Culture's Impact on Design: Redesigning the Costa Rican UPS Website

Prepared by Rachel Peters

Executive Summary

From a marketing-strategic perspective, a company that defines itself as cross-culturally aware knows (or should know) that creating appealing and efficient websites for other cultures is no longer just a matter of language and modification of time- and date-formats.

—Wurtz, 2005

Costa Rica is a high-context, collectivist culture with high uncertainty avoidance. Many Costa Rican sites emphasize nature, people, and government. A website designed for them should focus on the following:

- Clarity and predictability
- Cooperation and feminine characteristics
- Government authority and regulations, where applicable
- Nature and family

The UPS site for Costa Rica is well designed, but details were overlooked that could greatly improve the site. In this report, I review three pages: Home, Tracking, and Support. I suggest redesign options for each that will help to declutter content, place the focus where it belongs, and emphasize values important to Costa Rican users. When viewing and redesigning the current UPS pages, I considered the following questions:

- *Does the information hierarchy always highlight what's most important?* This design element is crucial for a high uncertainty-avoidance culture.

- *Do the images and animation focus on nature? On cooperation? And on feminine aspects?* These subtle details speak to the audience along cultural lines. For example, users may not explicitly state that they want to see images of nature, but research shows that they are drawn to it. Any design efforts should focus on incorporating values considered important by the target culture.

- *Is the page overwhelming?* Good design calls for creating pages that display information in a visually pleasing manner. Adequate use of whitespace, alignment, font style, and more all prevent a page from looking cluttered—even when a lot of content is present.

- *Can users guess what happens next?* Controls, links, videos, drop-downs—everything must be predictable. Users must have a good idea about what will happen when they click something on the page.

Screen shots are provided of the original pages and the suggested redesigns. The changes respect the corporate template employed by UPS, while offering a more culturally sensitive design. Culture is in design, and design is in the details. Understanding a culture's impact on design and its importance in reaching out to a global audience is essential to success in today's market.

References

Aaron Marcus and Associates. (2001). *Cultural dimensions and global web design: What? So what? Now what?* Retrieved from http://www.amanda.com/resources/hfweb2000/AMA_CultDim.pdf

Adlin, T., & Pruitt, J. (2010). *The essential persona lifecycle: Your guide to building and using personas.* Boston, MA: Morgan Kaufmann.

Albert, W., Tullis, T., & Tedesco, D. (2010). *Beyond the usability lab: Conducting large-scale online user experience studies.* Boston, MA: Morgan Kaufmann.

Anderson, C. (2008). ¿Habla Español? Testing and designing for U.S. Latino users. *User Experience, 7*(1), 25–28. Retrieved from http://www.upassoc.org/upa_publications/user_experience/past_issues/2008-1.html

Arar, Y. (2008, June 2). Most returned products work fine, study says. *PC World.* Retrieved from http://www.pcworld.com/article/146576/most_returned_products_work_fi ne_study_says.html

Aykin, N. (2005). *Usability and internationalization of information technology.* Mahwah, NJ: Lawrence Erlbaum.

Barnes, S. J., Bauer, H. H., Neumann, M. M., & Huber, F. (2007). Segmenting cyberspace: A customer typology of the Internet. *European Journal of Marketing, 41*(1–2), 71–93.

Barnum, C. M. (2002–3). The "magic number 5": Is it enough for web testing? *Information Design Journal, 11*(2–3), 160–170.

Beaton, J., & Kumar, R. (2010). Indian cultural effects on user research methodologies. *Proceedings of CHI 2010: Work-in-Progress.* Atlanta, GA: ACM.

Benedek, J., & Miner, T. (2002). Measuring desirability: New methods for evaluating desirability in a usability lab setting. Presentation at the Usability Professionals' Association Conference, Orlando, FL. Retrieved from http://www.microsoft.com/usability/UEPostings/DesirabilityToolkit.doc

Berkun, S. (2009). *Confessions of a public speaker*. Sebastopol, CA: O' Reilly Media.

Berry, D. C., & Broadbent, D. E. (1990). The role of instruction and verbalization in improving performance on complex search tasks. *Behaviour & Information Technology*, *9*, 175–190.

Beyer, H., & Holtzblatt, K. (1998). *Contextual design: Defining customer-centered systems*. Boston, MA: Morgan Kaufmann.

Bias, R. D., & Mayhew, D. J. (Eds.). (1994). *Cost-justifying usability*. Boston, MA: Academic Press.

Bias, R. J., & Mayhew, D. J. (Eds.). (2005). *Cost-justifying usability: An update for an Internet age* (2nd ed.). Boston, MA: Morgan Kaufmann.

Bolt, N., & Tulathimutte, T. (2010). *Remote research: Real users, real time, real research*. Brooklyn, NY: Rosenfeld Media.

Bowers, V., & Snyder, H. (1990). Concurrent versus retrospective verbal protocols for comparing window usability. *Proceedings of the Human Factors Society 34th Annual Meeting* (pp. 1270–1274). Santa Monica, CA: Human Factors and Ergonomics Society.

Chavan, A. L. (2007, October 11). *Around the world with 14 methods: Innovation and culture*. Human Factors International (white paper). Retrieved from http://www.humanfactors.com

Chisnell, D. E., Redish, J., & Lee, A. (2006). New heuristics for understanding older adults as web users. *Technical Communication*, *53*(1), 39–59.

Consumer Reports' Webwatch (2002). *How do people evaluate a web site's credibility? Results from a large study*. Retrieved from http://www.consumerwebwatch.org

Cooper, A. (1999). *The inmates are running the asylum*. Indianapolis, IN: SAMS.

Courage, C., & Baxter, K. (2005). *Understanding your users: A practical guide to user requirements methods, tools, & techniques*. Boston, MA: Morgan Kaufmann.

Dumas, J., & Loring, B. (2008). *Moderating usability tests: Principles and practices for interacting*. Boston, MA: Morgan Kaufmann.

Dumas, J. S., & Redish, J. C. (1999). *A practical guide to usability testing* (revised 2nd ed.). Portland, OR: Intellect.

Ericsson, E. K., & Simon, H. A. (1993). *Protocol analysis: Verbal report as data*. Cambridge, MA: MIT Press.

Faiola, A., & Matei, S. A. (2005). Cultural cognitive style and web design: Beyond a behavioral inquiry into computer-mediated communication. *Journal of Computer-Mediated Communication, 11*(1, article 18). Retrieved from http://jcmc.indiana.edu/vol11/issue1/faiola.html

Fink, A. (2008). *How to conduct surveys: A step-by-step guide*. Thousand Oaks, CA: Sage.

Finstad, K. (2006, August). The System Usability Scale and non-native English speakers. *Journal of Usability Studies, 1*(4), 185–188. Retrieved from http://www.upassoc.org/upa_publications/jus/jus_home.html

Frandsen-Thorlacius, O., Hornbaek, K., Hertzum, M., & Clemmensen, T. (2009). Non-universal usability? A survey of how usability is understood by Chinese and Danish users. *Proceedings of CHI 2009* (pp. 41–50). Boston, MA: ACM.

Gray, W. D., & Salzman, M. C. (1998). Damaged merchandise? A review of experiments that compare usability evaluation methods. *Human-Computer Interaction, 13*(3), 203–261.

Hackos, J. T., & Redish, J. C. (1998). *User and task analysis for interface design*. New York, NY: Wiley.

Hall, E. T. (1989). *Beyond culture* (2nd ed.). New York, NY: Anchor Books.

Hall, M., de Jong, M., & Steehouder, M. (2004, November). Cultural differences and usability evaluation: Individualistic and collectivistic participants compared. *Technical Communication, 51*(4), 489–503.

Henry, S. L. (2007). *Just ask: Integrating accessibility throughout design*. Lulu.com. Retrieved from http://www.uiAccess.com/JustAsk

Henry, S. L., & Arch, A. M. J. (Eds.). (2009, June). *Developing a web accessibility business case for your organization*. World Wide Web Consortium (MIT, ERCIM, Keio). Retrieved from http://www.w3.org/WAI/ bcase/

Hofstede, G., Hofstede, G. J., & Minkov, M. (2010). *Cultures and organizations: Software of the mind* (revised 3rd ed.). New York, NY: McGraw-Hill.

Howarth, J., Andre, T. S., & Hartson, R. (2007, November). A structured process for transforming usability data into usability information. *Journal of Usability Studies, 3*(1), 7–23. Retrieved from http://www.upassoc.org/upa_publications/jus/ jus_home.html

Huff, D. (1954). *How to lie with statistics*. New York, NY: Norton.

Information Behaviour of the Researcher of the Future. (2008, January 11). CIBER (Centre for Information Behaviour and the Evaluation of Research). London: University College Briefing paper. Retrieved from http://www.jisc.ac.uk/media/documents/programmes/reppres/gg_final_keynote_11012008.pdf

Jacobsen, N. E., Hertzum, M., & John, B. E. (1998). The evaluator effect in usability studies: Problem detection and severity judgments. *Proceedings of the Human Factors and Ergonomics Society 42nd Annual Meeting* (pp. 1336–1340). Santa Monica, CA.

Jones, S., & Fox, S. (2009, January). *Generations online in 2009.* Pew Internet & American Life Project. Retrieved from http://www.pewinternet.org/Reports/2009/Generations-Online-in-2009.aspx

Kuniavsky, M. (2003). *Observing the user experience: A practitioner's guide to user research.* Boston, MA: Morgan Kaufmann.

Landauer, T. (1997). Behavioral research methods in human-computer interaction. In M. Helander, T. K. Landauer, & P. Prabhu (Eds.), *Handbook of computer interaction* (2nd ed.) (pp. 203–228). Amsterdam, The Netherlands: Elsevier.

Lewis, J. R. (1995). IBM computer usability satisfaction questionnaires. Psychometric evaluation and instructions for use. *International Journal of Human-Computer Interaction, 7*(1), 57–78.

Lewis, J. R., & Sauro, J. (2009). The factor structure of the System Usability Scale. *Proceedings of the Human Computer Interaction International Conference,* San Diego, CA. Retrieved from http://www.measuringusability.com/papers/Lewis_Sauro_HCII2009.pdf

Light, A. (2009, January 19). Designing for other cultures: Putting Hofstede to bed. *Flow Interactive: The Think Blog.* Retrieved from http://www.thinkflowinteractive.com/2009/01/14/designing-for-other-cultures-putting-hofstede-to-bed/

Liu, Z., Coventry, L., Johnson, G., Zhang, H., & Chen, J. (2007). The people's money machines: Automatic teller machines in China. *User Experience, 6*(2), 18–22. Retrieved from http://www.upassoc.org/upa_publications/user_experience/past_issues/2007-2.html

Mahmood, M. A., Bagchi, K., & Ford, T. C. (2004, Fall). On-line shopping behavior: Cross-country empirical research. *International Journal of Electronic Commerce, 9*(1), 9–30.

McLuhan, M. (1964). *Understanding media: The extensions of man.* New York, NY: McGraw-Hill.

McSweeney, B. (2002, January). Hofstede's model of national cultural differences and their consequences: A triumph of faith—a failure of analysis. *Human Relations, 55*(1), 89–118.

Medlock, M. C., Wixon, D., McGee, M., & Welsh, D. (2006). The rapid iterative test and evaluation method: Better products in less time. In R. J. Bias & D. J. Mayhew (Eds.), *Cost-justifying usability: An update for an Internet age* (2nd ed.) (pp. 489–517). Boston, MA: Morgan Kaufmann.

Molich, R. (1999). CUE-2 (Comparative Usability Evaluation). Retrieved from http://www.dialogdesign.dk/cue.html

Molich, R., & Dumas, J. S. (2008). Comparative usability evaluation (CUE-4). *Behaviour & Information Technology, 27*(3), 263–281.

Molich, R., & Nielsen, J. (1990). Improving a human-computer dialogue. *Communications of the ACM, 33*(3), 338–348.

Morville, P. (2004, June 21). The user experience honeycomb. *User Experience Design*. Retrieved from http://semanticstudios.com/publications/semantics/000029.php

Morville, P., & Rosenfeld, L. (2006). *Information architecture for the world wide web: Designing large-scale web sites* (3rd ed.). Sebastopol, CA: O'Reilly Media.

Mulder, S., & Yaar, Z. (2006). *The user is always right: A practical guide to creating and using personas for the web*. Berkeley, CA: New Riders.

Nielsen, J. (1993). *Usability engineering*. Boston, MA: Morgan Kaufmann.

Nielsen, J. (2000, March 19). Why you only need to test with 5 users. *Alertbox*. Retrieved from http://www.useit.com/alertbox/20000319.html

Nielsen, J. (2002, April 12). Kids' corner: Website usability for children. *Alertbox*. Retrieved from http://www.useit.com/alertbox/children.html

Nielsen, J. (2006, April 17). F-shaped pattern for reading web content. *Alertbox*. Retrieved from http://www.useit.com/alertbox/reading_pattern.html

Nielsen, J. (2008, February 4). User skills improving, but only slightly. *Alertbox*. Retrieved from http://www.useit.com/alertbox/user-skills.html

Nielsen, J., & Mack, R. L. (Eds.). (1994). *Usability inspection methods*. New York, NY: Wiley.

Nielsen, J., & Pernice, K. (2010). *Eyetracking web usability*. Berkeley, CA: New Riders.

Nisbett, R. E. (2003). *The geography of thought: How Asians and Westerners think differently … and why*. New York, NY: Free Press.

Olmsted-Hawala, E. L., Hawala, S., Murphy, E. D., & Ashenfelter, K. T. (2010). Think-aloud protocols: A comparison of three think-aloud protocols for use in testing data-dissemination web sites for usability. *Proceedings of CHI 2010* (pp. 2381–2390). Atlanta, GA.

Pawson, M., & Greenberg, S. (2009, May). Extremely rapid usability testing. *Journal of Usability Studies*, *4*(3), 124–135. Retrieved from http://www.upassoc.org/upa_publications/jus/jus_home.html

Peracchio, L., & Luna, D. (2006). The role of thin-slice judgments in consumer psychology. *Journal of Consumer Psychology*, *16*(1), 25–32.

Quesenbery, W. (n.d.). Getting started: Using the 5Es to understand users. Retrieved from http://www.wqusability.com

Quesenbery, W. (2006, March 20). More alike than we think. *UX Matters*. Retrieved from http://www.uxmatters.com/mt/archives/2006/03/ more-alike-than-we-think.php

Quesenbery, W., & Brooks, K. (2010). *Storytelling for user experience: Crafting stories for better design*. Brooklyn, NY: Rosenfeld Media.

Redish, J. (2007). *Letting go of the words: Writing Web Content that Works*. Boston, MA: Morgan Kaufmann.

Redish, J., Chisnell, D. E., Laskowski, S. J., & Lowry, S. Plain language makes a difference when people vote. *Journal of Usability Studies, 5*(3), 81–103. Retrieved from http://www.upassoc.org/ upa_publications/jus/jus_home.html

Reynolds, G. (2008). *Presentation Zen: Simple ideas on presentation design and delivery*. Berkeley, CA: New Riders.

Reeves, B., & Nass, C. (1996). *The media equation: How people treat computers, television, and new media like real people and places*. New York, NY: Cambridge University Press.

Rhenius, D., & Deffner, G. (1990). Evaluation of concurrent thinking aloud using eye-tracking data. *Proceedings of the Human Factors Society 34th Annual Meeting* (pp. 1265–1269). Orlando, FL.

Rogers, K. (2008, May). The culture of China's Internet: Developing web content for the world's fastest growing online market. *Intercom*, 10–13.

Rubinstein, R., & Hersh, H. M. (1984). *The human factor: Designing computer systems for people*. Burlington, MA: Digital Press.

Salant, P., & Dillman, D. A. (1994). *How to conduct your own survey*. New York, NY: Wiley.

Schumacher, R. M. (Ed.). (2010). *Handbook of global research*. Boston, MA: Morgan Kaufmann.

Schulte-Mecklenbeck, M., & Huber, O. (2003). Information search in the laboratory and on the web: With or without an experimenter. *Behavior Research & Methods, Instruments & Computers, 35*(2), 227–235.

Shaikh, D., & Lenz, K. (2006, February). Where's the search? Re-examining user expectations of web objects. *Usability News, 8*(1). Retrieved from http://psychology.wichita.edu/surl/usabilitynews/81/webobjects.asp

Shi, Q., & Clemmensen, T. (2008). *Communication patterns and usability problem finding in cross-cultural thinking aloud usability testing. Proceedings of CHI 2008; Work-in-Progress* (pp. 2811–2816). Florence, Italy: ACM.

Singh, M., & Pereira, A. (2005). *The culturally customized web site: Customizing web sites for the global marketplace.* Amsterdam, The Netherlands: Elsevier.

Software Usability Research Laboratory. Wichita State University. *Usability News.* Retrieved from http://www.surl.org/usabilitynews

Spool, J., & Schroeder, W. (2001). *Testing web sites: Five users is nowhere near enough. Proceedings of CHI 2001: Extended Abstracts* (pp. 285–286). Seattle, WA: ACM.

Stanford Persuasive Technology Lab. Stanford Web Credibility Research. (2002, June). *Stanford guidelines for web credibility.* Retrieved from http://credibility.stanford.edu/guidelines/index.html

Sy, D. (2007, May). Adapting usability investigations for agile user-centered design. *Journal of Usability Studies, 2*(3), 112–132. Retrieved from http://www.upassoc.org/upa_publications/ jus/jus_home.html

Tamler, H. (1998, July). How (much) to intervene in a usability testing session. *Common Ground, 8*(3), 11–15. Retrieved from http://www.htamler.com/papers/intervene

Teague, R., De Jesus, K., & Nunes-Ueno, M. (2001). Concurrent vs. post-task usability test ratings. *Proceedings of CHI 2001: Extended Abstracts* (pp. 289–290). Seattle, WA: ACM.

Theophanos, M., & Quesenbery, W. (2005, November). Toward the design of effective formative reports. *Journal of Usability*

Studies, 1(1), 27–45. Retrieved from http://www.upassoc.org/upa_publications/jus/jus_home.html

Tobin, R., Hotchkiss, G., & Lee, P. (2008, January). Chinese search engine engagement. Retrieved from Enquiro Research website: http://www.enquiro.com/whitepapers/pdf/chinese-search-engine-engagement.pdf

Tullis, T., & Albert, B. (2008). *Measuring the user experience: Collecting, analyzing, and presenting usability metrics.* Boston, MA: Morgan Kaufmann.

Tullis, T. S., & Stetson, J. N. (2004). A comparison of questionnaires for assessing website usability. Presentation at the Usability Professionals' Association Conference, Minneapolis, MN. Slides retrieved from http://www.upassoc.org/usability_resources/conference/2004/UPA-2004-TullisStetson.pdf

van den Haak, M. J., de Jong, M. D. T., & Schellens, P. J. (2007). February). Evaluation of an informational web site: Three variants of the think-aloud method compared. *Technical Communication, 54*(1), 58–71.

Vatrapu, R., & Pérez-Quiñones, M. A. (2006, August). Culture and usability evaluation: The effects of culture in structured interviews. *Journal of Usability Studies, 1*(4), 156–170. Retrieved from http://www.upassoc.org/upa_publications/jus/jus_home.html

Virzi, R. (1992). Refining the test phase of usability evaluation: How many subjects is enough? *Human Factors, 34*(4), 457–468.

Virzi, R. A. (1990). Streamlining the design process: Running fewer subjects. *Proceedings of the Human Factors Society 34th Annual Meeting: Vol. 1* (pp. 291–294). Orlando, FL.

Williams, D., Kelly, G., Anderson, L., Zavislak, N., Wixon, D., & de los Reyes, A. (2004). *Proceedings of CHI 2004* (pp. 959–974). Vienna, Austria: ACM.

Wright, R. B., & Converse, S. A. (1992). Method bias and concurrent verbal protocol in software usability testing. *Proceedings of the Human Factors Society 36th Annual Meeting: Vol 2* (pp. 1220–1224). Atlanta, GA.

Wurman, R. S. (1989). *Information anxiety*. New York, NY: Doubleday.

Yammiyavar, P., Clemmensen, T., & Kumar, J. (2008). Influence of cultural background on non-verbal communication in a usability testing situation. *International Journal of Design, 2*(2), 31–40.

Young, I. (2008). *Mental models: Aligning design strategy with human behavior*. Brooklyn, NY: Rosenfeld Media.

Yunker, J. (2003). *Beyond borders: Web globalization strategies*. Berkeley, CA: New Riders.

Index

Note: Page numbers followed by *f* refer to figures.